Yaxcabá and the Caste War of Yucatán

Yaxcabá and the Caste War of Yucatán

An Archaeological Perspective

Rani T. Alexander

UNIVERSITY OF NEW MEXICO PRESS • ALBUQUERQUE

11 10 09 08 07 06 05 04   1 2 3 4 5 6 7

LIBRARY OF CONGRESS CATALOGING-IN-PUBLICATION DATA

Alexander, Rani T., 1962–
    Yaxcabá and the caste war of Yucatán : an archaeological perspective
/ Rani T. Alexander.— 1st ed.
        p. cm.
Includes bibliographical references and index.
    ISBN 0-8263-2962-4 (cloth : alk. paper)
    1. Mayas—Mexico—Yaxcabá—History—19th century. 2. Mayas—Mexico—
Yaxcabá—Antiquities. 3. Excavations (Archaeology)—Mexico—Yaxcabá.
4. Ethnoarchaeology—Mexico—Yaxcabá. 5. Yucatán (Mexico : State)—
History—Caste War, 1847–1855. 6. Yaxcabá (Mexico)—Politics and
government. 7. Yaxcabá (Mexico)—History—19th century. 8. Yaxcabá
(Mexico)—Antiquities. 9. Mexico—History—Spanish colony, 1540–1810.
I. Title.
F1435.1.Y27A54 2004
972'.6500497'427—dc22

                                                    2003018564

s

All drawings are by Rani Alexander, unless otherwise noted.
Interior design and typesetting: Kathleen Sparkes
Body type: Minion 10 / 13
Display: Akzidenz Grotesk

Contents

List of Figures

List of Tables

Preface

I n 1986 I was working on the Yaxuná Archaeological Survey, 17 km south of the site of Chichén Itzá on the Yucatán Peninsula. At that time the project's objectives were to acquire a greater understanding of the tenth- and eleventh-century conflicts that occurred between the city of Chichén Itzá and its east-coast rival, Cobá. The site of Yaxuná is connected to Cobá via a 60-km-long causeway, yet it is actually closer to Chichén, an observation that has led to archaeological speculation about the competitive relationship between the two centers. Ethnohistorians identify the site of Yaxuná with a place called Cetelac mentioned in the books of Chilam Balam, where it is said that the leaders of Chichén and Cetelac "agreed in their opinions" and thus established a boundary between the two polities.[1] Cetelac, which appears on two early colonial maps, the 1549 Map of Mani and the 1600 Map of the Tierras de Sotuta, also figured prominently in a sixteenth-century border dispute between the provinces of Sotuta and Cupul.[2] One day when we were mapping, I asked Emeterio Tamay, the *comisario ejidal* (a municipal official charged with overseeing the distribution, use, transfer, and cultivation of communal lands), if he knew of a place called Cetelac. "Ceteac," he corrected me, and off we went with our crew and the project director.[3]

A few hundred meters beyond our last grid-marker, we entered a corral enclosure containing a number of wooden beehives that were set in rows. A buckskin mare calmly grazed the *zacate* near the well outside the main gate. At the far end of the corral, an empty corn crib made of wood poles and tar paper and surrounded by corn husks was nestled into the corner of a large, vine-covered masonry structure. A few minutes of work removing the vegetation revealed a surprisingly ornate, two-story house of a landed estate, or hacienda, along with its *noria* (well) and water troughs. As we poked around, Don Emeterio commented, "*En el tiempo de esclavitud* [in the time of slavery], this hacienda and three others were owned by the same family, a group of brothers. Now, of course, it belongs to us; it is part of our ejido."

The nineteenth century in Yucatán was the crucible that fused agrarian change to Maya social identity. When people in Yaxuná and surrounding villages talk about "el tiempo de esclavitud," they are referring to the early nineteenth century, before the onset of the Caste War of Yucatán (1847–1901). It was a politically turbulent era, one which saw independence from Spain; attempts to establish an independent republic of Yucatán; conflict between elites in Mérida and Campeche; and the extension of Spanish-Creole entrepreneurial ventures to the countryside. Most important for the rural Maya were the changes created by the growth of the haciendas and new legislation governing land tenure. Following independence, Spanish Creoles came to dominate the local *ayuntamientos* (town councils), effectively disenfranchising Maya from most political processes (Cline 1947; Güemez Pineda 1994; Rugeley 1997). As a result, Creoles largely controlled the disposition of property within the municipalities, as well as open lands known as *terrenos baldíos*, which increasingly became concentrated in non-Maya hands as they were added to private estates. Depending on the region, haciendas used Indian labor to produce sugar, maize, cattle, and, later, henequen. The landlords contracted laborers through a number of arrangements, from salaries and sharecropping to debt peonage. The latter situation is a form of slavery, in that it constrained the mobility of Maya laborers by indebting them monetarily and socially to the hacienda's owner. Because debts were inherited and transferable, the patrimonial relationship could extend over several generations, and when the hacienda was sold, laborers' debts (and sometimes the laborers themselves) were passed to the new owner (Bracamonte y Sosa 1993).

The Caste War changed all this. The protracted conflict commonly is interpreted as a revitalization movement in which there was a "deliberate, organized, conscious effort by the members of a society to construct a more satisfying culture" (Bricker 1981: 5; Wallace 1956: 265). For the Maya, the Caste War was a way of coping with rapid change by attempting to throw off the yoke of foreign domination while at the same time reinterpreting Catholic symbols for indigenous use through the cult of the "talking cross" (Reed 1964, 2001). Scholars widely regarded the war as a classic case of peasant resistance and open rebellion designed to redress the excesses of a colonial state. The outcomes of the war included: (1) the emergence of an organized priesthood and new cult practices, often symbolized by the "dressed crosses" still common today in Yucatán (Dumond 1985, 1997: plate 4); (2) a degree of political and territorial autonomy for the rebel Maya, which eventually resulted in the partitioning of the state of Quintana Roo from Yucatán; (3) revision of the tax code and reduction of the most flagrant castelike social divisions between Indians and non-Indians; and (4) successful agrarian reform and reassertion of traditional patterns of Maya land use over most of the peninsula. Nevertheless, the struggle also produced a demographic decline of approximately 30 percent for the entire peninsula, but this figure ranged up to two-thirds in some regions (Cline 1947: 41–57; Dumond 1997: 411–12). Although early arguments about the Caste War emphasize the roles played by postindependence progressivism, land pressure, and hacienda expansion as causes of the rebellion, recent debate downplays these, largely because the revolt began in the eastern regions of the peninsula where conditions were less acute (cf. Cline 1947; Dumond 1997; Joseph 1998; Patch 1991, 1993; Rugeley 1997; Strickon 1965). Although current treatments of the conflict do not discard the agrarian-pressure argument, they focus on broader, multicausal explanations that include unfulfilled economic expectations among the peasantry, ineffective Maya leadership, taxation, changes in social and ethnic identity, political factionalism, and Yucatán's articulation to the global economy.

During the course of the war, the rebel Maya burned the hacienda Cetelac, and both the Maya rebels and the Spanish-Creole militia repeatedly attacked and pillaged villages such as Yaxuná. The parish of Yaxcabá, to which both Yaxuná and Cetelac belonged, would suffer in the words of one historian "almost Biblical destruction during the Caste War" (Rugeley 1997: 5).[4] Even though local oral history links agrarian reform and freedom from slavery to events of the rebellion, documentary evidence shows that the inhabitants of Yaxcabá and its surrounding region were caught in the crossfire. Yaxcabá was attacked, changed hands, and burned some nine times during the course of the war, and as late as 1880 parish priests, preferring to remain in the relative safety of Sotuta, relegated the region to the uncivilized rebel Maya frontier.[5] In view of the enormous loss of life, wholesale emigration, and destruction of property, the agrarian reform appears to be less a consequence of a successful campaign of Maya resistance than the economic ruin left to a vastly reduced population of survivors and returning refugees.

How does one resolve this contradiction between oral and documentary history? Are people's comments about the Caste War and the time of slavery part of the "myth of history," an ideological representation of current agrarian struggles (Bricker 1977)? Or do such comments describe a long-term process of Maya resistance in nineteenth-century Yaxcabá in which the rebel cause was adopted opportunistically, perhaps inadvisably, as a vehicle for advancing peasant interests within ongoing disputes? To evaluate these questions, I have turned to historical archaeology as a means to examine the behavior and practices of Yaxcabá's Maya agriculturalists and their relations with Spanish Creoles and the state in the late eighteenth and the nineteenth centuries.

This book is about the time of slavery and the transformation of agrarian structure in Yaxcabá before, during, and after the Caste War. The experiences of people in Yaxcabá parish are emblematic of vast numbers of nineteenth-century Maya, for whom open rebellion was not a realistic solution to their problems. More likely, Maya farmers used "everyday forms of resistance" (Scott 1985) to redress disputes over land with Spanish Creoles, difficulties in the allocation of labor and meeting tax obligations, and lack of political representation. Dispersal and flight (Farriss 1984) were two of their most important tactics. Although many Maya supported and joined the rebellion in its first years, many others later became victims of the war—killed in numerous massacres and raids; taken prisoner by the rebels and forced into agricultural labor; taken prisoner by the Creoles and sold into slavery in Cuba; or forced to flee when soldiers of both armies scoured the land for resources (Dumond 1997). Consequently, this study recasts the nineteenth-century agrarian reform in Yaxcabá as a long-term, dynamic process that included variable strategies of circumventing problems within particular structures of power and class relations, as well as the more eye-catching examples of armed resistance.

Evaluating resistance in the past proves to be a difficult task. Social scientists originally developed the concept of resistance, particularly its "everyday forms" and "weapons of the weak," by analyzing the discourse, intentions, and practices of the living (Scott 1985). The concept is widely overromanticized and culturally "thin," to the detriment of those striving to sort out the complex relationships between accommodation and insubordination, subalterns and their superiors, landlords and peasants, embedded within various systems of domination (see Abu-Lughod 1990; Guha 1983, 1997; Ortner 1995). Historians and anthropologists interested in the past typically have had to rely on relatively few sources that describe peasant grievances or express elites' dissatisfaction with the actions of their subordinates. By definition, everyday forms of resistance do not make the headlines, and they are difficult to distinguish from the quotidian coping mechanisms on which peasants typically rely for survival. Using documentary sources, we can identify the pressures and conflicts generated by political and economic change in Yucatán. But because the activities of ordinary Maya farmers in Yaxcabá seldom surmounted the barriers of class, literacy, and language to gain a foothold in the documentary record, history neglects to tell us how indigenous inhabitants coped with those pressures or settled disputes.

Within the arsenal of approaches used to study the Caste War, however, one body of evidence—archaeology—has not been brought to bear on the problem. Although Spanish Creoles dominate the historical record, the Maya agriculturalist monopolizes the archaeological record. Because archaeology encodes information about past human behavior for people who are not well represented in historical documents, as well as those who are, it can provide insight into the ways in which the Maya adjusted their agricultural strategies to accommodate or resist the changing conditions in Yaxcabá parish during the nineteenth century. Archaeology is ideally suited to the long-term study of agrarian strategies, household survival tactics, and their spatial patterning, an area of study known as "settlement" or "household ecology" (Stone 1996; Wilk 1991). Consequently, the analysis of archaeological settlement patterns in Yaxcabá, with the judicious use of appropriate analogies, yields interpretations of changing agrarian structure for whole communities that are barely mentioned in the historical record. Therefore, through archaeology it is possible to determine how parish inhabitants coped with the turbulent political and economic changes of their times. This book juxtaposes archaeological and historical evidence in order to assess the long-term processes of resistance and accommodation for Maya agriculturalists in Yaxcabá.

Diachronic analysis of agrarian change in Yaxcabá suggests some intriguing consistencies in the broad patterns of Maya resistance. Ironically, throughout its history Cetelac always has occupied a disputed location at the edge of various spheres of political-economic interaction. Today Cetelac and Yaxuná occupy the periphery of a zone of tourist development centered at Chichén Itzá (Castañeda 1996). As the inhabitants negotiate attempts to alienate their agricultural land in the name of preserving cultural patrimony, some patterns of adjustment and resistance likely will prove all too familiar.

Acknowledgments

Archaeological research is never a solitary endeavor. During the course of this investigation, I have accumulated many intellectual, academic, and personal debts, far too numerous to recount here. The archaeological and archival research for this project was funded by grants from the National Science Foundation (BNS-8813858), the Wenner Gren Foundation for Anthropological Research (Gr #5089 and Gr #6404), the Organization of American States, Tinker-Mellon Field Research Grants of the Latin American Institute, University of New Mexico, and Sigma Xi Grants-in-Aid of Research. Permission to conduct this investigation was granted by the Consejo de Arqueología, Instituto Nacional de Antropología e Historia (INAH) and the Centro-INAH Yucatán as a branch of the Yaxuná Archaeological Survey, directed by David Freidel of Southern Methodist University. I wish to express my appreciation to Rubén Maldonado Cárdenas, Fernando Robles Castellanos, Alfredo Barrera Rubio, and David Freidel for their support.

This book weaves together several strands of archaeological and ethnohistorical investigation that I have conducted since the mid-1980s. The archaeological data originally comprised my doctoral dissertation (Alexander 1993), although the present work bears little resemblance to it. Parts of Chapter 5 have appeared in modified form in Alexander 1998 and 1999; parts of Chapter 4 appeared in Alexander 1997a, 1997b, and 2003. My research since 1998 has focused on the development of theoretical frameworks, in-depth analysis of additional documentary sources, and several new analyses of the archaeological data that appear for the first time in this book.

Many academics, students, and friends have been instrumental in the development of this project. Victoria Bricker, E. Wyllys Andrews V, and Anthony Andrews inspired interest in Colonial-period Maya archaeology and ethnohistory early on, and this work owes much to their constant encouragement. I am equally indebted to the members of my doctoral committee—Robert Santley, Lewis Binford, David Freidel, and James Boone—whose questions fostered a more creative approach to this topic. The historical research presented here has benefited from the generosity and patience of several wonderful historians, who encouraged, rather than merely tolerated, the attempts of an archaeologist to come to grips with archival material. I especially thank Sergio Quezada, Robert Patch, and Pedro Bracamonte y Sosa. I am grateful to all of the archivists of the Archivo Notarial del Estado de Yucatán, the Biblioteca Cresencio Carrillo y Ancona, the Archivo de la Mitra Emeritense, and the Archivo General del Arquidiócesis, for their assistance, but special thanks are due to Piedad Peniche Rivero, director of the Archivo General del Estado de Yucatán, Guillermo Náñez Falcón, director of the Latin American Library at Tulane University, and their respective staffs. Rafael Cobos Palma at the

Facultad de Ciencias Antropológicas, Universidad Autónoma de Yucatán, first introduced me to his large cadre of students, and thanks to his support both the students and I benefited from our field experiences. I extend my sincerest appreciation to Eunice Uc González and Elena Canché Manzanero, who unselfishly worked as my field assistants and without whom the months of fieldwork in Yaxcabá would never have been completed. Rosalía Carrillo Sonda, Oana del Castillo, and Soco Jiménez Alvarez also participated in fieldwork as their studies permitted. These investigations would not have been possible but for the hospitality of people in Yaxcabá and the efforts of the field crew. I especially acknowledge the contributions of José Díaz Santiago, Jorge Campos González, and Benigno Poot Canul as well as their respective families.

Finally, this book would not have been written without the interest and encouragement of numerous colleagues, friends, and family. Anne Pyburn read the manuscript, and her insights about smallholder cultivation strategies greatly improved the final work. Evelyn Schlatter and Kathy Sparkes at the University of New Mexico Press did a wonderful job of taking the manuscript through editing and production. Scott Rushforth and Lois Stanford at New Mexico State University were supportive during the writing process and generously shared their views on resistance. Jeanne Randall still believes that one day I will learn to take a decent photograph; her friendship and her photos have improved this book. Thanks also to Robin Alexander for providing laughter and a roof over my head while finishing research in New Orleans. I am deeply grateful to my parents, Ron and Clara Alexander, who first took me to Yucatán many years ago. Finally, to Nigel Holman goes my heartfelt thanks for his constant support and encouragement; he has put up with this book for a very long time.

## CHAPTER ONE

Legacies of Resistance

Yaxcabá is located in central Yucatán, 100 km southeast of Mérida (Figure 1.1). To get there, one takes the old highway from Mérida heading toward Chichén Itzá, and turns south at Libre Unión. Farther down the road another 18 km, a new school and some industrial-size speed bumps greet one's arrival. During the day, the central square with its benches and shade trees is usually deserted; activity is invariably low-key as people go about their business. A large cenote, surrounded by a high concrete-block wall, occupies the plaza just north of the church, but it is unused, having been replaced during the program for rural electrification by a more modern pumping system for potable water. A few stores occupy parts of the old, high-ceilinged masonry buildings that line the square.

Today Yaxcabá is the seat of a municipality that covers 1,079 sq km that has a population of more than 8,500 inhabitants.[1] The pattern of settlement is dispersed. Only six other towns have more than 500 people—Kancabdzonot, Libre Unión, Tahdzibichen, Tiholop, Tixcacaltuyú, and Yokdzonot. Twenty-four hamlets and thirty-one small ranches contain the remainder of the population. Approximately 37 percent of the population engages economically in agriculture and stockraising. The region's principal products include maize, beans, watermelon, chile, jicama, cattle, pigs, poultry, and honey. Yaxcabá does not have a market and only hosts a few establishments, which sell prepared food, groceries, and miscellaneous sundries.

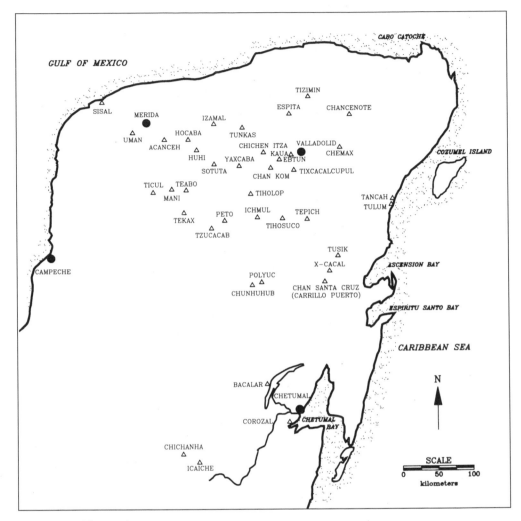

FIGURE 1.1. The study area.

Yaxcabá's colonial architecture seems decidedly oversized for its population, an effect made more noticeable by recent architectural restoration of the colonial facades (Figure 1.2a–d). Building exteriors have been repaired and painted in traditional pastel colors with white trim. The church, dedicated to San Francisco Asís, dominates the main plaza with its three towers and adjacent rectory and ossuary. Recently restored retablos, whose central altarpiece is completely gilded in 24-karat gold leaf, suit the elaborate exterior architectural decoration on the church's salomonic columns, archways, facades, and doorways.[2] A number of equally impressive structures surround the church, including the municipal building with its arched and colonnaded portico, the small church (or *hermita*) of Santa Cruz situated on a high limestone outcrop to the southeast, and the impressive former residence *(quinta)* of Claudio Padilla, a wealthy and prominent nineteenth-century citizen. The quinta's crumbling upper facade still retains traces of fading red and yellow

Figure 1.2a.
Yaxcabá town center:
San Francisco Yaxcabá,
from the roof, facing west.
(all Figure 1.2 photos by
Jeanne Randall).

Figure 1.2b.
Yaxcabá town center:
View of the Hermita de
Santa Cruz and the cenote
from the church roof.

Figure 1.2c.
Yaxcabá town center:
View of a defensive structure
from the palacio municipal.

Figure 1.2d.
Yaxcabá town center:
A quinta, west side.

paint. Although restoration has improved the look of the colonial buildings on the main square, masonry residences beyond any hope of repair litter the roads leading out of town. These structures lack roofs and parts of walls, and some appear to have burned. Sometimes the doorways are blocked with dry-laid stone walls to pen livestock and prevent trespass.

Most unusual, however, are the defensive features constructed at the corners of the churchyard. The local inhabitants say that these round pill boxes as well as the slits in the church towers were used to defend the town during the Caste War of Yucatán (1847–1901). Nevertheless, to the casual observer they suggest that something happened here to disconnect the present from the past.

In 1971 Victoria Bricker (1981: 255) recorded a story about the 1853 rebel Maya attack that accounts for Yaxcabá's current state of affairs. The storyteller was a ladino living in Sotuta, and when asked if the Caste War leaders had come to Sotuta itself, he responded:

> They came to Yaxcabá; yes, they came to Yaxcabá; yes, so that they always survived... and the suitcases were ready... the clothes were there. Ah, every minute there were people in the carts in order to fire shots in order to warn them that the people were coming. And the people, well, they went into the woods to protect themselves, because Cecilio Chi came, and Jacinto Canek. Well, they reached Yaxcabá, and they burned houses. That is why Yaxcabá was left in ruins. And Yaxcabá never raised its head, until even now. They fled.... Because Yaxcabá used to be a city; because Yaxcabá used to be a city. Yes those from here [Sotuta] bought soap and candles there. All kinds of things were manufactured there in Yaxcabá, isn't that so? But Yaxcabá was very—how shall I say it?—populated. Yes, there used to be much corn, then no.

This story and others about "the time of slavery" present an argument about the archaeological record. They attribute changes in settlement patterns to the violent activities of a group of principal actors—the Caste War rebels and their local supporters. Furthermore, changes in the material record are coupled with interpretations of the intent of these actors to resist the intrusion of foreigners (Spanish Creoles) and their market-based enterprises that would dispossess the Maya from their lands and way of life (see Bricker 1977). To local inhabitants the ruins of Yaxcabá and surrounding places constitute evidence of the revolt's success—the Creoles fled and Maya culture was preserved.

Throughout the twentieth century, Western scholars have been interested in questions of continuity or change for the Maya inhabitants of towns such as Yaxcabá (see, for example, Thompson 1970:xv). One prevailing theme in history, archaeology, and cultural anthropology is cultural survival and continuity, which portrays the Maya as tenaciously maintaining cultural traditions in the face of the Spanish conquest, colonial upheavals, and the inevitable march of globalization. The opposing view seeks to identify and explain myriad changes in Maya culture in light of the long-term history of resistance to colonialism and capitalism. Through astute negotiations with foreign invaders and manipulation of local conditions, the Maya creatively adjusted to political, economic, and ideological changes, at times resorting to armed rebellion in order to keep the worst ravages of the colonial and modern systems at bay. Both themes, sides of the same coin, posit an active role for the Maya agriculturalist; yet, in the popular imagination they have fostered a view of Maya culture that is at once "traditional and conservative" and "resistant to the inexorable forces of global progress."

The Caste War of Yucatán figures prominently in any assessment of cultural continuity for the Maya because it marks a period of rapid change between the Colonial and Modern periods. Although the nineteenth century was a watershed of culture change throughout Mexico, Yucatán's Caste War provides the archetypical case study of peasant resistance to expanding state authority and the shifts in macroregional political economy. Widely regarded as the most successful Indian rebellion in the New World, the conflict is interpreted as a nativistic movement in which the Maya attempted to rid themselves of foreign domination and revitalize traditional culture. The movement generated a new religion, focused on the worship of a prophetic, "talking" cross, with its own priesthood and cult practices (Bricker 1981). The aftermath of the war produced a successful agrarian reform and the reassertion of traditional patterns of Maya land use. The Caste War "explains" the disjuncture between the present and the recent past in Yaxcabá. Furthermore, the patterns of resistance before and after the conflict share several elements with peasants' struggles to retain control of agricultural land worldwide. The conditions and events of the nineteenth century supply a blueprint for understanding relations between Maya agriculturalists and the state in the present.

The experiences of the Maya in nineteenth-century Yaxcabá are important because they describe a process of economic transformation commonly associated with the expansion of capitalism to rural areas. To increase production and respond to market demands, elites typically monopolize the means of production (land, tools, labor, capital), thus disenfranchising small farmers from their land base and forming a rural workforce that is remunerated in wages or other patrimonial support. Typically this transformation increases economic stratification in the countryside such that smallholders become shareholders (Netting 1993). Smallholders are autonomous, subsistence-oriented agriculturalists who practice intensive and sustainable cultivation on land they own or control. Shareholders, by contrast, do not own their land and must negotiate share or wage-labor contracts with those who do in order to make a living. The widespread persistence and survival of smallholders around the globe in an era dominated by large-scale agribusiness and an expanding capitalist economy presents an enduring question. Some scholars see smallholders' survival as a product of isolation. Because world capitalism has expanded unevenly, some "pockets" remain untouched or are characterized by an incomplete transformation of the rural workforce. Other scholars emphasize smallholders' sustainability in responding to changes in macroregional economy, land tenure, population density, technology, environment, and subsistence risk. Smallholders have an active and conscious role in maintaining a resilient adaptation that successfully resists the blandishments of world capitalism.

If one considers why Maya smallholders in Yaxcabá still practice subsistence agriculture, however, the usual explanations seem singularly unsatisfying in light of the region's history. In the late eighteenth and early nineteenth centuries, Yaxcabá was hardly isolated from processes of economic transformation. To the contrary, the Caste War reversed the process of rural proletarianization in much of Yucatán. Moreover, the ways in which Yaxcabá's farmers retain control of the allocation of labor, resources, and household decision-making today, while no doubt effective, pale in comparison to the struggle for autonomy mounted by Maya smallholders of a century and a half ago. To explain in part how and why traditional patterns of Maya land use persist, this study examines the local strategies and tactics of resistance, accommodation, and survival through which the Maya coped with early processes of globalization before, during, and after the Caste War. This work draws on contemporary ethnography, ethnoarchaeology, history, and, most importantly, archaeology, to understand the workings, potential, and sustainability of the nineteenth-century agrarian system in Yaxcabá. The course of agrarian change in this region is instructive for those who would explain how and why smallholders succeed in today's global arena.

For much of its history Yaxcabá and its dependent settlements occupied a colonial hinterland. The Spanish conquest of Yucatán was a relatively unsuccessful endeavor. Only after multiple attempts at conquest were the conquistadors able to pacify and colonize the northwestern third of the peninsula. Yaxcabá was a principal town in the Maya province of Sotuta, whose leader, Nachi Cocom, was a key player in the Great Revolt of 1547 against the Spaniards. Rather than prolong a losing campaign for a marginally productive region, the Spaniards quelled the rebellion, declared victory, and focused subsequent efforts on more lucrative Peru (Restall 1998). The crown subjected the region to its routine program of colonization early on. In 1549 conquistadors rounded up the Maya and resettled them in Yaxcabá and its auxiliary town Mopilá; an absent Spaniard received their tribute payments *(encomienda)*. By 1582 the town became the parish seat *(cabecera de parroquia)* and a benefice for the secular clergy. To the south and east of the parish, however, lay the vast unpacified zone, where the Maya continued their existence unhindered by the benefits of Spanish civilization.

By the late eighteenth century, a second stage of colonization was underway. This time Spanish-Creole entrepreneurs flooded the countryside and established landed estates or haciendas. The edge of the colonial frontier expanded past Yaxcabá, down toward Tihosuco. From 1786 to the beginning of the Caste War in 1847, a spirit of progressivism prevailed. As Creoles assumed control of local politics, they increasingly diverted resources and labor to projects that would enrich them, increase production, and more fully "civilize" rural areas (Cline 1947; Güemez Pineda 1994). As Indians were dispossessed of land, the remaining Maya nobility were alienated from their traditional bases of power. Yaxcabá itself was a Creole success story. From the Maya perspective, however, restructuring of the conditions of domination only made Yaxcabá a prime target for attack.

Like the first Spanish conquest, the attempt to more fully harness the productive capacity of the peninsula to the authority of the state was not an unqualified success. As early as 1761 the perpetrators of the Canek revolt had planned to attack Yaxcabá as a means of reasserting Maya sovereignty (Bricker 1981:73–74; Patch 1998). By 1847 and the onset of the Caste War, Yaxcabá had become a strategic target as a gateway to the colonial heart of Yucatán. In the first two years of the war, the town changed hands four times (Dumond 1997; Reed 1964). The subsequent establishment of a military canton did little to prevent the rebel Maya from burning and pillaging the settlement five more times between 1853 and 1870. Throughout the second half of the nineteenth century, the rebel Maya largely succeeded in severing the ties between Yaxcabá and the rest of Creole-controlled Yucatán.

Does this aborted attempt at state integration suggest the Maya of Yaxcabá ultimately redressed the conditions of their oppression? Was a nineteenth-century campaign of Maya resistance responsible for restoring a more balanced agrarian pattern and reasserting traditional Maya values observed today in Yaxcabá? To answer these questions, it is necessary to disarticulate the concepts of resistance, adaptation, and peasant rebellion.

Current thinking in the social sciences conceptualizes resistance as a ranked series of strategies in which peasants attempt to "work the system to their minimum disadvantage" (Scott 1985). In an era where agribusiness readily would absorb independent farmers, disenfranchising them from their land to form a mobile and malleable rural proletariat, smallholders around the globe have developed a remarkable resilience. Their capacity to respond flexibly to changes in markets, land tenure, population density, technology, environment, and subsistence risk has allowed them to retain control over land and agricultural decision-making. These survival strategies, however, are coupled with established structures of defiance, which may vary from routine acts of petty resistance that include footdragging, dissimulation, pilfering, desertion, false compliance, sabotage, and the like (Scott 1985:xvi, 29) to open political activity and armed rebellion. Although the "everyday forms" of resistance are by far the most widespread, their organization and the degree to which they constitute a coherent and conscious strategy depends largely on regional and local differences in the structure of domination (Guha 1983; Joseph 1991). Rebellions such as the Caste War are only flashes in the pan. They constitute neither the beginning nor the end of long-term processes of resistance and adjustment that stem from normally adversarial relations between peasants and the state (Stanford 1991; Stern 1987). As the Yaxcabá case shows, accommodation and resistance have a history; to explain their relationship we need to look beyond the immediate conditions of the present.

Since its inception, however, the concept of everyday forms of resistance has been problematic for those who study the past (Joseph 1991; Stern 1987). Scott's (1976, 1985:29, 1990; see also Wolf 1969) original argument is that the historical emphasis on peasant uprisings and open political defiance as vehicles for political-economic change is misplaced. Large-scale rebellions are few and, more often than not, unsuccessful. Instead, the most common ways in which peasants achieve gains against a coercive and hegemonic state is through normal and routine forms of resistance that seldom make their way into the historical record. In order for activities to be considered acts of resistance they must run counter to the attempts of the state and dominant classes to appropriate labor, surplus, and resources from peasants, and *intentionally* mitigate or deny elite claims. Although acts of resistance need not manifest themselves as collective action and class consciousness, the development of a subculture of resistance within the moral economy of peasant communities serves to distinguish them from ordinary coping or survival mechanisms.

In an excellent review of the methodological problems that a concept of everyday resistance poses for historians, Gilbert Joseph (1991) demonstrates the difficulty of drawing the line among acts of resistance, common crime, and the routine tactics of peasant survival. Although the criterion of intentionality would seem to obviate the historical study of everyday resistance, he suggests that microhistorical research (Brannon and Joseph 1991; González y González 1973) holds the key to the diachronic study of forms of protest. Assessment of the local setting in which the interests of peasants conflict directly with their superordinates, especially regarding access to land, water, or primary resources, may permit the historian to infer intention, and thus resistance, even when documentary or oral evidence is scarce (Joseph 1991:29; see also Stanford 1991). This approach, however, runs the risk of confounding routine acts of everyday resistance with ordinary survival strategies. In order to create a strong case for resistance as opposed to survival, such inferences need to be contextualized within a holistic model of social, political, ecological, and ideological systems (Adas 1986; Joseph 1991:30).

In order to assess Maya resistance in Yaxcabá, it is necessary to know something about not only the conditions of domination and local political economy but also cultivators' responses and reactions to it. Not all dissatisfaction crystallizes as resistance—either the open and violent or the more passive varieties—nor is dissatisfaction always polarized between peasant and landlord. As Scott and others have pointed out, peasants frequently justify acts of routine resistance as a need for survival, rather than as collective class action or a coherent intention to resist. Any systematic investigation of resistance in the past, therefore, necessarily incorporates the range of local survival tactics practiced by peasants (Stern 1987).

For example, nowhere is the problem of separating resistance from survival greater than in the analysis of Maya mobility, long considered the archetypical strategy of both accommodation and resistance to colonial rule (Farriss 1978, 1984:199–214; Patch 1993:62–66; Robinson 1990). In her now-classic framework, Nancy Farriss categorized three related manifestations of mobility as dispersal, drift, and flight. Dispersal refers to the tendency for Maya to temporarily (or sometimes permanently) shift residence from town to outlying agricultural plots during seasons of peak agricultural activity. Drift is a more intense form of mobility where individuals or households may move between major towns and smaller, outlying settlements for a greater period of time, sometimes spanning a generation. Flight is the permanent movement beyond the boundaries of civil and ecclesiastical jurisdiction. While dispersal is regarded as a tactic of survival clearly related to the needs of extensive swidden agriculture and the lengthy fallow system for tropical soils, flight is regarded as resistance (see also Wilk 1991). Yet both tactics, as well as drift, are systemically related; they are part of an integrated strategy in which the importance or prevalence of one tactic relative to the others varies over time and in response to local conditions. The middle ground constitutes a vast gray area that is difficult to characterize clearly as resistance or survival unless it is evaluated against specific agricultural strategies.

A number of historians and anthropologists have taken up the challenge to understand resistance in nineteenth-century Yucatán (Dumond 1997; Güemez Pineda 1991, 1994; Joseph 1991, 1998; Patch 1991, 1998; Sullivan 1989). As this research progresses, however, two problems have emerged. The first problem is that the structure of defiance and forms of protest are highly variable in time and space both before the onset of the revolt and during the course of the war itself. Much of the current literature about the origins of the Caste War discusses a unilineal model of peasants' reactions to changing forms of domination and increasing oppression in nineteenth-century Yucatán. The Caste War was metaphorically viewed as a pot boiling over, and initially we had expected a simple progression and escalation in forms of resistance that paralleled increased hegemony—from simple coping, to everyday forms of resistance, to open litigation and political protest, and finally to armed rebellion.

Nevertheless, recent evidence suggests that everyday forms of resistance were not the precursors of armed rebellion in Yucatán; rather, they were most concisely articulated in areas where peasants failed to support the rebel's efforts (Güemez Pineda 1991). Similarly a number of scholars have remarked that the conflict began in parts of the peninsula where land pressure and the conditions of domination were less acute (Dumond 1997; Joseph 1998; cf. Patch 1991, 1993; Rugeley 1997). Although the intensity and duration of the rebellion were fiercest in areas where Spanish-Creole appropriation of land, resources, and political processes was most severe, the intensity of the conflict also waxed and waned in particular regions over time (Strickon 1965). Although the Maya rebels were consistent in their official demands throughout the course of the conflict, they hardly followed a uniform strategy for gaining acquiescence to those demands (Dumond 1997).

The second problem is that although a patchwork view of resistance has emerged, it has not been matched with an equivalent understanding of the local variability of the agrarian system or in the normal coping and survival mechanisms of Maya agriculturalists. Steve Stern (1987) has argued that understanding the development of "resistant adaptations" and long-term peasant survival strategies is predicated on the use of adequate frames of reference. Because the local structure of domination alone provides insufficient grounds for inferring resistance, researchers need to redirect their attention to the specific and local organization of political economy and cultural ecology in order to distinguish resistance from common survival strategies. Currently, extensive swidden or slash-and-burn agriculture is the assumed agrarian pattern (the frame of reference) for the entire peninsula throughout the nineteenth century. Consequently, although microhistorical research has demonstrated enormous variability in conditions and pressures that sparked resistance, it has assumed that the normal survival tactics of Maya agriculturalists must be relatively uniform.

This assumption is understandable given its source. The agricultural system is described incompletely in a few nineteenth-century historical sources that focus on the slash-and-burn techniques used to make milpa (Granado Baeza 1845; Regil and Peon 1853; see also Tozzer 1941). Twentieth-century ethnographies of Maya villages such as Chan Kom and Piste depict extensive swidden agriculture in the context of low population density (Redfield and Villa Rojas 1934; Steggerda 1941). Because the Maya farmer is not prominent in the historical record, Maya survival strategies and the intricacies of the agricultural system under conditions of greater population density in earlier periods are assumed to be similar to those observed in the early twentieth century.

The agrarian system and cultural ecology of nineteenth-century Yucatán are overdue for reconsideration. Although extensive shifting cultivation has long been considered the cornerstone of Maya subsistence, cultivation of milpa by means of slash-and-burn techniques clearly is embedded within a more complex and intensive system of production (Arias Reyes 1980; Arias Reyes et al. 1998; Faust 1998; Fedick 1996; Killion 1990, 1992; Marcus 1982; Nations and Nigh 1980; Vara Morán 1980; Wilk 1991). Other important components of the subsistence system include kitchen gardening and fruit-tree horticulture, animal husbandry, apiculture, and cultivation of infield plots containing mixed cultigens, medicinal plants, and nonstaples. Some Maya also cultivated cash crops such as sugarcane and henequen. Clearly, both intensive and extensive agricultural strategies were practiced alongside each other. Some Maya owned their land, whereas others did not. Differences in the kinds and amounts of tools, labor, resources, or land needed to practice extensive or intensive agriculture affected patterns of resistance and accommodation (see Netting 1993; Pyburn 1998; Stanford 1991), and especially the degree to which dispersal, drift, or flight were considered effective resistance tactics. Current research on tropical agriculture offers a multifaceted model of Maya farming that provides a much more sophisticated frame of reference with which to view the changes in nineteenth-century agrarian structure. The challenge is to examine how various productive activities and forms of resistance were organized within Maya communities and how their configuration varied over time in response to changes in the nineteenth-century political economy.

In anthropology, the household is regarded as a sensitive interface through which production, labor, coping mechanisms, resistance, and survival tactics are coordinated. Many studies examine the structure of "householding" that emerges as articulations change between social organization, production, the local environment, and the extractive measures imposed by the state and global economy (see, for example, Netting et al. 1984; Small and Tannenbaum 1999). Because states regulate their economies and interfere in local production in order to accrue resources necessary for their activities, peasant households maintain adversarial relations with its institutions and agents. In an attempt to keep surplus out of state hands, householders respond to extractive measures in a variety of ways, including migration, intensification, diversification, specialization, market participation, storage, and exchange. Among other things, households are activity groups in which the arrangement of different behaviors and economic tactics comprise the overall strategy of the coresidential unit (Netting et al. 1984; Wilk 1991:34–40). As a household undergoes change or its members try to avoid extraction of surplus, specific behaviors or productive activities may be dropped, added, or rearranged within the household repertoire. Furthermore, the spatial structure of settlements and their component residential units is intimately related to this interplay among social organization, production, labor, and the environment (Stone 1996).

Most historians immediately will recognize the difficulty of such an approach, because documentary sources seldom describe the subsistence strategies of individual peasant households in sufficient detail. Using a concept of "householding" to understand Maya survival strategies in the nineteenth century would appear to suffer from the same methodological difficulties as the concept of resistance. Unlike resistance, however, many aspects of household organization are behaviorally and ecologically defined. Furthermore, because previous studies have demonstrated a strong relationship between household organization, landscape ecology, and settlement patterns, a domain variously called household or settlement ecology, relevant information about nineteenth-century Maya agrarian strategies is available from an unusual quarter—archaeology. Although one cannot directly observe household activity sets and their organization in the past, the redundant sets of ordinary activities, behaviors, and practices left their mark in the archaeological record of Yucatán. Therefore, in order to assess the processes of agrarian change before, during, and after the Caste War, this study focuses on the archaeology of nineteenth-century settlements and the remains of household activities in Yaxcabá.

The results of the investigation presented here required an interdisciplinary and multistage research design. First, using documentary sources I created a model of production and labor organization for Yaxcabá parish that also described the differences between various kinds of communities. Important variables included population, length of occupation, amount and diversity of production, civil and ecclesiastical tax structure, and the prevalence of wage labor and craft specialization. Archival research was conducted in the Archivo Notarial del Estado de Yucatán, the Archivo de la Mitra Emeritense, the Archivo General del Estado de Yucatán, the Archivo General del Arzobispado, the Colección Alfredo Barrera Vásquez of the Centro INAH Yucatán, the Biblioteca de la Escuela de Ciencias Antropológicas of the Universidad de Yucatán, and the Biblioteca Cresencio Carrillo y Ancona in Mérida, Yucatán, during the summer months of 1987, 1988, 1989, and 1999. Other important sources were located in the University of New Mexico Scholes collection, the manuscript and rare-book collections of the Latin American Library of Tulane University, the University of Pennsylvania Berendt collection, and the manuscript collections of the British Museum and British Library.

Second, I defined the range of variation in settlement forms and established the changes in settlement patterns over time within the Yaxcabá region. This objective entailed an extensive archaeological survey, placing emphasis on site location, ecological setting, size, amount and kinds of architecture, evidence of specialized functions, and variability in site layout. With the assistance of local farmers from Yaxcabá and archaeology students from the Universidad Autónoma de Yucatán, the survey was carried out from October to December 1988. Additional brief reconnaissance was conducted in January and June 1999.

Next, I described the range of spatial variation among residential units within each type of settlement. My assistants and I chose three settlements, one from each level of the settlement hierarchy (Mopilá, Cetelac, and Cacalchén), for intensive archaeological survey and mapping. We paid particular attention to the internal spatial variation and organization of the house lots within each settlement, recording house-lot size and the numbers, sizes, and types of dwellings, features, and animal-penning structures.

Finally, in order to examine the variability in the spatial configurations within house lots, I chose a small random sample of lots from each settlement for intensive surface collection, placing transects to traverse different areas and features within the lots. Soil was removed from the surface of each unit within the transect and screened through 6-mm mesh.[3] The density, size, and types of artifacts were analyzed to reveal differences in the arrangement of patios, garden areas, and dwellings within the house lots. The intensive surveys and surface collections were conducted from January through June 1989.

In Yaxcabá, political-economic changes implemented in the late eighteenth and early nineteenth centuries renewed the struggle over the control and allocation of land and labor between Maya agriculturalists and Spanish-Creole elites. The complex network of adversarial relations among Maya households, elites, the Catholic Church, and the state produced multifaceted coping mechanisms, survival strategies, and forms of resistance among these principal actors. The Caste War notwithstanding, documentary evidence of intentional forms of resistance is limited in Yaxcabá. Litigation over the management of municipal resources more commonly was implemented as a strategy of domination used by Creoles against other Creoles, by Creoles against Maya peasants, and by Creoles against the church. For the Maya farmer, forms of mobility that distanced agricultural produce, labor, and other clandestine activities from the eyes of civil and ecclesiastical authorities were the principal strategies of escaping the worst exigencies of church and state taxation.

The archaeological evidence, however, demonstrates that agrarian production among the communities of the parish was not uniform; rather, the responses to economic changes, particularly the distribution of land, were variable and flexible. As revealed by differences in the spatial patterns among and within house lots in Yaxcabá parish, variation in production strategies and the choice of tactics that minimized subsistence risk among Maya householders were largely dependent on their ownership of land and the degree to which Maya community institutions controlled its disposition. The structure of domination and the efficiency of resource extraction varied locally. Differences in spatial organization among the settlements of Yaxcabá parish can be linked specifically to variation in population growth, tax structure, and land stress coincident with changes in the local political economy. These coping and survival mechanisms contextualize and explain the progress and outcome of the Caste War in Yaxcabá.

Ultimately the explanation for the agrarian reform in Yaxcabá and the changes that occurred during the Caste War rest not with the rebellion itself but with the long-term processes that link tactics of accommodation, survival, and resistance to agrarian structure. Attempts on the part of the state, the church, and the elite to extract surpluses and to dispossess Maya farmers from their land failed. In the end the Maya of Yaxcabá maintained control of the allocation of resources and labor necessary to sustain agricultural production and a smallholding way of life, no small feat considering its final cost.

## CHAPTER TWO

Agrarian Change and the Caste War

Howard Cline completed a manuscript in 1947 that rooted the Caste War's origins in postindependence progressivism, changing relations between Indians and non-Indians, and the transformation of Yucatán from a colonial backwater to an autonomous agrarian state. He argued that the hallmarks of the progressive agenda, namely a cultural and literary renaissance, secularized thought, a move toward political autonomy, the assertion of civil over ecclesiastical authority, and the expansion of a hacienda economy based on sugar, cattle, and henequen, entailed other rural changes (Cline 1947:659). These included difficulties in controlling and stabilizing a relatively mobile agricultural labor force, the emergence of new frontiers, and the movement of population into areas inhabited by Maya who previously had experienced relatively little contact with outsiders. One of the key elements of Cline's (1947:663) argument was that the state's preference that land be placed in commercial production (especially of sugar) and its extension of incentives and concessions that permitted entrepreneurs to do so created complex frictions between Spanish Creoles and Mayas. Furthermore, because the Maya had few options for legal redress or compensation for their lands, their exploitation under the progressive agenda became the principal source of grievances voiced during the Caste War.

Since Cline disseminated his manuscript, numerous researchers have reiterated his fundamental conclusion—that the origins of the Caste War were exceedingly complex and multicausal (see Bricker 1981; Dumond 1997;

Joseph 1985; Patch 1985, 1991; Reed 1964; Rugeley 1997; Strickon 1965). Although some scholars have delved all the more deeply into the economic history of the late eighteenth and nineteenth centuries (Patch 1993; Wells and Joseph 1996), others have eschewed economic and materialist perspectives in favor of social-historical and social-psychological approaches (Dumond 1997:135; Restall 1997; Rugeley 1997; Sullivan 1989). To understand more about Maya attitudes during the conflict, particularly their relationships with outsiders, a few recent studies have de-emphasized the agrarian, "land pressure" arguments in an effort to move beyond the progressive thesis and avoid "reductionism" (Rugeley 1997:xviii).

Nevertheless, I return to the agrarian debate as a vehicle for understanding the relationship between the Caste War and the transformation of rural Maya communities. The loss or retention of a community's autonomy to shape its field of political and economic relations—or structural power (Wolf 1990:587)—is an important theme in exploring the effects of state expansion, transitions in the social relations of production, and the process of globalization. I suggest that further progress in understanding Maya resistance is predicated on a more sophisticated understanding of the agricultural system, the ways in which the state interfered in domestic production, and the strategies that Maya householders employed to circumvent such interference. Over the last twenty years, research in ethnography and archaeology steadily has advanced our knowledge of tropical agriculture and the impact of globalization on rural communities. Collectively, these studies supply a frame of reference for looking at resistance, survival, and agrarian change that illuminate the processes of rural transformation in nineteenth-century Yucatán.

Below I briefly review the status of the agrarian arguments in the literature on the Caste War, suggesting that the issue of land pressure and its relation to the onset of the rebellion have been mischaracterized. Next I place the postindependence progressivism of nineteenth-century Yucatán in the context of a broader body of research on colonization, globalization, and state-rural relations. Finally, I discuss an area of study known as settlement or household ecology, and specifically a model of settlement agriculture, as a framework for examining the variability of Maya household strategies in Yaxcabá before the Caste War.

Explaining Caste War Origins

One long-standing theory about why peasants revolt is that the intrusion of the global, capitalist economic system radically alters local economic and social values such that individual and community decision-making are increasingly constrained. Community members lose the power to manipulate their fields of social, political, and economic relations relative to the larger society, and they resort to violent protest to restore traditional patterns and lifeways (Wolf 1969, 1990). Peasant insurrections are a general feature of transitions to capitalist relations of production spawned by the collapse of colonial regimes.

This approach incorporates a number of questionable assertions that pervade historical studies of the Caste War and peasant resistance (Stern 1987:5–7). First, modernization is destructive to the traditional fabric of peasant communities. Second, the spread of capitalism exacerbates class differences between rich and poor because it constrains the mechanisms that level and redistribute wealth in traditional corporate communities. Third, the ways in which agrarian crises are resolved, either by conflict or diplomacy, strongly affect the political trajectories of modern nation-states and their capacity for industrial development. Finally, peasants are political actors (not just reactors) who commonly operate at the local level. Their success in forming a national political movement depends on their articulation with broader political arenas and on systemic conditions operating within society at large.

According to Dumond (1997:134) two specific explanations for the origins of the Caste War have long held sway in the historical and anthropological literature: (1) Maya hatred of outsiders, a condition dating to the conquest (see Restall 1998); and (2) oppression of the Maya by non-Maya elite, abetted by both the Catholic Church and the state, in the manner in which taxes were imposed, labor was extracted, and land was removed from the control of indigenous communities. Over the years different scholars have employed widely divergent approaches to examine these explanations. Oral history and documentary sources produced by Maya rebels and written in Yucatec Maya have been used in some masterful treatments of Maya attitudes toward progressive policies, change of leadership, and outsiders (Bricker 1981; Sullivan 1989). These studies suggest that Maya revolts and revitalization movements are deep-seated phenomena and share key cultural characteristics among regions and over time. Indeed, animosity toward outsiders, resistance to state oppression, and self-determination are hallmarks of the Zapatista rebellion in Chiapas.

Others have situated the issue of Maya oppression and Caste War origins within the long-term historical process of nation-state formation and globalization (Güemez Pineda 1991, 1994; Joseph 1985, 1998; Joseph and Nugent 1994; Patch 1991, 1993; Rugeley 1997; Wells and Joseph 1996). For example, in the mid-1980s, Joseph (1985:116) treated the agrarian basis for the Caste War as given: "Rather than being isolated as an apocalyptic race war, the 1847 revolt is now conceived as the terrible outcome of an extended dialectical process of commercial agricultural expansion and Maya response that began late in the Colonial period." Much of this literature builds on Cline's original arguments and research on peasant rebellions in general, to examine the structural causes of resistance within Yucatecan agrarian society (Joseph 1998). Lately, however, identifying the subaltern has become a common goal, and numerous studies focus on how the passive, everyday forms of footdragging and noncompliance were linked to the explosive 1847 revolt (Güemez Pineda 1991; Joseph 1991; Patch 1998; see also Restall 1997; Rugeley 1997; Wells and Joseph 1996). The idea that peasants are effective political actors has become something of a lightning rod for stimulating further research in Yucatán.

Efforts to illuminate political action and resistance among nineteenth-century Maya agriculturalists consequently have taken several methodological tacks. One direction, represented by the earlier works of Robert Patch (1993), Manuela Cristina Garcia Bernal (1972, 1978), Marta Espejo-Ponce Hunt (1974), Nancy Farriss (1984), Pedro Bracamonte (1993), and Arnold Strickon (1965), is consonant with Joseph's (1985, 1998; see also Stern 1987:9–12; Wells and Joseph 1996) emphasis on the structure of agrarian society and state-rural relations over the long term. These works constitute the foundation for the study of political-economic change from the Spanish conquest through the nineteenth century in Yucatán. They reveal substantial subregional variability in political-economic structure and in the pressures that were brought to bear on Maya agriculturalists. Patch (1985; 1991; 1993), in particular, presents the strongest argument for the agrarian basis of the Caste War. Documentary evidence for his interpretation is quite robust and includes land sales, hacienda tithe records and inventories, censuses, and claims of vacant land that demonstrate the transfer of land from Maya to non-Maya hands. Although these sources are subject to reinterpretation by scholars working from different perspectives, they constitute the basis for a regional model of hegemonic structure, including its social, political, ecological, and ideological subsystems.

Previous work on Yucatecan political economy nevertheless has propelled new trends in research on Maya resistance. Although historians could demonstrate significant variability in agrarian structure and processes between regions, many remained unsatisfied with explanations that portrayed the Maya as simply reacting to economic conditions. In searching for ways that did not treat peasants as an undifferentiated mass—"as potatoes in a sack form a sack of potatoes"—they began to work with sources that could inform them specifically about Maya behavior and the ways in which rural community members conceptualized sociopolitical relations.[1] One course of investigation emphasizes the analysis of documents written in Yucatec Maya, an approach that resonated with earlier efforts to create documentary ethnographies, using Maya-language documents as replacements for live consultants (Bricker 1977, 1981; Cline 1972; Farriss 1984; Restall 1997, 1998; Thompson 1978, 2000). A second direction of inquiry was to use penal court cases to document incidents of Maya resistance, behaviors that would be recorded as "crimes" by the state (Güemez Pineda 1991; Joseph 1991; Patch 1998). Another tactic was to focus explicitly on Maya social history and political relations with Creoles in distinct regions and communities in Yucatán (Rugeley 1997). While not denying that land pressure was an important variable in many areas, some scholars suggest that local data only partly support the notion that agriculturalists' reaction to land stress and hacienda expansion was a principal cause of the Caste War (Rugeley 1997:xvi). The tactics and strategies of Maya resistance depended on the local configuration of hegemony and the strength of indigenous leadership. The key to understanding resistance, variation among subaltern groups, and the consequent rebellion lay in microhistorical research that matched the scale of study commonly used by ethnographers (Adas 1986; González y González 1973; Joseph 1991).

Dumond (1997) established a different path to explaining the Caste War by examining the social-psychological aspects of the arguments for Maya oppression and hatred of outsiders. He focused on the origins and progress of the conflict itself, not on processes of capitalist expansion or globalization. Through an exhaustive and rigorous historiographical analysis of the documentary sources pertaining to the era (not only from Yucatán but also from Belize), Dumond explored changes in the mind-sets of Caste War leaders, participants, and Creole antagonists over the course of the conflict.[2] He attributes the origins of the war to the long-standing subjugation and exploitation of the lower classes, the rise in their expectations after independence from Spain in 1821, and the unexpected arrest and reversal of those expectations under the progressive political agenda.[3] In contrast to Patch and others, Dumond (1997:407) refutes the role of land pressure in the origins of the Caste War. The area in which the revolt began lacks strong historical evidence that Maya agriculturalists were deprived of land (Dumond

1997:136–37, 451). Furthermore, the official demands of the rebels never mention land specifically. Demographic processes, the war's deleterious effect on economic infrastructure, and the difficulties of economic recovery figure more prominently than "land pressure" as explanations for the agrarian transformation on the peninsula.

Nevertheless, large-scale peasant political revolts like the Caste War are infrequent and usually unsuccessful. Social researchers have tried to reconcile this seeming contradiction by focusing on other, less obvious kinds of political action in rural communities. They argue that the absence of active and conscious defiance does not signal acquiescence to the prevailing system of domination. Peasants are not duped by prevailing progressive ideologies, nor do they accept their subordinate economic situation as legitimate. As a result, the passive, poorly organized, "everyday" acts of resistance and noncompliance are far more pervasive, and in some cases these may supply effective alternatives to revolt (Scott 1985:304–50). According to Scott (1977, 1985:311–12; Stanford 1991), the inability of local elites to provide the basic resources, insurance, protection, and services expected by peasants who have entered into patron-client relationships with them spark active and violent peasant rebellions. This explanation resonates both with Dumond's emphasis on unfulfilled expectations and with Joseph's work on nineteenth-century agrarian structure. But, can resistance help explain the origins and progress of the Caste War?

Alternatively, loss of legitimacy among local patrons may prompt forms of "avoidance protest," instead of violence (Adas 1981:73, 1986). Avoidance protest and similar defensive acts include (1) transfer of the client's labor, goods, or political support to another patron or to another institution (for example, state to church or vice versa); (2) flight beyond the boundaries of state control; (3) abandonment of normal subsistence activities to join a sectarian community, cult, or millenarian movement; and (4) switching occupations entirely to become a bandit, a member of a traveling theater/circus troupe, a domestic servant, or a wage laborer. These tactics diminish the potential for direct conflict between peasants and oppressive elites and ameliorate resource stress on the individual or household by stemming dependence on a patron.

Consequently, escalation of forms of protest from passive footdragging to violent confrontation is not a unilineal process. The timing and the methods of resistance by which peasants manage state and elite intrusion into the local economy depend on several variables. First, the extent to which peasants retain control over different factors of the production process (land, labor, capital, and product) and the extent to which control over one or more factors is threatened will influence the methods and process of resistance (Stanford 1991:71). For example, sabotage of a landlord's mechanical harvester was an effective tactic employed by semiproletarian farmers in Malaysia (Scott 1985:248–49), because mechanization would obviate the need for human labor, a production factor that peasants controlled. Smallholding agriculturalists, however, are more concerned over loss of land ownership (Netting 1993). Autonomous control of land is essential for practicing the micromanagerial strategies that enable self-sufficiency and prevent smallholders from being squeezed into tenancy or other shareholding arrangements.

Alienation of land or any other production factor, however, is more than just a threat to household subsistence. Systems of production and cultivation are inextricably linked to meaning, peasant identity, sociopolitical relations, and the ritual cycles and religious fabric of rural agricultural communities. Systems of hegemony intersect, interweave, and even conflict across these dimensions as power is exercised in different forms and at different levels within a community (Ortner 1995:179). Specific forms of resistance are not always diagnostic of a single, overarching power structure (Abu-Lughod 1990), but resistance tactics and strategies may signal broader arenas or "sites" of struggle.

Second, the degree to which the patron-client relationship satisfies peasant expectations of physical security and subsistence is important (see also Johnson 1971; Scott and Kerkvliet 1977). When the balance of resource flows becomes too lopsided, or when the nature, number, or cost of reciprocal services shifts, clients may exercise several options. Where demand for labor is high and factional competition among elites is prevalent, clients may switch their loyalties to different patrons. If coercion is exercised to enforce the asymmetry of resource flows or to extort compliance in return for protection, client loyalty suffers, and patrons rapidly lose legitimacy (Scott and Kerkvliet 1977:449). Where open frontiers are located nearby or where the social boundaries of surrounding communities are open, migration and flight are options that often permit disenfranchised peasant households to improve access to means of production. The costs of such moves are weighed against the value of existing horizontal and vertical ties within the community of origin and against the risk of personal danger on the frontier. Direct confrontation and violent rebellion develop as patrons lose legitimacy, avoidance protest becomes less effective, and the growth of dissident ideologies garners outside support and promotes peasant mobilization over wide areas (Adas 1981:246–47).

In this context the debates about land pressure acquire renewed importance. As Cline (1947:430) points out, "The single most important agricultural activity in Yucatán was the production of maize. Whether measured by value, by acreage, or by its place in the thoughts of laborers, the ancient cereal was still pre-eminent." The principal method for producing maize in Maya communities was the cultivation of milpa, a sustainable agro-ecological system in which micromanagement of household and community land and labor permitted long-term harvest of the greatest diversity of tropical forest products with the lowest risk of ecological depletion (Arias Reyes et al. 1998; Faust 1998; Gómez-Pompa et al. 1990; Hernández Xolocotzi 1980; Nations and Nigh 1980; Re-Cruz 1996; Rico-Gray et al. 1990; Turner and Miksicek 1984). Milpa cultivation also is inextricably linked to household autonomy, ethnic identity, local politics, and religion and ritual. Its practice transforms the landscape, the built environment within settlements, and the meanings attached to spatial structure, spatial grammars, and the movement and actions of individuals among various contexts (Hanks 1990). Whether planted in maize *(col)* or reserved in states of subsequent vegetative succession *(kax)*, land is the key factor of milpa production. Its sale, inheritance, usufruct rights, measurement, and transfer are principal topics of every major collection of Maya-language documents discovered on the Yucatán peninsula (Restall 1997; Roys 1939; Thompson 1978, 2000). Given that Maya agriculture has never been a purely economic activity, arguments that relate resistance to land use are hardly unidimensional.

Because property rights, land ownership, and alienation of produce through rents, taxes, or labor services directly affect smallholders' control over milpa cultivation, they are important variables for understanding propensity of different forms of resistance across the peninsula (see Netting 1993:326–29). The structure and autonomy of agricultural practice is linked to land ownership, which helps explain why avoidance protest was the norm for some peasants and cultivators in Yaxcabá, whereas violent confrontation was preferred among smallholders in areas to the east. Dumond (1997), however, is correct in concluding that land pressure was not a cause of the Caste War. To a large extent, the issue has been conceptualized too simplistically. The ordinary response to land stress is not rebellion but intensification. Land pressure is a function of population, agricultural technology, and ecology and cannot be characterized as either present or absent. Smallholders and extensive shifting cultivators respond differently to land availability. Furthermore, intensification, like resistance, also takes many forms and is not a unilinear process (Boserup 1965; Kirch 1994; Morrison 1994, 1996; Stone 1996). Increased labor inputs, introduction or development of new or hybrid crops or animals, alteration of microwatersheds for irrigation or drainage, field dispersal, overproduction, storage, exchange, and migration are all tactics (singly or combined) by which the Maya have managed the balance of population to resources through the ages. Smallholders may respond to stress through intensification, but generally the ability and willingness to intensify and the choice of tactics depends not on stress but on the security of property rights to the land improvements that underwrite intensification (Netting 1993). In contrast, for extensive or shifting cultivators for whom land is plentiful, decisions to intensify production are predicated on size and composition of the household, especially the ratio of workers to dependents (Chayanov 1986; Netting 1993:305, 318). The origins of the Caste War aside, I contend that land use and intensification remain critically important for explaining the transformation of agrarian structure in nineteenth-century Yucatán. Understanding why Maya farmers in Yaxcabá abandoned forms of avoidance protest, embraced the Caste War, and consequently still retain control over agricultural production implies an understanding of tropical agro-ecology.

Long-term Perspectives on Resistance

To formulate an adequate theory about the role of peasant resistance and rebellion in the process of globalization is a methodological challenge for those who study the past. Early on, most social scientists that studied the relationship between peasant agrarian conflict and the expansion of capitalism worked with present-day or at least recent, twentieth-century cases (Scott 1976, 1985, 1990; Skocpol 1979; Tilly 1978; Wolf 1969). As this research progressed, there was a growing recognition that such studies were too synchronic. Capitalist expansion was a variable process conditioned by the history of a specific region's articulation with the larger world (Wolf 1982). Historical perspectives and the analysis of resistance as a long-term process have much to offer in understanding the relation of agrarian change to peasant rebellion.

The progressivism described by Cline in Yucatán was a local manifestation of a larger, long-term culture process in nineteenth-century Latin America (Charlton 1986, 2003; Wolf 1956). Charlton (2003:224; see also Charlton 1986), for example, has summarized the process as a series of general stages, widely comparable across most regions in Mexico:

(1) contact, political and economic conquest, and depopulation (c. 1521–1650);
(2) continuing depressed indigenous populations and stagnant economies (c. 1650–1750);

(3) the gradual increase in indigenous population leading to pressure on lands, a surplus of indigenous labor, accompanied by politically directed economic reforms and economic growth, increasing outside pressure on indigenous lands (c. 1750–1821);

(4) the wars of independence, the accompanying loss of crown protection for indigenous rights, the development of a national Mexican economy, and the integration of that economy into a world economy particularly during the late nineteenth century (c. 1821–1910); and

(5) the socialist revolution of the early twentieth century, which recognized the development of a national agrarian production system for urban areas and for export that had effectively supplied an alternative to the hacienda system, which was then eliminated for political expediency (c. 1910–40).

Characteristics of the process include indigenous population growth; modification of rural production and landholding under the pressure of market forces; removal of legal protection for Indian lands, which consequently came under pressure by nonindigenous persons; and inadequate native resistance undermined by conflicts of interest between elites and commoners within indigenous societies (Charlton 2003). As Mexico was severed from Spain, fledgling state institutions had to find new ways to realign themselves with world economy, deal with U.S. aggression, satisfy innumerable factions of feuding elites, and find new ways to make the hinterlands productive. Although in Yucatán the march of globalization was severely retarded by a successful native rebellion, the Caste War was not the lone indigenous conflict of the era. The period leading up to the Mexican revolution was punctuated by a number of revolts such as the 1840s peasant wars in Guerrero, the Yaqui rebellion in Sonora, the Sierra Gorda revolt in Central Mexico, and the Cora rebellion (Joseph 1988, 1985:119; Kyle 2003; Nugent 1998). Trajectories of agrarian change in these areas were consequently altered by violent, grassroots protest.

The demand for diachronic and comparative studies of resistance has resulted in two trends: (1) working with expanded time frames; and (2) specifying regional and subregional patterns. Stern (1987:9–12), for example, recommends that historians and social scientists look at the development of long-term patterns by which peasants politically engage the state—what he calls resistant adaptations—for times of quiescence as well as rebellion. Without detailed analysis of preexisting structures of resistance and accommodation, he argues, explanations of the causes of rebellion remain superficial, and is it impossible to develop an adequate theory about the use of violence as a form of resistance. Stern's recommendation entails the selection and study of longer time frames—centuries rather than decades—in order to contextualize resistance.

Joseph (1991; see also Adas 1986, 1991; Ortner 1995), by contrast, acknowledges that distinguishing acts of resistance from common crime or survival tactics is problematic for historians. Because subaltern groups interact multidimensionally, the "intentional" quality of resistance is difficult to infer. Indeed, intentionality may not be a very useful distinction when focusing on variation in global transformations in space and time (Ortner 1995:175). Joseph recommends microhistorical research and in-depth assessment of local hegemonic settings as a remedy for addressing past structures of defiance.

As intellectually appealing as these newer trends are, several problems in studying historical resistance have emerged. First, as the unit of analysis becomes smaller, either in time or space, available historical data often diminish. Documents written in Yucatec Maya are rare, and only in a few cases are there sufficient numbers of them to permit one to write the historical ethnography of a specific community.[4] In Yaxcabá, for example, only two Maya-language documents survive. One records the sale of land from a Maya family to a Creole. The other disputes the sale of a plot located on the main plaza in Yaxcabá on which the *audiencia* of the *república de indios* (administrative councils) once stood. Although the documents are interesting, they do not provide sufficient evidence to characterize Maya attitudes toward the causes of their economic subordination on a microhistorical level.

Second, although numerous Spanish-language documents may be available for a specific community or region, they may be uneven, clustered in time, and present only the discourse of the dominant Creole class. A holistic view of community organization that includes the Maya agriculturalist remains elusive. For example, in Yaxcabá and other communities of central Yucatán, most recorded acts of defiance are those that presented a challenge to Creole authority, such as disrespect for the mayor and assaults or insult to justices of the peace. These "crimes" or acts of resistance occurred at a time when local town councils systematically sought to dismantle the authority of the Maya *cacique* or *batab* (Rugeley 1997). Other forms of Maya resistance, such as flight, however, were only briefly mentioned or undocumented, because these acts were less threatening to Creoles. Although the historical record informs us of individual acts that run contrary to the prevailing system of domination, it fails to provide insight into the organization of those behaviors, a system of resistance, or in Stern's terms, "a resistant adaptation."

Although the combination of expanded time frames and a focus on individual communities is impractical for many social researchers, it is precisely these spatial and temporal scales that most archaeologists work with on a regular basis. Like recent trends among historians, a chief concern for archaeologists is the agency and autonomy of different groups of political actors that inhabit the countryside relative to the institutions of domination. Long-term studies risk losing sight of rural people, assuming they are swept along with the tide of regional political-economic forces. For this reason, archaeologists have focused on the household as a suitable unit of analysis for assessing the interplay of state intervention and the arrangement of different behaviors and activities that comprise the overall strategy of the coresidential unit (see Wilk 1991:34–40). Because Cline's progressive thesis specifically concerns relations between state institutions and rural areas in Yucatán, household archaeology has a unique ability to shed light on the agrarian transformation of the nineteenth century.

Nevertheless, resistance (as defined by social researchers who work in the present) is a difficult concept for archaeologists to implement. The archaeological record reflects redundant sets of past behaviors and their organization, rather than the intentions that lay behind them. Household organization follows from the mixture of defensive, survival, accommodative, and resistant activities regularly performed by its members. The meaning or intention attached to any particular activity may shift relative to the individual performing it or to its context at different points in time. Because the criterion of intention determines whether a particular action is "resistant," archaeologists generally infer resistance only for specific situations where the system of domination is already well understood and where material culture occurs in contexts that clearly indicate clandestine behavior.[5] Because resistance has been conceptualized mentalistically rather than behaviorally, its application in archaeology (as in history) would seem to be limited in its current form.

By contrast, many specific acts of defiance, forms of avoidance protest, and conditions that spark transitions from noncompliance to confrontation are readily identifiable in the archaeological record. Acts of vandalism and destruction directed against particular institutions often target the buildings and infrastructure that house their operations (Fry 1985).[6] Roofless and crumbling churches and chapels, burned-out haciendas, and the wreckage of elite houses still scar the architectural landscape in Yaxcabá. Even cattle rustling has its material consequences. Disposing of remains, such as the head, in cenotes or shallow limestone caves often hid the clandestine killing and consumption of the animals.[7]

Other sources of archaeological data are useful for contextualizing arenas of resistance or "sites" of struggle. Archaeological settlement patterns can help assess tendencies for dispersal, drift, and flight. Similarly, the location, size, and internal arrangement of sectarian communities, such as the estates of religious confraternities, can enlighten views of this kind of avoidance protest. Land stress and agricultural intensification are empirical questions in archaeology. The disposition of human settlement and its spatial structure strongly reflects how strategies of production and consumption are connected to their ecological underpinnings. Advances in spatial analysis, often referred to as site structure, further inform investigators about ordinary quotidian activities such as labor organization, production, or consumption within residential locales.

Finally, insights into patron-client relationships and class structure are provided by the study of architecture and material culture (Allison 1999; Hayden and Cannon 1984; Hayden and Gargett 1990; Santley 1993). Consumption and display of nonlocal items, symbols and motifs, ostentatious architectural elements, or the restricted distribution of scarce resources (that is, particular foods or technology) may signal differences in class, division of labor, ethnicity, identity, or gender roles within communities. Although such investigations are not geared to "infer resistance," they convey contextual information about potential areas of struggle and thus the propensity for various resistant practices to develop.

Consequently, further progress in understanding Maya behavioral organization and resistant activities in Yaxcabá can be obtained through archaeological investigation. The results, however, rely on comparison of archaeological spatial variability against two independent theoretical frameworks (sensu Binford 2001): (1) detailed historical control, drawn from the analysis of documentary sources, over the hegemonic structure of state and rural relations in Yucatán, especially those that affected household organization in Yaxcabá; and (2) a general analogy developed from the study of settlement ecology for smallholders living in tropical settings, specifically a model called settlement agriculture (Killion 1992; Netting 1993; Stone 1996; Wilk 1991).

State and Rural Relations

Understanding the development of resistant adaptations, though they are not normally termed as such in anthropology, is strongly related to the comparative archaeological research on state and rural relations. Processes by which states, empires, or other macroregional systems expand and collapse are predicated on the ways in which the activities of rural inhabitants articulate with its central political, economic, and ideological institutions (Brumfiel 1993; Schwartz and Falconer 1994). In general, states and colonial regimes are extractive. Political institutions regulate the state's economy in order to accrue resources such as weaponry, means of communication, agricultural staples, and prestige goods so that they may deploy them in state-sponsored activities that include the use of coercive power, expensive construction ventures, long-distance trade, alliance formation, and maintenance of political control (Brumfiel 1993; Brumfiel and Earle 1987; Claessen and van de Velde 1991; Wolf 1956). They interfere in local production because agrarian households as a rule do not generate large amounts of produce in excess of that needed for their own consumption and the avoidance of local conditions that produce shortage (Brumfiel 1993; Chayanov 1986:5; Sahlins 1972:101; Schwartz and Falconer 1994; Wolf 1956; cf. Netting 1993:297–319). The extent of state interference depends on its capacity to control labor and resource flows over distance (Cowgill 1988; Hassig 1985; Stein 1998, 1999). The efficiency and capacity of transportation systems, military organization, the ease with which new technology may be replicated in rural areas, and the ability of rural elites and bureaucracies to retain resources within the provinces all affect state success. In the process of modern global expansion, these variables have been manipulated to foster a worldwide division of labor such that rural peripheries that supply raw materials become dependent on an industrialized, manufacturing core (Braudel 1984; Smith et al. 1984; Wallerstein 1974; Wallerstein and Smith 1992).

When states or empires politically and economically incorporate hinterlands, however, they do so selectively (Brumfiel 1993; Morrison 2001; Small and Tannenbaum 1999). In general, where sources of food, labor, and specific products are critical for state operations, the degree of central management is heavy-handed. Conversely, some goods and forms of daily subsistence production spark little notice or supervision by civil or religious officials. Furthermore, production in rural areas is not clearly divided between the urban state/elites and rural subsistence agriculturalists. Rather, a number of elite and nonelite interest groups have a hand in organizing production, distribution, and consumption in rural areas.

Although the ways in which states manipulate the relations of production vary widely, historically known colonial regimes extract resources from distant peripheries by establishing a dual economy. Most colonial systems follow a general pattern in which indigenous land, labor, or other primary resources are appropriated from subsistence producers and channeled into the production of cash crops or other commodities that can be lucratively exported (Geertz 1963; Wolf 1982). In Latin America colonial policies usually created a series of scheduling conflicts between the amounts of land and labor needed for subsistence production and that needed for the production of cash crops. This produced ecological crises in some areas as indigenous groups were deprived of the capacity to respond to shortage (Gibson 1964; Gross et al. 1979; Halstead and O'Shea 1989; MacLeod 1973; Strickon 1965). Labor shortages, whether the result of indigenous demographic decline or an increase in the demand for labor, frequently led to the transformation of productive institutions (Borah 1951; Wolf 1956, 1982).

From the perspective of the farmer, however, the expansion of colonial regimes is a variable process in which the structure and allocation of social labor are negotiated over time (Wolf 1982:74–75, 1990). Changes in the use of primary resources and access to the means of production (labor, tools, land) may entail significant modifications to production strategies at the household and community levels (see, for example, Little 1987; Netting 1993; Stier 1982). Households respond to economic change through migration, intensification, diversification, specialization, market participation, storage, and exchange. Nevertheless, their members select appropriate responses by assessing the availability of labor and resources. Smallholders, for example, generally intensify production and develop markets for their produce whenever and wherever possible, regardless of the extractive measures employed by authorities (Netting 1993:288–94, 239). The aim of these activities is to create an inheritance that keeps filial generations tied to the household and community.

The idea that colonial and capitalist expansion results in an inevitable polarization between landlord commercial farmers and landless, poverty-stricken workers is not demonstrated in recent studies of agriculturalists and their relations to the global economy. Rather, the process produces peasant economic stratification and differentiation in the ownership of farmland, producing a spectrum ranging from noncultivating landlords to landless laborers (Hayami and Kikuchi 1982; Netting 1993:214–21). Where further intensification of production is limited or where land and produce are alienated from the household's control, wage labor, cash cropping, or nonagricultural production can provide crucial income that may ameliorate shortage and subsistence risk (Chayanov 1986). Participation in the global economy is often, but not always, accompanied by increased consumption of nonlocal secondary products (Charlton 1972; Wilk 1991).

Households and Colonialism in Yucatán

The relationship between individual households and colonial states is generally adversarial. Households attempt to retain the fruits of their labor for their own use, whereas the state attempts to extract resources from them. The adversarial relationship, whether resources are ceded to a centralized authority or whether resource use remains locally autonomous, is continually negotiated at the household, community, and regional levels. The household constitutes an interface for this process of negotiation; it is the level at which social groups articulate directly with economic and ecological processes (Netting 1993; Wilk 1991; Wilk and Rathje 1982). Originally defined as observable coresidential units (Murdock 1949), households lately have been categorized on the basis of their function, including production, consumption, pooling of resources, coresidence, reproduction, transmission, and shared ownership (Ashmore and Wilk 1988; Blanton 1994; Netting et al. 1984). They form a nexus of actions and behaviors that are continually reorganized on short-term and long-term bases.

The imposition of the Spanish colonial regime and the later policies of the independent national government severely affected the economic and household organizational strategies of the indigenous communities in Yucatán. The effectiveness with which the state penetrated rural areas and extracted resources, however, was variable. Interaction between households and the state over time produced a resistant adaptation—a pattern of interaction that successfully prevented the most excessive forms of state intrusion. Because households were able to maintain various degrees of self-sufficiency and autonomy, extractive claims by elites, the state, and the church were partially denied, and these individuals and institutions were ineffective in fostering peasant dependency (see Wolf 1990).

Two major sources of risk are associated with agriculture in Yucatán: (1) a propensity for frequent crop failures due to catastrophes such as drought, tropical storms, and insects; and (2) the likelihood of reduced yields due to overcultivation of the land under conditions of increased population density and shortened fallow (Farriss 1984; Sanders and Webster 1978). In light of the relationship among agricultural risk, population density, and the environment in the Maya Lowlands, a dispersed pattern of settlements and house lots was the preferred solution to improving or at least maintaining agricultural productivity under conditions of increasing population (Drennan 1988; Sharer 1994). After the conquest, however, conditions imposed by the Spanish colonial regime altered Maya settlement patterns.

Three critical changes occurred following the Spanish conquest that altered settlement, land use, and agricultural risk in Yucatán. First, the introduction of European pathogens initiated a drastic decline of the indigenous population. Epidemics alternated with episodes of famine, and from 1545 to 1750 the population fluctuated, eventually reaching a low point—an estimated decline of half to two-thirds—in the late 1600s (Cook and Borah 1979; Farriss 1984; Garcia Bernal 1978; Patch 1993). Second, civil and ecclesiastical authorities imposed tribute and labor drafts in which the production of exportable goods was placed in competition with subsistence production for land and labor resources. Third, the policy of *congregación* forcibly aggregated Maya settlements. The Maya population was removed from hamlets and villages and forced to reside in designated cabeceras (municipal seats) and visitas (auxiliary towns) under the supervision of Spanish authorities (Relaciones Histórico-Geográficos 1983; Scholes and Adams 1938; Scholes et al. 1938).

These changes affected household production strategies in several ways. Demographic decline, for instance, could produce a shortage of labor within the household itself, within the community, and among communities within a region. Fluctuations in the ratio of producers to dependents within the household may have affected patterns of intensification, labor exchange, and the potential for surplus production. The forced aggregation of settlement may have restricted options of field placement and probably altered the amounts and locations of maize storage (in the house lot or in the field). Although towns were relocated, the inhabitants retained the right to cultivate lands near their former residences (Roys 1939). Retention of cultivation rights in places of former residence was problematic since information about other cultivators in the area, ecological and crop conditions, and trespassers was not as readily available to farmers. Distance to agricultural plots was often far, resulting in an increase in travel time and a reduction in labor efficiency.

Attempts to redisperse settlement occurred early after congregación and continued gradually throughout the Colonial period in response to local population growth. With the increased demand on resources brought by tribute payments and the introduction of new domesticated animals and cultigens, the exploitation of a more heterogeneous range of resources occurred. Subsistence activities that supplemented agriculture in Yucatán included the cultivation of citrus and other fruit trees, hunting, beekeeping, raising poultry, and occasionally raising horses and goats. In some cases the colonial regime regulated diversification, particularly in raising large livestock *(ganado mayor)* and through miscellaneous obventions assessed for the sale of goods.

During the late eighteenth and early nineteenth centuries, the relationship between population and land changed again. After 1750, the indigenous population of Yucatán began to grow rapidly; this episode of population increase corresponded to the growth and establishment of haciendas. These were large, Spanish-American-owned estates that produced agricultural products, livestock, or other goods for market by attracting and binding a large resident Maya labor force to the estate through debt peonage. Maya labor was incorporated onto the haciendas to varying degrees (Bracamonte y Sosa 1984; Patch 1993; Strickon 1965). Sugarcane- and henequen-producing haciendas had large resident labor forces, whereas small numbers of permanent employees operated cattle estates. The extent to which specific cash crops were compatible with maize cultivation also differed. Sugar and cattle estates directly competed for land needed for milpa cultivation, whereas henequen could be grown without encroaching on land needed for maize (Cline 1947; Strickon 1965). Land availability combined with population increase and the varying potential for haciendas to absorb the population dramatically altered local agrarian autonomy.

Disenfranchisement and Credit

In nineteenth-century Yucatán, two processes were particularly important in determining the articulations between rural households and the state: disenfranchisement from land, and the formation of vertical economic relationships that extended credit. "Disenfranchisement" is defined here as a process by which access to the means of production is restricted. In Yucatán ownership of land is critical to agricultural production and intensification. Extension of credit allows farmers to overcome subsistence shortfalls by borrowing either the subsistence resources themselves or the means to produce them from others. Economic relationships that provide credit in time of need may be established horizontally or vertically (see Johnson 1971; Scott and Kerkvliet 1977). Relationships established among members of the same social class, particularly between real or fictive kin, are horizontal and often long-term, whereas economic relationships between individuals of unequal social class constitute vertical exchange contracts of varying duration. These dyadic contracts acquire a different dynamic with the introduction of a cash economy. Opportunities to form vertical economic relations involving monetary-based credit became increasingly available in the context of hacienda expansion after 1821. They probably had a significant effect on the convertibility and liquidity of exchange contracts, and they altered existing patron-client relations, horizontal and reciprocal labor obligations between households, and labor organization within the household.

Restriction of ownership and access to land in Yucatán directly affected subsistence productivity and the household's ability to pay tribute and taxes. Dispersal was a response that avoided both problems; it conferred greater access to land and potential for agricultural intensification while avoiding tribute. In the early nineteenth century continued dispersal was not an option, and partial disenfranchisement resulted in the need to adopt additional productive strategies to compensate for potentially lower yields. Several options were available: (1) intensification and diversification of production within the privately owned house lot; (2) wage labor; and (3) renting land or sharecropping for a patron. Whether individuals' choices among these options created factional and ideological tensions within communities, as they do today, can only be surmised (see Re-Cruz 1996).

Before the Caste War, central Yucatán did not have a diversified, broad-spectrum economy, and conversion of specie to produce was frequently difficult. Money was useful for meeting tribute obligations, and acquiring it usually required the establishment of a vertical exchange contract. Although some religious taxes were paid in maize, tribute obligations were increasingly met in silver or in specific products such as cotton cloth, honey, or beeswax. The expansion of the cash economy complicated the relations of production in the region. Loans of cash, produce, or the means of production could be subsequently remunerated in a variety of ways, including cash, produce, labor, or political support. The frequency of such transactions, the direction of the relationship between parties, and the duration of the contract or relationship were also variable, and they determined whether each of the aforementioned tactics were useful for ameliorating periodic shortages.

In nineteenth-century Yucatán, property rights could be maintained through individual ownership or by entering into credit arrangements of varying degrees of intensity, duration, and commitment. Creoles who owned large tracts of land, however, did not always use them principally for agricultural production. Cattle raising provided little impetus for hacienda owners to seek subsistence agriculturalist clients. Instead the land was used to produce a more lucrative, more liquid, and easily convertible asset that permitted hacienda owners to participate more fully in the emerging market economy. Cattle raising with subsidiary maize cultivation was a non-labor-intensive activity and, ultimately, it incorporated only a small proportion of the regional population as a permanent or semipermanent resident labor force. Consequently, Maya farmers often faced conditions of disenfranchisement from land coupled with limited possibilities for establishing vertical economic relationships that ensured the extension of credit. The range of tactics that could potentially compensate for shortfalls in household production effectively prohibited them from participating in the macroregional economy rather than fostering it.

Settlement Ecology and Settlement Agriculture

Milpa cultivation in all of its forms creates a recognizable signature in the archaeological record. Thanks to the intensive research efforts of ethnographers, ethnoarchaeologists, ethnohistorians, and biologists, we now have firm ideas about how variation in agricultural intensity in the humid tropics affects spatial patterning within settlements and across regional landscapes. This area of study is known as "settlement" or "household ecology." It examines the relationship between patterns of settlement and household production by analyzing the ecological substrate on which strategies of production and consumption are based (Stone 1996:11). Collectively these studies supply a frame of reference (sensu Binford 2001) for analyzing and interpreting archaeological patterns. Understanding range of variability in milpa cultivation, or any other system of behavioral organization, such that one can specify how a limited number of variables structure the spatial distribution of material culture, creates a solid basis for the exercise of analogical reasoning and archaeological interpretation.

In lowland Mesoamerica, the risks of overexploitation of fragile soils present great challenges for resource management in tropical forest ecosystems. The cultivation of milpa is the cornerstone of agricultural strategies in the humid tropics, in which a plot is cleared, burned, and planted in corn, beans, squash, and other cultigens. Traditional views of Maya agriculture identify the milpa with extensive swidden cultivation of uniformly poor, shallow soils. Under conditions of low population density, the tendency toward declining yields on plots cultivated two to three consecutive years is offset by shifting the plot to a new area and allowing the original field to lie fallow for at least two years for every year of cultivation (Sharer 1994:435). Farmers may cultivate a number of widely dispersed milpa plots, some of primary forest land (*milpa roza*) and others of secondary growth (*milpa de caña*) (Granado Baeza 1845; Redfield and Villa Rojas 1934). Because one-third or more of the available land is likely fallow at any one time, however, the broad distribution of agricultural plots was thought to encourage dispersal of settlement (Morley and Brainerd 1956).

In seasons of peak agricultural activity, farmers may move their family residence to the milpa, establishing *milperíos* or *rancherías* (outlying hamlets). Under conditions of population growth, the milperíos may become permanent settlements, especially if they improve farmers' access to uncultivated, primary forest lands (Redfield and Villa Rojas 1934). Because dispersed settlement, communal land tenure, and swidden cultivation do not encourage agricultural intensification or land conservation, these techniques have been decried as wasteful and detrimental to Yucatecan economic development since the mid-nineteenth century (Regil and Peon 1853).

During the last twenty-five years, however, research in archaeology, ethnohistory, and ethnography has demonstrated that the swidden hypothesis mischaracterizes the complexity and intensity of Maya subsistence (Faust 1998; Fedick 1996; Flannery 1982; Turner and Harrison 1978; Wilken 1971). First, archaeological investigations show that milpa cultivation occurred on continuously cultivated fields as well within fallow systems. The evidence points to the intensive use of permanent raised fields, terraces, fenced plots improved by furrows, and household gardens in the pre-Hispanic period. Furthermore, the soils of the Yucatán peninsula are not uniformly poor and shallow. Farmers differentially exploited the microenvironmental diversity of wetlands, upland zones, coastal areas, and geomorphologic features such as cenotes and *rejolladas* (Dunning 1996; Gómez-Pompa et al. 1990; Kepecs and Boucher 1996; Schmidt 1980). Hillside terraces, horticulture in moisture-retaining rejolladas, and raised fields at the edges of wetlands provided opportunities for "locational intensification" where farmers could modify natural landscape features to improve production (see Stone 1996:52–53).

Second, ethnohistorical research indicates that Landa's description of milpa cultivation has been inadequately contextualized (Sharer 1994). Although he described a slash-and-burn technique for making milpa, additional historical sources indicate the prevalence of household gardens, orchards, and specialized cultivation of cash crops, such as cacao (Marcus 1982; Restall 1997; Tozzer 1941). Taken together these sources attest that sixteenth-century subsistence was not based solely on shifting cultivation. Not surprisingly, the evidence also points to diverse forms of land tenure that include private ownership, joint ownership, and complex usufruct arrangements in the sixteenth through eighteenth centuries. Communal land tenure (in the strict sense of the term) was comparatively rare (Restall 1997; Thompson 1978, 2000).

Finally, ethnographic research demonstrates that the milpa is not the sole source of subsistence. Rather, it is embedded within a more diverse strategy that includes household gardening, tree horticulture, hunting and gathering, fishing, and animal husbandry (Faust 1998; Hellmuth 1977; Hernández Xolocotzi 1980; McAnany 1995; Nations and Nigh 1980). Milpa cultivation takes place within the forest and modifies rather than replaces the natural ecosystem. In addition to planting traditional cultigens, farmers may protect and tend wild resources, leave a portion of the crop unharvested as a means to attract game, and plant fruit trees to improve a plot's utility during fallow periods. The house lot, or *solar,* also is a crucial component of the subsistence system. In the area surrounding the dwelling, Maya householders raise domestic animals and cultivate gardens sown in maize, herbs, chilies, squash, fruit trees, and other agricultural products. According to Re-Cruz (1996:109–10), Faust (1998), and others, the milpa is an agronomic system that permits household self-sufficiency by satisfying its basic consumption needs. A large variety of necessary items are produced in small quantities, a practice that absorbs resources, time, and knowledge that otherwise would go to waste.

Practice of the most extensive system of swidden cultivation probably dates to the early nineteenth through the mid-twentieth centuries when settlement nucleation was enforced and metal tools became increasingly available (Granado Baeza 1845; Nations and Nigh 1980; Sharer 1994: 437). Radical demographic fluctuation and experiments in agrarian policy under the Constitution of Cadiz, the War for Mexican Independence, and the Mexican Revolution characterize the era (Cline 1947; Dumond 1997; Güemez Pineda 1994). Various policies encouraged settlement nucleation, imposed communal status on lands around communities, deprived Maya authorities of control over land tenure, and legitimated Creole colonization and privatization of open crown lands. Between 1847 and 1900 the Caste War of Yucatán prompted significant demographic decline (30 to 60 percent) and massive displacement of the indigenous population. Following the Mexican Revolution, rural farmers acquired land in the form of grants of communal ejidos and established numerous pioneer settlements (Joseph 1988; Redfield and Villa Rojas 1934; Steggerda 1941). Under conditions of low population density, swidden was a reasonable subsistence strategy, which gave way to more intensive forms of cultivation as the population increased in the late twentieth century.

Current ethnographic investigations in the realm of "household ecology" have improved our understanding of milpa agriculture and its relationship to Maya household organization. The particular balance of agricultural tactics and their scheduling affects household form, optimum work group size, and labor efficiency (Wilk 1983, 1984, 1991:180–203). Among the Kekchi Maya who practice swidden cultivation under conditions of low population density, Richard Wilk (1991) has shown that household and community organization are strongly related to the diversification of labor strategies within a mobile subsistence cycle. The ecological requirements of swidden cultivation place constraints on viable organizations of labor, which in turn is reflected in the spatial patterns among dwellings.

Farmers inhabiting relatively new settlements and cultivating milpa within primary forest according to a linear labor schedule with few bottlenecks tend to reside in individual household units consisting of a single principal dwelling. As the radius of primary forest land becomes more distant from the settlement, farmers begin to cultivate mixtures of primary and secondary forest and diversify productive activities within the house lot. In villages where farmers cultivate primary and secondary forest, grow dry-season crops, practice cash cropping, or pursue craft specialties or wage labor, the agricultural calendar is more complex, and bottlenecks in the sequencing of tasks become problematic. Households in these villages tend to form clusters, consisting of two or more principal dwellings, creating intermediate-size labor groups (beyond the nuclear family) capable of performing subsistence tasks simultaneously. Ultimately the domestic cycle and strategies of diversification and intensification reach a threshold where the household fissions, and sometimes farmers migrate to new primary forest land, establishing a new community. Under these conditions, dispersed settlement is a form of agricultural intensification (Drennan 1988; see also Stone 1996). As the radius of cultivation expands around a settlement, relocation of household labor nearer to one's fields enhances oversight and management of microenvironmental variability within agricultural plots.

Contemporary investigations of settlement ecology in tropical Mesoamerica have developed a new model that reconciles extensive swidden practices with the evidence for more intensive cultivation. This model, known as "settlement agriculture," explains the relationships among the organization of agriculture, the social organization of the household, and the spatial patterns of domestic residential compounds (Hanks 1990; Killion 1990, 1992:5–6; Killion et al. 1989; Sanders and Killion 1992; Santley and Hirth 1993; Smyth 1990). The intensity of land use is viewed as a continuum, divided between monocropped outfields located more than 45 minutes from the residence, multicropped infields located less than 45 minutes from the residence, and kitchen gardens. Cultivators in the tropics often employ short-fallow and intensive agricultural techniques on infields close to the settlement, whereas they practice long-fallow and extensive techniques on more distant outfield plots and on other marginal lands. The settlement zone itself harbors "dooryard" or house-lot gardens and constitutes the permanently and intensively cultivated sector within the system.

Within settlements throughout Mesoamerica, the basic unit of residence is the house lot, or solar. It constitutes the focal point where households perform fundamental activities of production, consumption, pooling of resources, coresidence, reproduction, transmission, and shared ownership (Ashmore and Wilk 1988; Netting et al. 1984). Household activity groups are linked to places and spaces where actions are carried out—the house lot, the settlement, and the region. As an archaeological unit of analysis, the household becomes a nested series of spatial contexts through which actions, behaviors, and interactions are performed. As households change, the arrangement of activities varies. Some behaviors may be dropped from practice or added to the household repertoire, or the importance and amount of labor dedicated to one or more productive activities may increase or decrease relative to others (Chayanov 1986).

Defining households on the basis of "what they do" is a workable concept for archaeologists investigating the relationships among settlement ecology, site structure, production, and labor organization (Hammel 1984; Santley and Hirth 1993; Stone 1996; Wilk 1991; Wilk and Netting 1984; Wilk and Rathje 1982).

Although modifications to the household repertoire are not always accompanied by new technology, variation in the organization of activities is reflected faithfully in the spatial patterning of the house lot. House-lot space is differentiated and concentrically arranged; a patio and garden surround the dwelling. Because the patio serves as a staging area for agricultural activities, the relative size of patios and gardens within house lots reflects varying intensity among the components of the settlement agriculture continuum, especially cultivation of fields at varying distances from the residence (Killion 1987, 1990). In situations where infield cultivation was intensified, patios were large, reflecting a need to conduct preparatory activities close to home, whereas in situations where outfield cultivation was emphasized, patios were small. In the latter case, agricultural staging activities were usually relocated to field houses.

The arrangement of house lots within settlements may be dispersed or aggregated. Dispersal clearly is related to agricultural intensification. Establishment of a milperío transforms extensively cultivated outfields to permanently and intensively cultivated house-lot gardens. Although dispersal is the norm, aggregation may occur where local conditions override this tendency. Overriding conditions include the need for defense, an uneven or clustered distribution of water sources, availability of arable land, or greater efficiency in exploiting widely distributed ecozones from a central location (Killion 1992; Stone 1996; Wilk 1991).

Aggregated settlement patterns also may be imposed by state bureaucracies, as occurred under the policy of congregación in the Early Colonial period and again in the 1840s with the implementation of new land legislation in Yucatán (see discussion below in Chapter 3). When aggregation is accompanied by changes in the size and spatial organization of the house lot, it usually indicates change in household composition and the strategies of agricultural production.

By focusing on the house lot, "settlement agriculture" can be applied to most time periods in the Maya Lowlands. Today in Yucatán, house lots are bounded by dry-laid stone walls (albarradas) and contain dwelling structures surrounded by a patio and refuse-laden garden. The garden zone is used for a variety of activities including cultivation of dry-season corn crops, tree horticulture, beekeeping, and small livestock raising. Milpa plots are cultivated at varying distances from the settlement, between 1 and 7 km, and the diversity of cultigens in different plots varies depending on soil characteristics (Arias Reyes 1980; Arias Reyes et al. 1998; Smyth 1990). At pre-Hispanic sites in Yucatán, dwellings and outbuildings were situated on large platforms that served as patios and work areas, while house-lot gardens occupied interstitial space between dispersed residential platforms (Killion et al. 1989; Tourtellot et al. 1989). Archaeological remains of house lots also have been identified in Colonial-period sites such as Mopilá and Hunactí (Alexander 1998, 1999; Hanson 1996; Roys 1952), at Postclassic-period sites such as Cozumel (Freidel and Sabloff 1984), and at Classic-period sites, especially Cobá, Chunchucmíl, Dzibilchaltún, and Calakmúl (Garza Tarzona de González and Kurjack 1980; Manzanilla and Barba 1990).

Summary

The following archaeological study examines the long-term structure of agrarian households in Yaxcabá in order to enlighten more general questions about the process of globalization in nineteenth-century Yucatán. Although this approach does not specify the origins of the Caste War itself, it does describe a cultural process by which rural communities of a single parish, the parroquia of Yaxcabá, developed systems of defense and resistance to the intrusion of a colonial state. For the purposes of archaeological study, resistance is reconceptualized along the lines suggested by Stern (1987), as a system of tactics and strategies practiced by rural inhabitants that presents obstacles to state intervention and the exercise of hegemony. Individual inhabitants may remain nameless, but archaeology enhances understanding of their household strategies and practices without denying the decision-making or agency of rural people.

If the course of political and economic change in nineteenth-century Yaxcabá was at all similar to processes of globalization elsewhere, it should have had a radical impact on peasant household organization and resistant practices. Specific configurations of behavior, whether justified in the minds of the actors as survival or resistance, should be visible in the archaeological patterns in settlements, house lots, and distribution of material culture. The failure of liberal and progressive policies in Yucatán and the consequent trajectory of nation-state formation are partly explained by the success of the Maya farmer in subverting processes of state and rural integration.

The theoretical and methodological literature discussed above suggests several variables that are sensitive indictors of the transformation in agrarian structure in Yucatán. First, the extent to which Maya agriculturalists retained control over different factors of the production process (land, labor, capital, and product) and the extent to which control over one or more factors was threatened under systems of hegemony exercised by the state, the church, or groups of Spanish Creoles was of particular importance. Because some Maya agriculturalists in eighteenth- and nineteenth-century Yaxcabá were smallholders, ownership of land was key in determining the propensity for different forms of resistance to develop. Second, the degree to which rural Maya clients were satisfied with their patrons' ability to meet subsistence needs and to protect them from the predations of other elites or institutions was vital. The structure of patron-client relations, the degree of coercion, and the extent of client dependency were critical variables for assessing the likelihood that methods of defiance and protest would turn violent.

In Yaxcabá's historical record, we should look for consistent, long-term patterns of Maya behavior (or complaints about such behavior) that run counter to the efforts of institutions or elites to exercise domination. Analytical procedures should be particularly sensitive to locating incidents or resistances that might signal arenas of struggle involving land, local authority, or patron-client relations.

In Yaxcabá's archaeological record we should look for variability in regional settlement patterns over time and for variation in spatial patterning that would indicate changes in household organization, production, and labor—the everyday arrangement of tactics of survival, accommodation, and resistance that comprise the household or community system. Important archaeological variables include the size of solares, patios, and gardens, the locations and diversity of features and sites serving specialized productive functions, the degree of aggregation of residential units, and the distribution of nonlocal material culture among residential units. These variables inform us about organization of "normal" survival activities such as mobility, the family cycle, agricultural intensification, diversification, and craft specialization. Nevertheless, only by understanding such mundane behaviors can resistant practices be contextualized within the overall organization of household activities.

Analysis and interpretation of archaeological settlement and spatial patterning also depends on understanding the ways in which tropical agriculturalists "map onto" the landscape. Thus, settlement agriculture, settlement ecology, and the Mesoamerican house-lot models supply appropriate frames of reference for describing the variability in the intensity of use of different parts of the landscape. These frameworks and models permit one to assign interpretations to archaeological patterns that reflect the transformation of household strategies and the development of different forms of resistance in Yaxcabá.

## CHAPTER THREE

The Political Economy of Yaxcabá

For most of the Colonial period, Yucatán was an economic backwater of the Spanish overseas empire. The conquest had been a more protracted and less lucrative endeavor than most colonizers admitted (Restall 1998). The declining Maya population and the tendency for flight beyond the boundaries of the colonial system effectively limited profits, and both the church and the crown encountered difficulty in extracting sufficient labor and resources from the peninsula. This situation often led to abuse and prompted authorities to develop additional ways of appropriating surplus. Ideological conformity was another matter, and the church's attempts to convert the Maya masses and to reduce the political influence of native leaders and priests were not greeted with easy compliance.

In the late eighteenth century, the crown made a final attempt to recoup some returns from the colony by stimulating the economy with free trade and more efficient fiscal management. These efforts eventually failed, and Mexico gained independence from Spain in 1821. Liberalism and progressive reforms, however, continued to dominate the postindependence period, as Yucatecan Creoles attempted to make the new republic economically viable within the global economy. Their efforts at decolonization, reducing the power and influence of the church, and expanding landed estates, however, only created an agrarian crisis in the countryside. The liberal experiment ended abruptly in 1847 with the onset of the Caste War.

The purpose of this chapter is to use documentary sources to specify the conditions of domination and locate potential arenas of struggle in Yaxcabá over the long term. The following discussion describes how the collapse of the Spanish overseas empire and the program of decolonization reworked the methods of extraction in the countryside. When compared to the Early Colonial period, the organization of Yaxcabá's political economy in the nineteenth century reveals a drastic restructuring in the relations of production. New forms of exploitation altered the pressures and stresses on the agrarian system. Although the documentary evidence implies a range of "resistant" practices, such actions clearly occurred within a broad social milieu of Spanish Creoles, clergy, Maya agriculturalists, and Maya leaders. Individuals within these groups had varying interests, and seldom was one group consistently and diametrically pitted against another. Most importantly, not all Maya communities in the parish faced the same set of pressures, nor did they present a unified response.

The Early Colonial Period

In the sixteenth century, the inhabitants of Yaxcabá experienced wrenching changes in their way of life. Spanish colonization ushered in political reorganization, settlement relocation, drastic population loss, and a dual system of tribute and taxation by the church and state. These policies, in turn, caused radical changes in local leadership, agricultural production, religious practices, and the strategies by which households and communities managed their relationships with the Spanish administration.

At the time of the Spanish conquest, the people of Yaxcabá lived within the Province of Sotuta and owed loyalty and tribute to Nachi Cocom, the *halach uinic,* or native leader of the province (Roys 1939, 1957).[1] The Province of Sotuta was hierarchically organized. The halach uinic resided in the capital and presided over individual batabs, who were members of the Maya nobility that governed the constituent towns within the jurisdiction. Each batab was assisted by a council of *ahcuchcabs* (later known as *principales*), leaders of the extended family groupings or wards that together comprised the jurisdiction of the batab. Before the arrival of the Spaniards, Sotuta was quite effective in making war on its neighbors, especially the Xiu of Mani, and this bellicose stance continued throughout the conquest. Between 1532 and 1534 Sotuta had united with its eastern neighbors to defeat the Spaniards at Chichén Itzá (Chamberlain 1948:237). Consequently, it was not one of the provinces that allied itself with the Spanish forces during the final conquest. In 1542 Montejo the Younger moved against Sotuta and rapidly subjugated the area, but Nachi Cocom, along with the leaders of neighboring provinces of Cupul, Cochuah, and Uaymil, again rose against the Spaniards in the Great Maya Revolt of 1546–47. After the suppression of the revolt, Nachi Cocom was baptized Juan Cocom and continued to rule under Spanish authority as the batab (or cacique) in the pueblo of Sotuta until his death in 1561 (Roys 1939; Scholes and Roys 1938).

Even before the Spaniards consolidated their control over the peninsula, however, the crown distributed grants of encomienda, a heritable seigniorial privilege, to subjects who had distinguished themselves in its service. An encomienda was a grant of the tribute owed by specified Indian towns to an individual Spaniard. Most of the encomiendas assigned between 1541 and 1545 did not coincide with previous indigenous political and territorial divisions, and as such they constituted the vanguard of political change that during the next seventy years would dismantle the indigenous provinces in Yucatán (Farriss 1984:149; Quezada 1985, 1993). More often than not, the encomiendas grouped tributary villages from disparate jurisdictions under the authority of different Maya nobles. Because the batab (cacique) and ahcuchcabs (principales) of each village were responsible for delivering the tribute to the *encomendero,* this tended to circumvent the ties between the batabs and the halach uinic (Quezada 1985:667). By 1549 Yaxcabá and Mopilá were granted in encomienda to different Spaniards (Roys 1957:99). Consequently, tribute from Yaxcabá's and Mopilá's inhabitants no longer flowed into the hands of the Cocoms.

With the arrival in 1552 of Tomás López Medel, an administrator of the audiencia of Guatemala, the Spanish authorities began a program of forced resettlement called congregación. Under this policy, hamlets were combined into villages, villages into towns, and subordinate towns into local centers, leaving a two-tiered hierarchy of cabeceras (municipal seats) and *subjetos* (auxiliary towns) (Farriss 1984:158; Roys 1939). Sometimes two or more communities were combined within a single settlement, as was the case for the congregación of Yaxcabá in which a single municipal organization was formed from two communities, Yaxcabá and Tanuz (Roys 1939, 1957; Scholes et al. 1938.).[2] Between 1552 and 1562, Yaxcabá was established as a cabecera within the jurisdiction of the Partido of Sotuta. Its auxiliaries were Mopilá, Tixcacaltuyú, and Taccibichén (Gerhard 1979; Relaciones Histórico-Geográficas 1983; López de Cogolludo 1954). In accordance with López Medel's decrees, the internal arrangement of settlements also changed. Relocated populations were required to dispose themselves along the colonial grid plan centered on a church and central plaza. The inhabitants also retained rights to cultivate lands near their former residences (Roys 1939).

The difficulties posed by congregación for the inhabitants of Yaxcabá are illustrated in a series of land records known as the Titles of Ebtun (Roys 1939). In the late sixteenth century, the removal of people from dispersed settlements along the boundary shared by the native provinces of Sotuta, Cupul, and Cochuah had resulted in incursions of agriculturalists from Sotuta, especially from the Yaxcabá area, on lands originally worked by the inhabitants of Cupul. By 1600 the dispute had come to a head, and the governor of Yucatán, Diego Fernández de Velazco, ordered the authorities of Yaxcabá, Tinum, and Kaua to present documentation of their lands. Leaders in Yaxcabá presented a survey of the boundaries of the Province of Sotuta made by Nachi Cocom in 1545. The leaders of the five principle Cupul towns (including Ebtun) presented a record based on the visit of López Medel to Tekom that listed the names and locations of the abandoned towns from which their congregated populations were drawn. After several meetings, they reached an agreement in which the Cupul boundary was accepted with the proviso that individuals from Yaxcabá would be permitted to continue to farm tracts east of the boundary. Compared to Nachi Cocom's survey, the agreement ceded a substantial area of the cenote belt to the Cupul towns (Roys 1939:13–15). Additional litigation of lands bordering the Cupul, Cochuah, and Sotuta jurisdictions continued through the late eighteenth century.

Further political change swept the peninsula under the administration of Don Diego Quijada, and oversight of the countryside by both civil and ecclesiastical authorities became more invasive (Scholes and Adams 1938). Until the 1560s, the hereditary caciques or batabs were appointed as local governors. Although repúblicas de indios were established within the congregated towns,

Spanish policy had little altered indigenous politics at the local level (Quezada 1985). With the advent of the new administration, however, the governor himself began to appoint new positions with greater frequency. Positions for *alcaldes* and *regidores* proliferated, and some of the newly appointed local governors were not hereditary rulers. The interference was strongly opposed by original caciques. Quijada's appointments are a frequent source of confusion in the documentary record. For example, the Quijada administrative records list Don Juan Hau as the local governor of Yaxcabá in the late 1550s, whereas other documents indicate that the cacique of Yaxcabá was Diego Pech during that time (Quezada 1985; Roys 1957; Scholes and Adams 1938). Roys (1957:99) suggests that Hau may not have been the hereditary cacique, but the governor's appointee.

Increased oversight in the countryside led to the perhaps inevitable discovery in 1562 of widespread idolatry in Mani, Hocaba, and Sotuta (Scholes and Roys 1938). The outcome of the proceedings of the Office of the Inquisition only served to erode further the power of native leaders. Maya caciques, principales, and *ahkines* (priests) were accused of practicing human and animal sacrifices in the churches in opposition to the clergy's missionary efforts. Inquisitors coerced original testimony through the use of torture, and many Maya went to extremes to avoid prosecution. Lorenzo Cocom, Nachi Cocom's brother and successor, committed suicide. Others actively looted pre-Hispanic sites (particularly Cobá) for clay *incensarios* so that they would have some "idols" on hand to deliver to the priests, as evidence that they had forsaken previous practices. A number of individuals were sentenced in the *auto de fé* held in Mani in July, but other cases involving several caciques and principales, a number of whom were from Yaxcabá and Mopilá, were transferred to Mérida for further investigation.

Fortunately, in August 1562 the overzealous Bishop Diego de Landa was replaced by the more moderate Bishop Francisco de Toral, who ordered a reinvestigation. This time officials were under strict orders to avoid coercion. Although many scholars correctly question the veracity of the original testimony (Chuchiak 1994; Scholes and Roys 1938; Scholes and Adams 1938; Tedlock 1993), Scholes and Roys (1938:600) indicate that with respect to the reinvestigation of the Sotuta cases some elements may be valid. Although most witnesses admitted falsifying testimony during the reinvestigation, particularly human sacrifice, the consistency of the accounts among different people many years after their original occurrence, as well as parallels with pre-Hispanic religion, argues against wholesale rejection of the alleged behaviors.[3] The details are interesting, not only because they pertain specifically to Yaxcabá and Mopilá, but also because they illustrate the activities and functions of the caciques.

Leaders both in Yaxcabá and in Mopilá confessed to conducting clandestine human sacrifice at night in the churches (Scholes and Adams 1938:70–114). Usually, the perpetrators included the cacique, ahkines, the schoolmaster, and other principales. They would collect "idols," large anthropomorphic incense burners made of clay or wood, from the cacique's house or milpa and arrange them within the church. Alleged sacrifices performed in front of the incensarios occurred within the church itself or more often in milpas or at the feet of crosses that marked entrances to the town. They usually consisted of offerings of food and drink, or animals such as dogs, deer, or peccaries, and in several cases participants consumed the sacrifice. Human sacrifice, if it occurred at all, was a last resort. According to the testimony, human sacrifice was performed in order to end severe drought, to remedy the damage of a hurricane, or to aid the health of the halach uinic of Sotuta. It is clear that caciques called for such sacrifices, in one case circulating a letter. Victims of human sacrifice were mostly young children who were kidnapped or purchased from other communities. Sacrifice allegedly was performed by heart excision, and the bodies were disposed of in caves and cenotes.[4] Most telling were the caciques' insistence that "what the friars said was not true and not to be believed" (Scholes and Adams 1938:103–14).

Accusation of idolatry became the principle weapon by which the church expanded its influence at the expense of native caciques. Neither the Office of the Inquisition nor the ecclesiastical courts actually managed to stamp out idolatrous activity, but such accusations justified the appropriation of resources from native governors and the extension of ecclesiastical authority in the countryside (Chuchiak 1994; López de Cogolludo 1954). The church finally gained a solid foothold in Sotuta when it established a Franciscan mission in 1576. When the secular clergy assumed control of the parish in 1581, Yaxcabá was established as an independent benefice. This pattern continued in Yucatán throughout the seventeenth century. Whenever idolatrous activity was denounced, parishes were divided, thus increasing supervision and the efficient collection of religious taxes.

According to Ana Luisa Izquierdo (1988), Yaxcabá was divided again in 1686 when another accusation of idolatry prompted ecclesiastical authorities to elevate Tixcacaltuyú to the rank of cabecera. In this case, an incensario and figurines were found in the possession of a Maya couple from Tixcacaltuyú, who confessed to burning incense in order to bring rain and a good harvest. They were convicted and punished along with the cacique and the choirmaster. Tixcacaltuyú and its auxiliary, Taccibichén, with a combined population of 1,300 people (more lucrative than Yaxcabá and Mopilá), became an independent benefice under the control of Dr. Alonso Padilla, the ecclesiastical judge who had tried the case.

Throughout Yucatán, indigenous population loss exacerbated the changes in political structure, settlement patterns, attempts to limit the power and influence of native caciques, and efforts to extract sufficient resources. The introduction of European pathogens initiated a drastic decline of the Indian population, yet tribute burdens often were not adjusted with equal frequency. Epidemics, especially yellow fever, alternated with episodes of famine, and from 1545 to 1750 the population fluctuated, reaching its nadir in the late 1600s. Population loss undoubtedly began with the first Spanish contact in the region in 1511, and the smallpox pandemic of 1521 likely affected Yucatán as well as central Mexico. From the conquest to 1700, Cook and Borah (1979; see also Farriss 1984:61; Garcia Bernal 1978; Patch 1993) estimate the decline of the indigenous population in Yucatán at one-half to two-thirds of the preconquest total. The list of disasters is substantial: in 1568, famine; in 1569–70, plague; in 1571–72, drought, famine and plague; in 1575–76, smallpox, drought, and famine; and finally in 1580, measles and *tabardillo* (typhus). Yucatán was particularly hard-hit in the mid-1600s, when the appearance of yellow fever retarded the recovery of the population (Patch 1993).

Caciques were not immune to such hazards, and epidemics caused significant disruptions of local political authority (Quezada 1985:682). Declining village populations also meant declining tribute, and attempts to reconsolidate Maya villages occurred with or without official sanction throughout the seventeenth century (Hunt 1974; López de Cogolludo 1954). Although Indians frequently were excused from tribute after such disasters, more often than not they responded with flight from the villages. The encomenderos would organize manhunts to round up runaway Indians, sometimes from as far away as the unpacified frontier (Hunt 1974:304).

Population estimates for Yaxcabá and Mopilá drawn from the number of tributaries listed on colonial tax lists (Garcia Bernal 1978:94–95; G. Jones 1989:110–13) suggest that they follow the peninsular profile (see Figures 3.1 and 3.2). The population of Yaxcabá and Mopilá increased slightly between 1549 and 1607, mirroring the modest growth for the peninsula as a whole, possibly due to migration and congregación. The population profile for the seventeenth century, however, shows declines of 46 and 64 percent in Yaxcabá and Mopilá respectively (Garcia Bernal 1978). When one considers that the burden of tribute was born by a total parish population of less than 1,000 people in 1688, epidemics, famines, and the methods of resource extraction seem particularly damaging. The population of the parish did not begin its recovery until the mid-eighteenth century.

Tribute and Taxation

For much of the Colonial period, tribute was owed both to the encomendero and to the church, and the presence of the clergy and civil officials in Indian villages made taxation difficult to avoid. As early as 1549 the tribute of Yaxcabá's inhabitants was assigned as the encomienda Hayan of Martín de Leguizamo. Likewise, Mopilá (later Yaxcabá's auxiliary town) became a part of the encomienda called Cacauacá of Gerónimo de Campos (Garcia Bernal 1978; Gerhard 1979; Paso y Troncoso 1939; Roys 1957:99). From this date onward, the encomienda tribute was a fixed rate equivalent to 14 reales for men and 11 reales for women.[5] Maya often paid tribute in kind, in the form of cotton cloth *(patí)*, maize, and poultry. Crown representatives collected twice per year, once at Christmas and on the Day of St. John (June 24). In 1549 Yaxcabá provided 390 mantas, 300 chickens, 6 fanegas of maize, 0.5 fanegas of beans, 10 arrobas of beeswax, 2 arrobas of honey, and 4 Indians per week to provide personal service to the encomendero. Mopilá provided 180 mantas, 150 chickens, 3 fanegas of maize, 0.5 fanegas of beans, and 2 Indians per week for personal service.[6] On the tax list of 1562 both Yaxcabá and Mopilá appear under their current names (Roys 1939, 1957; Scholes and Adams 1938). Tribute became increasingly burdensome as additional taxes were imposed and abuses escalated. Other civil taxes included the *comunidades* tax, the Holpatan, and the Bula de la Santa Cruzada, which brought the total civil taxes paid per year by an Indian couple to 38 reales (Farriss 1984:41).

In 1581 Yaxcabá was established as a benefice of the secular clergy, thus initiating the regime of ecclesiastical exactions that paralleled those of the crown. By 1636 it had become one of the largest and most lucrative parishes on the peninsula (Hunt 1974:311). Even in the early nineteenth century, when many parishes suffered declining rents, Yaxcabá still was ranked ninth with an annual income of 5,900 pesos (Harrington 1982:187). Tribute paid to the church was called *limosnas* (alms), or *obvención* (stipend), and the amounts only became more or less standardized in the second half of the eighteenth century. Scheduled payments in particular products were spread throughout the year and often remitted in maize, beans, honey, wax, chile,

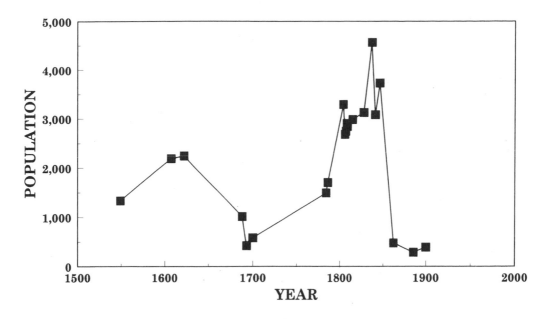

FIGURE 3.1. Population of Yaxcabá, 1549–1900.

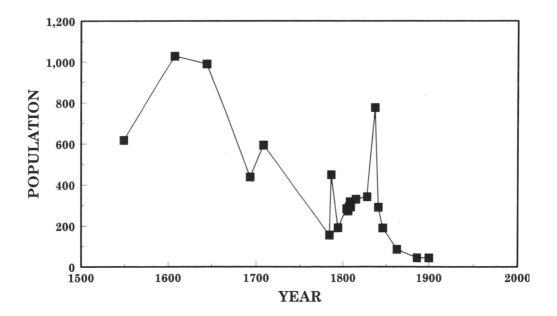

FIGURE 3.2. Population of Mopilá, 1549–1900.

salt, and cotton cloth, as well as silver. For the *obvención mayor,* males paid 12.5 reales, and women 9 reales. In addition, minor obventions were paid for baptisms (3 reales), confirmations (8 reales), marriages (10 reales), burials (infants 4 reales; adults 8–20 reales, depending on whether the mass was sung), wills (4 reales), and matrimonial inquiries (4 reales) (Dumond and Dumond 1982; Farriss 1984:41). Children who attended catechism paid a fee consisting of one egg and one jar of oil for the lamps each week. Farriss (1984:41) calculates the total contributions to the church paid per year by an Indian couple with three surviving children and three dying in infancy as 34.5 reales, almost as much as the civil taxes. The total of civil and religious taxes for an Indian couple totaled about 72.5 reales per year, which may have amounted to half of the family's annual income (Dumond 1997:33).

Unlike tribute paid for encomienda, ecclesiastical taxes were subject to local variation and abuse resulting from the protracted conflicts among parish priests, local Maya officials, and civil authorities. Although by 1784 Yaxcabá's curate had carefully balanced the schedule of obventions so as not to exceed the stipulated totals, previous abuses in the parish had been contested.[7] Garcia Bernal (1972:104) describes a case where in 1723 the *defensor de los indios* denounced the curate of Yaxcabá for exacting an additional 15 pesos 6 reales, purportedly to pay for the mass and sermon, and to purchase chickens and a pound of wax for the altar needed for the fiesta of Yaxcabá's patron saint, San Francisco. Additionally, the priest regularly obliged the Indians to work for Spaniards living in Yaxcabá in order that they might contribute 8 pesos for the feast of Corpus Christi and 3 pesos for Pentecost. Payments in specie and in kind were manipulated by the priests to exploit disparities in the value of the goods occurring within the annual cycle or during times of abundance and scarcity (Garcia Bernal 1972:103). The burden of religious taxes and the excesses of the priests were cited as the principle causes of Indians abandoning their pueblos to become fugitives in the forests in the mid-eighteenth century.[8]

In addition, the residents of Yaxcabá paid a tithe *(diezmo)* equivalent to 10 percent of their income. Theoretically the church tithed Spaniards not Indians, but by the mid-eighteenth century tithes were collected on minor livestock *(ganado menor)* raised by Indians for their own consumption in the pueblos and ranchos and for religious confraternities *(cofradías).*[9] In Yaxcabá the cacique was primarily responsible for delivering tithes to the curate. The incompetence of the cacique in this task and the nonpayment of tithes by those who had fled were the subject of frequent complaints by the curate to the bishop.[10]

In the seventeenth and eighteenth centuries, civil taxes were augmented further by the *repartimiento* for cloth and wax (Hunt 1974). Although in other regions of New Spain the repartimiento was instituted as a form of labor rationing in which laborers were partitioned among various Spanish enterprises, in Yucatán it became an extension of the tribute system. Local products were obtained for market by middlemen (often governors' agents) who forced unreasonably small advances of cash and materials on Indians in return for the delivery of cotton cloth and beeswax twice per year (Garcia Bernal 1972; Hunt 1974). The advances were funneled through the authority of the Maya caciques. Because the caciques were required to collect the repartimiento goods for individuals who had died or migrated, they frequently compensated for lost labor by passing the cost on to their constituents and short-weighting the raw materials and using a long measure for the goods delivered. Indians were repaid in relatively useless, cheap manufactures including Spanish cloth, china, dishes, silk scarves, wine, olive oil, religious articles, and occasional silver or gold ornaments (Hunt 1974:476–83). Indian migration away from the pueblos was blamed on the excesses within the system, which prompted the bishop to protest. In 1731 the crown reduced the amounts of repartimiento and imposed more control (Garcia Bernal 1972:129).

Finally, in addition to civil and religious taxes and repartimiento, the inhabitants of Yaxcabá were subject to three forms of labor drafts: community *tequios,* state labor drafts, and personal service (Dumond 1997:33; Farriss 1984:47–52). According to Nancy Farriss, the tequio was a community service assessment of one day's labor per week to build or repair local buildings (including churches) or to serve local leaders. The state imposed labor levees for the construction of public buildings, roads, the official transport of people or goods, maintenance of facilities for travelers, or the relay of post. Personal service, however, provided labor to private citizens. Each community was required to fill a weekly quota of workers who were assigned to individual Spaniards holding official permits. The work was to be paid for by a minimum wage, originally 2 reales per week. In practice, workers were paid far less than the minimum wage, not paid at all, or worked far longer than one week. In 1723, the crown granted the church the right to reform the abuses of *servicio personal* (Garcia Bernal 1972:109). The bishop proceeded to place control on repartimientos and loan of Indians for post, vigil, transport, and other works in which they were exploited.

Although the historical record regarding labor drafts is somewhat sparse for Yaxcabá, one incident stands out as a clear case of resistance. Marta Hunt (1974:546–47; G. Jones 1998:263) describes the occasion in 1700 in which the Indians of Yaxcabá and Sotuta were conscripted for opening the road to the Peten and carrying supplies. This contingent of laborers flatly refused to work and returned to their villages. Most additional information about labor drafts in Yaxcabá comes from ecclesiastical sources. A visit by Bishop Padilla to Yaxcabá in 1757 suggests that the Maya were employed in rebuilding the church in Yaxcabá. Although the bishop indicated that the project had not been a burden to the Indians, the size and elaboration of the church, its oratory, and the rectory indicate that labor requirements were substantial.[11] By the late eighteenth century, the efforts to stem labor abuses had had some effect. The *visita pastoral* of 1784 indicates that services for transport had only been contracted once to carry two cargas over the 60 leagues of bad roads and deserted countryside down to the town of Bacalar.[12] Those involved were paid the princely sum of 1 peso. Personal service also was provided as tribute to the encomendero, and Yaxcabá's parishioners provided similar service to the curate. Aside from the curate, however, only a few Spaniards and outsiders lived in Yaxcabá during the seventeenth century (Hunt 1974). As the Spanish population grew in the second half of the eighteenth century, personal service and wage labor became more common (Granado Baeza 1845).

Political and Economic Change, 1750–1821

At the turn of the eighteenth century, Yaxcabá parish consisted of about one thousand people concentrated in the cabecera and in Mopilá, its only remaining auxiliary town following the division of the benefice in 1686. Most of the population was Maya, but increasing numbers of Spanish Creoles and mestizos active in the church, commerce, and the collection of tribute resided in Yaxcabá (Hunt 1974:430, 521). According to Hunt (1974:429), rural estates, or *estancias*, in the Sotuta-Yaxcabá region prior to the mid-eighteenth century consisted of little more than a site with a few goats, pigs, cows, and, sometimes, horses. Agricultural and commercial infrastructure was undeveloped. Most inhabitants practiced subsistence agriculture, and civil and ecclesiastical tribute remained the basic method of surplus extraction. For these reasons, Patch (1979, 1993) places Yaxcabá at the edge of Mérida's marketing sphere in 1750.

In the second half of the eighteenth century, however, this picture had changed radically. The parish's population rebounded, totaling 4,332 people in 1784.[13] Parish inhabitants had dispersed from the cabecera, Yaxcabá, and its auxiliary town, Mopilá, to settle eleven independent ranchos and six cattle-raising estates (Table 3.1). Independent ranchos were small communities, usually containing several families, established near outlying milpa plots away from civil and ecclesiastical jurisdiction (Dumond and Dumond 1982). In the first two decades of the nineteenth century, three of these ranchos, Kancabdzonot, Yaxuná, and Santa María, were elevated to the status of auxiliary towns. At least three of the ranchos in Yaxcabá were properties of cofradías, which operated such estates in order to generate agricultural produce used for the annual celebration of the cofradía's patron saint. The six cattle-raising estates, variously called haciendas or ranchos, were the private property of Spanish Creoles.

In 1761 an incident occurred in the neighboring parish of Tixcacaltuyú, which is widely regarded as a classic case of Maya resistance to the expansion of cattle raising (Bricker 1981; Dumond 1997:57–60; Patch 1998; Rugeley 1997:14–16). The Cisteil revolt has been analyzed in detail, most thoroughly by Robert Patch (1998), and the summary presented here follows his work. According to Patch, in 1755 people from surrounding communities founded the village of Cisteil, located near Hacienda Huntulchac in the parish of Tixcacaltuyú. In 1761 a man known as Jacinto Uc de los Santos from Campeche, later crowned king as Jacinto Canek (invoking the name of the last Itza Maya king of Nohpeten), appeared in Cisteil to inform local Maya leaders that he was Montezuma and the legitimate Christ. Patch (1998:74) indicates that Uc demanded and burned tribute receipts and confiscated all repartimiento goods. He ordered people to kill all their pigs (because swine had Spanish souls), conducted night-long rituals, ate jasmine flowers, refused all meat, and claimed to be able to fly. Through his bizarre behavior, Uc eventually convinced the inhabitants of Cisteil and Maya religious leaders of surrounding communities that he was the true Maya king. Inhabitants of Yaxcabá, however, apparently declined his invitation to join the movement (Bricker 1981).

The ensuing revolt contained numerous hallmarks of revitalization movements, including the presence of a charismatic leader who mixed Spanish-Christian with non-Christian Maya elements in order to restore an idealized "traditional" way of life. As people from around the peninsula converged on the town to see Uc, a Creole merchant staying in the community was shot and killed as a demonstration of Uc's authority. The event was reported in nearby Tixcacaltuyú, and a detachment of twenty men under Sotuta's *capitán a guerra*, Tiburcio de Cosgaya, entered the village to restore order. All but four were killed. Captain Cosgaya was dismembered, and several of his anatomical parts were distributed among the rebels. A second detachment of Spanish militia was called in. Jacinto Uc, or Canek, prepared for the conflict by requesting aid from various communities around the peninsula (including Uxmal), claiming

TABLE 3.1: Population Distribution by Settlement Class in Yaxcabá Parish, 1784–1886

Year	Cabecera	Pueblos	Independent Ranchos	Haciendas	Sitios	Total
1784						
#	1	1	11	6	0	19
Population	1,491	155	2,556	139	0	4,341
%	34	4	59	3	0	
1804						
#	1	2	7	7	0	17
Population	3,292	876	2,522	632	0	7,322
%	45	12	34	9	0	
1828						
#	1	4	6	15	0	26
Population	3,128	4,625	2,241	1,058	0	11,052
%	28	42	20	10	0	
1841						
#	1	4	6	15	4	30
Population	3,084	3,385	2,250	270	66	9,055
%	34	37	25	3	1	
1862						
#	1	3	1	6	0	11
Population	478	206	31	164	0	879
%	54	23	4	19	0	
1886						
#	1	2	3	0	0	6
Population	288	199	64	0	0	551
%	52	36	12	0	0	

that the English would send supplies, and encouraging his followers to believe they could not be killed if they did not cry out. In the ensuing battle, more than five hundred Maya were killed. The ringleaders, including Canek, were captured and brought to trial. Nine were sentenced to death and mutilation; 115 were given two hundred lashes and six years of forced labor; and 134 others were sentenced to various combinations of lashes, exile, and forced labor. Cisteil was destroyed, and Cosgaya's remains were interred in the church in Yaxcabá to commemorate his heroic efforts (Bretos 1992).

The Cisteil revolt illustrates the severity of local tensions produced by even the earliest development of commercial agriculture and stockraising in the region. The increased integration of Yaxcabá to the peninsular market economy and the subsequent expansion of commercial enterprises, however, were the product of the Bourbon political reforms (Patch 1993). The Bourbon reforms and their effects in Yucatán have been summarized succinctly elsewhere (Dumond 1997;

Farriss 1984; Patch 1993), therefore only a cursory review is merited here. The two principle achievements of the Bourbon regime—the policy of free trade (*comercio libre*) and the imposition of fiscal management under the intendancy system—had repercussions in Yaxcabá.

The policy of free trade not only stimulated agricultural production but also unleashed a flood of Spanish Creoles on the countryside. As the Creole population dispersed from the traditional centers of Mérida, Campeche, and Valladolid, a variety of commercial, real estate, and investment activities also were extended to rural villages (Nichols 2003). Consequently, opportunities for wage labor increased in rural areas. Cattle estancias, later called haciendas, appeared in Yaxcabá, often absorbing land from subsistence agriculturalists and ushering in new kinds of labor contracts. In many areas of the peninsula, Maya became resident laborers on the haciendas. Labor arrangements varied and included debt peonage, simple sharecropping, and salaried posts. Positions on the estates were ranked. The owner usually employed one or two foremen (*mayoral/mayordomo*) as salaried workers, cowboys and horse wranglers, and sharecroppers (either as permanent residents or *luneros*). In some cases, the hacienda's owner paid an individual's tribute and obventions. Because these amounts, as well as other loans and patrimonial support, were recorded as debts, however, the laborer was bound to the hacienda, often for life (Bracamonte y Sosa 1993; Rugeley 1997:70–72). In other cases, an individual labored on a hacienda as a semipermanent worker, a lunero, or sharecropper. In return for the use of the land and water of the estate, one could provide labor rent, one day per week (usually on Monday, *lunes,* thus the term "lunero") to the estate's owner or cultivate a parcel (20 mecates; 1 mecate = 20 m or 400 sq m) whose produce was ceded to the estate owner.[14]

The Bourbon intendancy exercised direct oversight in the collection of tribute and taxes, a move paralleled by the church. The crown installed governmental representatives in every cabecera in Yucatán. These officials were responsible for extracting tribute and taxes directly from the Indians. Whereas previously the Maya cacique and officials of the república de indios collected resources destined for the crown, for the encomendero, for repartimiento, and for the local community, the direct administration of tax collection removed discretionary funds and operating expenses from their control (Rugeley 1997). By the end of the eighteenth century, Maya caciques' control of appreciable sources of village income had diminished.

The crown abolished the repartimiento in 1783 and began to phase out encomiendas in 1785. The grants expired with the death of the current incumbent. In place of the encomienda, the crown instituted a head tax of 13 reales.[15] The encomienda in Yaxcabá was phased out rather slowly, and some evidence suggests an overlap in encomienda and head-tax payments. In 1786 Yaxcabá's tribute amounted to 90 mantas and 0.5 *piernas de patí,* valued at 1,261 pesos and 6 reales. Mopilá was assessed a total of 16 mantas and 1.5 piernas valued at 229 pesos and 2 reales.[16] With the establishment of the head tax, however, taxes were collected not only from Yaxcabá and Mopilá, but also from sizeable ranchos that had been newly designated as pueblos. Consequently, amounts paid to the crown well exceeded those collected under encomienda, and the burden of tribute became heavier on the parish as a whole. In 1809 Yaxcabá, Mopilá, Kancabdzonot, and Santa María paid as half of their annual contribution a total of 1104 pesos to the treasury.[17] The revenue formerly paid as encomienda was finally ceded to the state in 1815 when the encomendero's heir was able to verify and notarize his death.[18]

During this period, the bishop also instituted a plan for the confiscation and sale of cofradía estates, thus removing them from the control of the Indian caciques and the repúblicas de indios. Although the church had long exercised direct supervision over the collection of obventions and tithes, tithe farming became a preferred method for collecting and converting revenue to usable specie. Collection of tithes was delegated to entrepreneurs who paid a percentage for the right to collect them in specified parishes (Patch 1993:170). Because the tithe farmers would put the goods up for auction *(remates de diezmos),* ecclesiastical authorities would then receive most religious taxes in the form of cash rather than agricultural resources.

In the early nineteenth century, the Napoleonic wars exiled the king from Spain for a short time. In the interim, a legislative body known as the Spanish Cortes assembled at Cadiz and drafted a liberal constitution (the Constitution of Cadiz), which took effect on March 19, 1812 (Dumond 1997:52–54; Güemez Pineda 1994). They proposed sweeping changes in keeping with liberal, Enlightenment ideas (Güemez Pineda 1994). According to Don Dumond (1997), from 1812 to 1814 the provisions of the constitution and various decrees of the Cortes were implemented in Yucatán. First, colonial tribute, including the head tax to the crown, was abolished. Second, all persons of free birth and living in Spain or its colonies were declared Spaniards; Indians became *vecinos,* or citizens, overnight. Third, town councils *(ayuntamientos)* were to be elected in all sizeable towns, and the repúblicas de indios were automatically abolished. This provision provided rural Creoles with the opportunity to monopolize local politics to the exclusion of native leaders. Fourth, personal service was abolished for Indians, and rates of parish fees and labor drafts were equalized among all classes. The result was a severe disruption of ecclesiastical operations as Indian parishioners refused to work or send children to catechism or pay obventions. When punishment for noncompliance was eliminated, many people migrated away from the pueblos to the surrounding countryside. When the king returned in May 1814, he revoked the Constitution of Cadiz and reinstated tribute and obventions (Dumond 1997:52–54).

The results of the Bourbon reforms and the proclamation of the Cortes were tangible in Yaxcabá. The population of the parish grew dramatically during this period, rising from a total of 4,332 in 1784 to 10,832 in 1828 (Figure 3.3).[19] Immigration to the interior regions from areas around Mérida fueled most of the increase (Remmers 1981).[20] The influx of Spanish Creoles and Indians not only prompted economic expansion but also altered the ethnic composition of the parish (Table 3.2; see also Granado Baeza 1845).

An ayuntamiento was duly elected in Yaxcabá in 1813, and it consisted entirely of Creoles. One of its first orders of business was to draft and approve a schedule of *arbitrios municipales,* taxes on products and commercial enterprises, which would cover municipal expenses.[21] The list provides a view of the community's economy. Taxes covered the production and importation of pigs, cattle, horses, rough cotton cloth (patí), sales of house lots, lard, cotton, wax, aguardiente, and sugar. Commercial establishments and occupations mentioned in the tax schedule included blacksmiths, carpenters, silversmiths, tailors, cobblers, and stores (some of which sold liquor). Hacienda owners with more than one hundred head of cattle were exempt, whereas prisoners kept in jail for more than twenty-four hours were taxed. In contrast, economic activity in the auxiliary town, Kancabdzonot, was much less diversified. The ayuntamiento stated that because agriculture and commerce were insufficient to support the expenses of the community, it would impose an annual

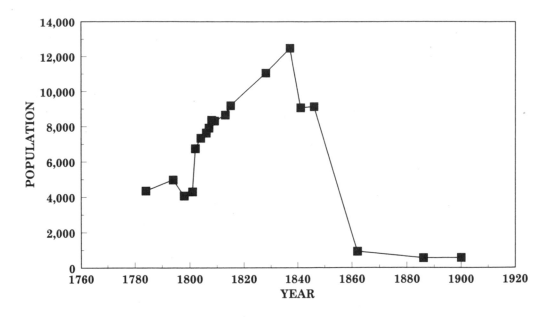

FIGURE 3.3. Population of Yaxcabá Parish, 1784–1900.

contribution of 6 reales for each male aged fifteen to sixty, payable in two installments in June and December.[22]

Ecclesiastical sources also provide a glimpse of the official side of Yaxcabá's economy. A book of tithes, or diezmos, for the year 1778 has survived (see Patch 1985, 1993).[23] Individuals paid tithes on maize, beans, cotton cloth (patí), cotton, cucumbers, horses, mules, pigs, chickens, honey, wax, and chile. Declarations of diezmos for haciendas also appear on the list, as do those of cofradías. Although Indians were theoretically exempt from this tax, the book from Yaxcabá demonstrates that they paid tithes on pigs and occasionally horses, forwarding the amounts to the church through the cacique or through the foremen (mayorales) of ranchos and haciendas. Goods declared for tithe by the haciendas included cattle, horses, mules, maize, cotton, cucumbers, honey, and wax. Cattle appear only on the hacienda tithe declarations and not on individual's inventories. Production for two cofradías, Kancabdzonot and Nuestra Señora del Rosario, was declared in maize, beans, goats, and silver. Yaxcabá was a lucrative parish, and resident Creoles regularly participated in tithe farming. During the period 1812 through 1836, the diezmos of Yaxcabá were put up for auction seven times.[24] The values range from a low figure of 300 pesos in 1815 to a high of 715 pesos in 1831.

Attempts to eliminate the cofradías were also underway. In 1782 the estate of cofradía Kancabdzonot was sold amid protest from the community's inhabitants (Farriss 1984:537n82). A 1797 document, however, suggests that the cofradía was reinstated after handing over 56 pesos in revenue owed to the church.[25] Furthermore, in the visita pastoral of 1804, Yaxcabá's long-term resident curate still classified the community as a hacienda de cofradía. By 1809, the settlement was acknowledged as a pueblo.

TABLE 3.2: Ethnic Change in Yaxcabá, 1798–1815

Year	Españoles y Mestizos	Negros y Pardos	Indios	Total
1798	438	166	3,452	4,056
1802	786	208	5,735	6,729
1806	931	220	6,468	7,619
1807	949	258	6,694	7,901
1808	940	269	7,145	8,354
1809	1,003	276	7,020	8,299
1815	916	253	8,009	9,178

Source: AME, Visitas Pastorales 1798–1815.

Notarial records suggest that no less than five religious confraternities were active in the parish throughout the early nineteenth century: Cofradía Kancabdzonot, Cofradía Xiat, Cofradía Nuestra Señora del Rosario, Cofradía Sohiste, and Cofradía Animas. During the 1830s several of these confraternities were supported by Florencia del Castillo. Her hacienda San José Yaxleulá was mortgaged for 600 pesos, and part of the interest from this sum benefited the Cofradía Sohiste. From a 250-peso mortgage on a house, she used 135 pesos to benefit the Cofradía Animas and 115 pesos for the Cofradía de Nuestra Señora del Rosario.[26] The documentary evidence suggests that cofradías survived in modified form under different patronage after the church ordered them sold. Although only three settlements, Kancabdzonot, Xiat, and Kulimché, can be linked as estates of these cofradías, it is apparent that such communities thrived and grew into the mid-nineteenth century.[27]

From 1780 to 1830 Yaxcabá's curate was José Bartólome del Granado Baeza, a remarkable priest known for careful attention to his parish.[28] In 1813 he responded to a questionnaire of thirty-six items circulated by the bishop regarding the subsistence, customs, and way of life of the Indians in his parish and assessing the impact of the Constitution of Cadiz. Granado Baeza's account corroborates information from the book of tithes on agricultural production but also adds details on the parish's racial composition, economic stratification, literacy and language, labor arrangements, and non-Christian religious practices. For example, in addition to agricultural pursuits, he stated that the inhabitants of Yaxcabá were dedicated to simple manufacturing, especially weaving baskets, mats, and hats. Before 1812, the duties of men contributing personal service included cutting firewood, collecting fodder and supplying water for the horses, attending the table, cooking, and caring for gardens and orchards. Women were employed to cook and grind maize and prepare tortillas. Sometimes personal service laborers would work in agricultural fields or collect salt.[29] Granado Baeza claimed that the parish lacked "rich men" and even the caciques led a simple life. Nevertheless, Indians "of means" could hire wage laborers to work in their milpas.

TABLE 3.3: Population Distribution in Yaxcabá Parish, 1784–1886

Settlement	1784	1804	1806	1807	1808	1809	1815	1828	1841	1846	1862	1886
Cabecera	1,491	3,292	2,682	2,746	2,902	2,843	2,984	3,128	3,084	3,730	478	288
%	34.3	45.0	35.2	34.8	34.7	34.3	32.5	28.3	34.0	40.9	54.5	52.3
Pueblos	155	876	939	982	2,279	2,345	3,320	4,625	3,385	3,379	206	199
%	3.6	12.0	12.3	12.4	27.3	28.2	36.2	41.8	37.4	37.1	23.4	36.1
Haciendas & Ranchos	2,695	3,145	3,998	4,173	3,173	3,111	2,874	3,299	2,586	2,008	195	64
%	62.1	43.0	52.5	52.8	38.0	37.5	31.3	29.9	28.6	22.0	22.1	11.6
Total	4,341	7,313	7,619	7,901	8,354	8,299	9,178	11,052	9,055	9,117	879	551

He also described non-Christian religious practices. Although his parishioners were well instructed in Catholic doctrine and devoutly took the sacraments, penances and punishments were ineffective in completely stamping out "superstition" and "idolatry." During this period the Maya widely used the *zaztun* (or *saastun*), a small piece of clear crystalline stone, for sorcery, divination, and diagnosis of various illnesses.[30] Similarly Granado Baeza describes the "mass of the milpa," known as the *primisia* (Redfield and Villa Rojas 1934), involving *balche* (fermented honey beverage) and the sacrifice and preparation of a turkey and thick maize tortillas in an underground oven *(pib)*, as a means of petitioning the Pahahtunes, the custodians of rain, for a good harvest.

As Spanish Creoles actively developed commercial agriculture and stockraising, land holdings and labor relations in the parish began to shift (Table 3.3, see also Table 3.1). Sales of land for establishing haciendas created confusion along the old boundary between Sotuta and Cupul. The line was resurveyed in 1775 by Antonio de Arze under the orders of the governor on behalf of the Cupul towns of Ebtun, Cuncunul, Tekom, Tixcacalcupul, and Kaua, which were engaged in litigation with Yaxcabá (Roys 1939:105–17). Three of the earliest and largest estates, Nohitzá, Popolá, and Cetelac, were located along the contested boundary.[31] Maya officials in both provinces manipulated land sales along the boundary to remedy trespass and uncomfortable usufruct arrangements. For example, hacienda Nohitzá spanned the Sotuta-Cupul boundary. Some of the lands for the estate had been sold by people of Cupul, but because the original documents had been lost, the exact boundary was blurred.[32] People from the town of Kaua sold the land for hacienda Popolá, thus evicting cultivators from Yaxcabá who farmed the tract under the provisions of the agreement of 1600. The lands for hacienda Cetelac, located just on the Cupul side of the boundary, likely were sold by people from Yaxcabá who had recently colonized the rancho Santa María, trespassing on Cupul lands.[33]

By 1815, the parish contained eight haciendas, and the development of mixed stockraising and agriculture continued apace. In at least one case, the transfer of land from Maya to non-Maya hands is clearly documented. In 1815 Leandra and Juana Kantun sold a cenote and two cuadras (1 cuadra = 100 m) of land to D. José Francisco del Castillo for 85 pesos, which later became the hacienda San José Yaxleulá.[34] The protracted process of sale documented previous Maya owners back through 1787. Less than ten years later, however, the estate was appraised at more than 1,000 pesos, having over two hundred head of cattle, two hundred beehives, a train of twenty-four mules, and "various" horses.[35] In other cases, the expansion of haciendas was contested. In 1818 the owner of hacienda Cetelac, Miguel Francisco Carrillo, was engaged in litigation with the adjacent Indian communities of Yaxuná and Santa María.[36] He apparently sought a license to place livestock at Yaxuná, claiming the parcel as his own and neglecting to acknowledge the claims of the rancho inhabitants.[37] Although the outcome of the dispute is not explicitly recorded, it appears to have been unsuccessful. The "rancho" Yaxuná is referred to as a pueblo or auxiliary town in later documents.

Concurrent with the development of cattle estates, three independent rancho communities were reclassified as pueblos or auxiliary towns. Construction dates on the churches in Santa María, Kancabdzonot, and Yaxuná correspond closely with Granado Baeza's reclassification of the settlements in the visitas pastorales. Although it is likely that pueblo status conferred legitimate land rights for these communities, more people were also drawn "into the fold," making them subject to church and civil jurisdiction and corresponding tax payments.

Unlike other areas of the peninsula, the haciendas in Yaxcabá never attracted large numbers of landless laborers. Cattle raising with subsidiary maize cultivation was not a labor-intensive activity and required relatively few cowboys and farmers to produce the list of goods mentioned in the tithe records.[38] Most hacienda laborers were either salaried workers (the mayoral) or luneros (sharecroppers), not debt peons (Bracamonte y Sosa 1993; Granado Baeza 1845). According to Granado Baeza, in return for the use of land and water on an estate, luneros cultivated 20 mecates of milpa with the produce owed to the hacienda owner, or (less commonly) provided the owner with one day of labor per week, or paid the owner 1 real in silver per week. Tithes and encomienda tribute payments were supposed to be made by the hacienda owner on behalf of his workers, including luneros.[39] For this reason Farriss (1984:216) suggests that the owners of cattle estates discouraged nonsalaried tenant farmers from attaching themselves to haciendas. Although their agricultural activities did not interfere with cattle raising, the estate owner was liable for tribute payments and obliged to provide loans or other forms of patronage that did not always offset the rents (returned in agricultural produce) paid by tenants.

Individuals needing to supplement their land base or household income also had other, more appealing options. Wage labor, available in Yaxcabá but less so in outlying communities, was well remunerated. A wage laborer was paid 4 reales in silver or the equivalent in produce and provided with food. Farmers could also cultivate land belonging to another individual, in which case the land owner was paid 5 cargas of maize or 10 reales in silver per 100 mecates as rent (Granado Baeza 1845). Finally, although the parish population and the numbers of haciendas increased rapidly during this period, no more than 10 percent of the total parish population was resident on haciendas. Most of the population growth occurred in the cabecera, in the pueblos, and in the independent ranchos. The haciendas never replaced the indigenous community as the principal social or productive entity in the parish (see discussion below in Chapter 4).

Independence and the Emergence of
an Agrarian Problem

Mexican independence from Spain in 1821 marked an era of accelerated change in Yucatán and in Yaxcabá. Liberal reforms originally instituted with the Constitution of Cadiz prevailed locally (Güemez Pineda 1994), even as the new republic of Yucatán scrambled to meet crises of state finance and international market competition. The cattle industry's market share, previously supported under the Bourbons, was curtailed by competition with markets in Havana and Veracruz. In this economic climate, Yucatecan elites sought to develop other more lucrative exports, most notably sugar and henequen. Three distinct economic regions developed after independence: (1) a sugar-growing region in the southwest; (2) a northern henequen-producing region; and (3) a central and eastern mixed cattle-raising and maize-producing region (Bracamonte y Sosa 1984, 1993; Patch 1993; Strickon 1965).

Growth of these enterprises required land and capital, prompting legislation favorable to economic expansion. According to Dumond (1997:64; see also Cline 1947), three different classes of land were recognized after 1821: Indian community lands received as colonial grants or purchased by the repúblicas de indios (including lands of cofradías); village ejido lands serving as the commons for each municipality; and *terrenos baldíos,* or vacant lands. In 1833 the remaining cofradía lands were sold, with proceeds returned to the church. By 1841 village ejidos were restricted to an area of 4 sq leagues (69.4 sq km) measured from the church in the town center. Terrenos baldíos, previously known as the *tierras realengas* or *monte del Rey* and open to agriculturalists for use, were declared alienable public property. Although their sale at public auction was intended to augment state finances, colonization and purchase of these lands did not become common until the 1840s when the state used the lands to repay government loans and military personnel (Dumond 1997:63–66; Rugeley 1997:63–68).

Taxes and international trade were the principle sources of capital for the new republic. In 1823 the head tax to the crown was replaced by the *contribución patriótica,* later to become the *contribución personal,* a tax of 12 reales paid by all adult males in two annual installments.[40] The debate over whether Yucatán should become part of Mexico prompted the federalist and centralist political swings of the 1820s, which largely concerned the advantages and disadvantages of tariffs, free trade, and embargo of Spanish ports. Consequently Mérida was at odds with Campeche during this time, over differing economic interests of elites in both cities. Obventions paid by Indians to the church remained in effect, and the repúblicas de indios were reinstated (Dumond 1997:68).

Postindependence policies and legislation had a profound effect in Yaxcabá and allowed Spanish Creoles to gain the upper hand in almost every instance. In the decades before the Caste War, two Creole factions fought for control over the ayuntamiento of Yaxcabá, challenged the activities of Yaxcabá's curate on a regular basis, progressively limited the activities and authority of the república de indios, and rapidly laid claim to available terrenos baldíos by establishing numerous sitios and haciendas. The Creoles no longer restricted their activities to Yaxcabá and assumed control of the local council in the auxiliary town of Kancabdzonot.

One of the first casualties of the new political arrangements was the república de indios in Yaxcabá. In 1825 members of the república de indios filed a lawsuit against the municipal authorities opposing the sale of the lot facing the church on which the audiencia of the república had stood.[41] They filed a document in Maya describing how earlier that year (1824) the audiencia, a thatched-roof structure, had burned to the ground during a large assembly involving singing, aguardiente, and a fight.[42] Rather than encouraging the república to rebuild, the alcalde of Yaxcabá, Claudio Padilla, sold the lot to Juan Péres without notifying república officials. The sale was opposed with the claim that the site of the audiencia had belonged to the república since the conquest. The república's petition was unsuccessful. They were offered another lot, several blocks away from the town center for 32 pesos. Soon after, the ayuntamiento constructed a new municipal building, granary, militia barracks, and a school (all of masonry) across from the church.

Eviction of the república de indios was the beginning of the end of the cacique's power in Yaxcabá. The postindependence era inaugurated a nominally electoral process for the selection of caciques across the peninsula (Rugeley 1997). Whereas previously the batab or cacique ruled for a term of twenty years (Thompson 2000), the república was required to submit a slate of candidates for the ayuntamiento's approval. Although the Creoles usually ratified the república's first choice, the new conditions initiated a pattern of interference that led to instability, ineffective native leadership, and loss of the república's control of land ownership. Terry Rugeley (1997:110–12) provides a cogent analysis of the destabilizing effects of cacique elections in Yaxcabá. It started in 1827 when alcalde Padilla removed the cacique, Lazaro Caamal, for ineptitude in collecting the contribución personal. In the next twenty years following the removal of Caamal, six different caciques presided over the república de indios in Yaxcabá.[43] Some died in office; some resigned citing ill health or the heavy financial burdens of the office as a cause; others were removed if they landed on the wrong side of Yaxcabá's factional political struggles. Similar elections and political turnovers occurred in Kancabdzonot.

Some evidence suggests that the Maya did not merely acquiesce to Creole authority.[44] In 1833 Manuel May and associates, from Kancabdzonot, were charged with riot and tumultuous assembly. According to the Creole testimony, the cacique of Santa María, Dionicio Camal, was conducting a meeting of forty to fifty Maya men and several women at his house when the situation got out of hand. When the justice of the peace arrived to restore order, the participants "had the temerity" to strip him of a document, his insignia of office, and to carry off his hat. Four of the women present were sentenced to three days in jail. In another incident in 1844, Domingo Uitz was sentenced to jail time for lack of respect for the deputy municipal alcalde of Kancabdzonot.[45]

Although these few incidents suggest that friction between the Indian and Creole leadership produced sporadic and poorly organized acts of defiance, another form of resistance was more prevalent. In 1825 and again in 1828, Granado Baeza reported that removal of the fear of punishment and bouts of sickness prompted widespread nonpayment of obventions, nonattendance at mass and catechism, and flight to ranchos and undeveloped *monte,* or forest. The parish rents had declined severely. In the 1830s and 1840s, this trend continued for Granado Baeza's successor, Eusebio Villamil, who excused obvention payments in 1833 and 1835 during the cholera epidemic. The increasing dispersal of the Indian population also impelled greater church expenditures in the ranchos rather than in the cabecera, a situation that did not suit Yaxcabá's Creoles.

The second casualty of postindependence politics in Yaxcabá was the church. Granado Baeza was an individual of modest lifestyle who owned neither houses, haciendas, lands, nor personal property and consequently did not compete with Creole merchants and landowners in Yaxcabá (Rugeley 1997:110). In 1830, however, he was succeeded by Eusebio Villamil, an extremely wealthy cleric whose property included several houses, house lots, slaves, and stores in Mérida (Harrington 1982:236, 311, 305, 315; Rugeley 1997:110–12). He frequently loaned considerable sums of money to other individuals, and his various enterprises often kept him away from his parish.[46] In 1842 the ayuntamiento of Yaxcabá filed a complaint against Villamil alleging "irregularities in the cemetery."[47] At that time the principal cemetery in Yaxcabá was the large and ornate ossuary adjacent to the north side of the church. Yaxcabá's alcalde, José Tiburcio Días, and other signatories of the ayuntamiento charged that the recent epidemic had produced an average of eight burials per day in the month of February. To keep abreast of the problem, Villamil was exhuming cadavers from the soil after only four months, before they had completely decomposed.[48] The Creoles attributed the cause of the recent epidemic to the "fetid corruption" that had spread to Yaxcabá's water supply as a result of rainwater draining from the cemetery into the cenote in the main plaza. Furthermore they charged Villamil with abuse of the Indians, claiming that his parishioners were "selling the sweat of their brow" in order to maintain their priest, while he abandoned the parish for long periods. The ayuntamiento requested Villamil provide funds to construct a new cemetery on the southeastern edge of town.

Villamil's response to the charges was the work of a master politician. First, he claimed, the sickness had not produced an average of eight cadavers per day, but a total of thirty-five in two months. The charge that his staff were exhuming cadavers after four months was a lie, especially since a provisional cemetery was available. Furthermore, water draining from the cemetery could not be responsible for the epidemic. Water from the cemetery was channeled away from the cenote, and the cenote was used only as a water source for livestock. As for abuse of the Indians and neglect of his parish, Villamil indicated that observance of none of the sacraments suffered. He had suspended obvention payments during the cholera epidemic of 1833 and 1835 and had just incurred major expenditures for repairing the church in Yaxuná and constructing chapels/shrines in rancho Cacalchén. Finally he refused to finance the construction of a new cemetery. Although the ayuntamiento later obtained funds to construct the new cemetery, the dispute was not immediately resolved. Yaxcabá's Creoles, along with three Maya functionaries of the república de indios, filed a second complaint to the bishop in 1845.[49] They requested that Don Juan Pablo Ancona, the *"cura coadjutor"* (adjunct priest), replace Villamil, whose constant absence was badly affecting the parish. The request was denied, and in 1850 Villamil became dean of the cathedral chapter in Mérida (Harrington 1982).

Nevertheless, clashes with Yaxcabá's Creole leadership were not limited to the church or the república de indios. Other Creoles living in the parish were perhaps the most outspoken critics of various political officeholders. Between 1825 and 1846 the ayuntamiento implemented several projects focused on civic improvements, public health, and beautification of the town, the tangible results of which included construction of a new municipal building and the new cemetery.[50] In order to maintain their improvements, the ayuntamiento also passed punitive ordinances. For example, in 1840, after the main plaza and streets had been refurbished with a new layer of *sascab*, the ayuntamiento ordered the streets closed to wandering livestock, especially pigs.[51] These activities required officials to obtain contributions of material from surrounding communities, to organize community labor, and to account for all expenses, no doubt rubbing the wrong way those providing labor and materials (as well as hog farmers).

In a political climate where individuals strove to implement their vision for the community through local office, friction escalated between two groups headed by the Días family and Claudio Padilla. Ayuntamiento records reveal that these factional disputes were long-standing and intensely personal. The first example occurred in 1826 when members of the Días family, claiming that "[the citizens] having suffered for much time the iron yoke of the most obstinate despotism with such scandalous infractions of the law," accused Claudio Padilla, then the alcalde, of abuse of power.[52] Specifically he was accused of whipping a prisoner, imposing excessive fines, and selling the goods of deceased and in testate community members without verifying next of kin. Although Padilla excused himself by blaming these oversteps on his political subordinates, the incident was not forgotten. In 1829, Claudio Padilla and Juan Péres Alvarado filed a complaint against Sebastian Días, then the alcalde and head of the civic militia, for excesses and insult against the citizenry, in which a rowdy mob went so far as to jail unjustly the schoolmaster.[53] In his defense, Días stated that he and the group had been gambling and things got a little loud.

Later in 1842, José Tiburcio Días was elected alcalde of the ayuntamiento. Some of his "enemies" complained that he was not old enough (twenty-five years) to assume office.[54] Testimony on both sides of the question was offered by a number of individuals until church officials produced his baptismal certificate, proving Días was only twenty-three at the time. The governor annulled the election. The proceedings, which took place in nearby Tabi, generated considerable excitement and had Días's supporters up in arms. The "disorder" was sufficient to make people in nearby villages nervous, to the extent that they called out the militia in Tabi.[55] Finally, in 1846 when José Tiburcio Días legitimately was elected alcalde, he and his associates were charged with riot and tumultuous assembly.[56] The postelection celebration apparently was too jubilant to suit the tastes of the losing candidates.

Although disputes over the control of the ayuntamiento may seem petty and personal, they were founded in real self-interest. Municipal office conferred not only prestige but also control of local taxes (arbitrios), town real estate, material appropriations and labor hiring for public works, and the registration of claims to terrenos baldíos. Those competing for office were merchants and landowners, and both the Días family and Claudio Padilla owned multiple cattle estates. Although the costs associated with holding the position of alcalde were substantial, the power and wealth that accrued to the officeholder through the daily business of the ayuntamiento was hardly negligible.[57]

During the postindependence era, population peaked at over 11,000 in Yaxcabá parish (Table 3.4, Figure 3.3). By the 1840s, however, it had leveled off between 9,000 and 10,000. In addition to the total numbers of parish inhabitants, the censuses of this period also provide a view of the distribution of population among different kinds of settlements in the parish, as well as production and occupational information (Tables 3.5 and 3.6).[58] These data reveal an important trend. Although

TABLE 3.4: 1841 Census

Settlement	Men 1–15	Men 16–40	Men 40+	Women (all ages)	Total
Yaxcabá	649	644	131	1,660	3,084
Mopilá	67	42	32	150	291
Kancabdzonot	462	386	56	941	1,845
Santa María	322	230	68	629	1,249
R. Canakóm	151	56	49	242	498
R. Xiat	53	41	18	101	213
R. Kulimché	67	40	3	131	241
R. Santa Cruz	78	60	21	165	324
R. Cacalchén	171	150	0	283	604
R. Chimay	75	35	31	229	370
H. Yaxleulá	3	2	2	8	15
H. Yximché	10	7	1	12	30
H. Xul	12	11	1	25	49
H. Kambul	24	19	15	32	90
H. Xbac	9	9	4	11	33
H. Yaxleulá	3	2	1	6	12
H. Xkopteil	6	5	1	7	19
H. ?	2	2	1	5	10
S. Santa Cruz	2	2	2	8	14
S. Kuxubche	3	7	1	12	23
S. Kancabchen	1	1	1	3	6
Sitio Chenche	5	5	1	12	23
? chen	6	3	2	1	12
Total	2,181	1,759	442	4,673	9,055

the numbers of haciendas had nearly doubled over late-eighteenth-century figures, they did not support a corresponding proportion of the parish's burgeoning population. Population growth was absorbed mostly by the pueblos and ranchos, whereas the growth of cattle raising increasingly alienated land from the hands of agriculturalists. No new independent ranchos were founded, and population became increasingly concentrated in existing settlements. The tendency for dispersal virtually ceased.

Furthermore, in the 1840s Spanish Creoles founded a number of sitios, small and relatively unimproved privately owned parcels, measuring 1 sq league, used for farming and low-level livestock raising. Some of these became classified as haciendas immediately before the Caste War (see Table 3.1 above).[59] In their 1853 *Estadística de Yucatán*, Regil and Peon estimate that

TABLE 3.5: Occupational Information for Cabecera and Pueblos, 1841

Occupation	Yaxcabá	Mopilá	Kancabdzonot	Santa María	Total
Abactereo	1				1
Abasteidor	6		2		8
Albañil	1				1
Albarradero	1				1
Arendador	1				1
Arriero	27		9		36
Asalariado	19				19
Cantero	3		2	1	6
Carpintero	2				2
Cohetero	2				2
Comerciante	27		6		33
Curtidor	4				4
Hacendado	1				1
Herrero	6		1		7
Jornalero	11		1	18	30
Labrador	643	74	421	279	1,417
Mayordomo	2				2
Musico	3				3
Preseptor	1				1
Sacador	3				3
Sastre	1				1
Zapatero	10				10
Total Men 16–40+	775	74	442	298	1,589

before the Caste War the Yaxcabá-Sotuta region contained some 24,934 head of cattle and 3,183 horses, the most numerous of any partido in Yucatán.[60] Indeed, the largest hacienda in Yaxcabá parish, Nohitzá, had 379 animals, comprising 36 percent of its value (Bracamonte y Sosa 1993:anexo 5, 6). The pattern suggests that a disproportionate amount of land was used to support cattle, to the detriment of Maya agriculturalists who increasingly had to make due with crowded communal village lands or rent land from others, usually as a lunero.

The growing imbalance in the distribution of population within the parish was undoubtedly exacerbated in the years just before the Caste War when Creoles claimed and purchased sizeable tracts of terrenos baldíos (Cline 1947:393–96; Patch 1985; Reed 1964:8–9).[61] Yaxcabá's citizens made a total of twenty-four claims for 12 sq leagues of land (1 sq league = 1,736 ha), one cenote, and six claims of unspecified size. Many of these claims were intended to enlarge

TABLE 3.6: Occupational Information for Haciendas, Sitios, and Ranchos, 1841

Settlement	Labrador	Jornalero	Lunero	Carpintero	Cantero	Mayoral	Arriero	Vaquero	Caporal	Total Men 16–40+
R. Canakóm	105									105
R. Xiat	59									59
R. Kulimché	42						1			43
R. Santa Cruz	77						4			81
R. Cacalchén	149						1			150
R. Chimay	63	1			1		1			66
H. Yaxleulá	0					2		2		4
H. Yximché	3			2		1		1	1	8
H. Xul	10					1		1		12
H. Kambul	0		28			2		4		34
H. Xbac	0		8			2		2	1	13
H. Yaxleulá	1					1		1		3
H. Xkopteil	0		4			1		1		6
H. ?	1					1		1		3
S. Santa Cruz	1		1			1		1		4
S. Kuxubche	0		4			1		2	1	8
S. Kancabchen	2									2
Sitio Chenche	4					1		1		6
? chen	5									5
Total	522	1	45	2	1	14	7	17	3	612

existing haciendas and bordered Maya milpas and ejidos of pueblos and ranchos. Only three claims were made by persons with Maya surnames, one of whom (Vicente Pech) was the cacique of Yaxcabá in 1841. If one arbitrarily bounds Yaxcabá parish based on the locations of settlements, a total of 700 sq km comprises the parish. Specified claims of terreno baldío therefore amounted to 210 sq km, about 30 percent of the total available land of the parish (for more detailed calculations, see Chapter 4 below).

The 1841 census also provides occupational information for adult males listed on the rolls in each settlement (Tables 3.5 and 3.6). Although overall the vast majority of parish inhabitants were farmers *(labradores)*, Yaxcabá was economically diverse and contained a number of specialists, including merchants, suppliers, mule drivers *(arrieros)*, stone workers, masons, *albarrada*-makers, blacksmiths, tanners, carpenters, cobblers, a tailor, a teacher, and even a musician. A number of individuals described themselves as wage laborers *(asalariado, jornalero)*.

Spanish Creoles who owned haciendas usually described themselves as merchants *(comerciante)*; only Claudio Padilla listed his occupation as "hacendado." Although there were a number of occupations related to livestock production (tanners, blacksmiths, mule drivers), cattle raising and the production of secondary products were not of sufficient scale to prompt significant development of support industries. For example, Yaxcabá apparently did not have a full-time butcher. Estate production emphasized the sale of live animals rather than their conversion into meat and hides. In the independent ranchos, most inhabitants were farmers, but mule drivers specializing in transportation were present in settlements located along key roads. Whereas luneros lived in some of the haciendas and sitios, the most common occupations in these communities were foremen, cowboys, and horse-wranglers.[62]

The 1841 census also lists women in Yaxcabá. Names of individuals were broken down into age and sex categories (Table 3.4). Men are listed in three age grades: from one to fifteen years old, from sixteen to forty years old, and over forty years old. Women are listed as "women of all ages," which together with the lack of any occupational information suggests that the authorities viewed them as household dependents. In a demographically stable population, women slightly outnumber men. Deviations from a 50:50 ratio suggest that some individuals of each group were undercounted. In Yaxcabá, in the pueblos, and in the independent ranchos, men are undercounted between 1 and 4 percent, in keeping with expectations for slightly greater numbers of women. This same pattern holds for the sitios and several haciendas and falls within the range of normal variability. At Rancho Chimay, however, men are underrepresented by 12 percent, suggesting that this rancho contained an unusually high number of women. At four haciendas all belonging to Claudio Padilla (Yximché, Kambul, Xbac, and Xkopteil), a different pattern emerges. The ratio of men to women was unbalanced in favor of men. Women were underrepresented by more than 10 percent, suggesting that the owner employed more single and unattached males. Some resident workers did not have or did not bring their families. This departure from the norm suggests that production on Padilla's estates may have been somewhat different, possibly indicating a different attitude toward patronage. The data for Rancho Chimay and Claudio Padilla's haciendas tentatively suggests that a small, mobile, male wage-labor force, whose individuals resided apart from their households, was emerging in the parish.

The Caste War and Its Aftermath

On July 30, 1847, the rebel Maya attacked Tepich, launching the first and most successful offensive of the Caste War. Five months later, they had entered the Yaxcabá-Sotuta region and attacked and burned Kancabdzonot. By February 1848 the population of Yaxcabá was evacuated first to Sotuta and then beyond as the rebels occupied the region. Nelson Reed (1964) points out that the rebels' success depended in large part on the support they received in the Sotuta region, long known for its resistance to the Spanish colonial regime in earlier eras. The rebels held Yaxcabá for six months, but in July 1848, following the ratification of the Treaty of Tzucacab, they abandoned it to the advancing Creole army.

As the initial Maya offensive was repulsed to the south and east, the conflict between the Creole militia and the rebels took on a different pattern. Yaxcabá was attacked by the rebels twice more in 1848, but retaken each time by the Creole army within a day or so. The garrison was a prime target for opportunistic raids in the later years of the war, and such attacks were most often accompanied by pillaging and burning. In all, the rebel Maya attacked Yaxcabá and/or its dependent settlements a total of nine times between 1847 and 1869 (Table 3.7). The pattern of violence continued into the early twentieth century when the liberalist-socialist disputes following the 1910 revolution prompted yet another strike against Yaxcabá and nearby towns in 1924 (Redfield and Villa Rojas 1934:25–27).

The destruction of Yaxcabá in the mid-nineteenth century is most tangibly evident in archaeology and in oral history.[63] The Caste War left an indelible imprint on the landscape. Buildings were destroyed, and settlements were abandoned. The 1862 census, the first following the Caste War, indicates that of the original twenty-nine settlements of the parish, only seven retained any population. A total of 879 people lived in the parish, a decline of more than 90 percent of the pre-Caste War total. Likewise the Caste War is important in the historical memory of Yaxcabá's modern inhabitants. People still talk about the Caste War, the time of slavery, and seldom distinguish the conflicts of the nineteenth century from those related to the aftermath of the Mexican Revolution.[64] Such destruction, however, took a negative toll on the historical record. Locally produced documentary sources are extremely sparse for this period, and it is difficult to reconstruct local events and conditions.

Between 1848 and 1862 the ayuntamiento conducted business on an attenuated schedule in conjunction with the garrison. Reports and resolutions consisted mostly of descriptions of rebel activity in the region, the condition and amounts of food supplies and material, or leaves and discharges for sick and wounded soldiers. In 1850 Taccibichén requested the government establish a garrison in their community. The request was declined. The military also oversaw Indian travel and migration, as in the case of Manuel Chi and his family who returned to Kancabdzonot from Rancho Nohdzonot, in rebel territory, in 1851.[65] During this time, the Días faction, including Pascual Espejo and Juan E. Castillo, was active in Yaxcabá's ayuntamiento. The documents contain the occasional florid complaint about the desolation of a remaining hacienda, Nohitzá, or the population's consequent inability to pay taxes or contribute supplies.[66] For example, Pascual Espejo complained "of much greater concern [is] for the sum of misery of this unhappy county, that after having suffered from the barbarians a most horrible war, to remain absolutely without houses or goods to maintain itself."

For the most part, however, the documentation in the 1850s consists of ratification of cacique elections. In 1851 cacique elections were held in several towns. In Yaxcabá, the reason for the election of Bernardo Tzakum was the death of the previous officeholder, Alejandro Couoh. Other towns such as Tabi, Kancabdzonot, and Taccibichén simply did not have a cacique, because all the Indians had fled the war.[67] A year later Pascual Espejo expressed his reservations regarding the elected cacique of Kancabdzonot, Marcos Canche, and suggested his removal.[68] Although Canche had previously served as lieutenant cacique before the uprising, it was alleged that he was the indebted servant of Don Pablo González, had fled among the rebels, and was only recently returned. Unstable Maya political leadership continued during the Caste War years. In 1857, Bernardo

TABLE 3.7: Events of the Caste War in Yaxcabá

Date	Description	Reference
July 30, 1847	Maya attack Tepich, official beginning of the Caste War	Reed 1964:59
Dec. 1847	Kancabdzonot burned, recaptured by Creoles, and lost again several days later; Creoles fall back to Yaxcabá	Reed 1964:71
Feb. 12, 1848	The rebel Maya attack Yaxcabá; the battalion retreats; and the population is evacuated to Sotuta and beyond	Reed 1964:71, 289; Dumond 1997:111
Apr. 23, 1848	Governor of Yucatán ratifies Treaty of Tzucacab in Ticul	Reed 1964:79; Dumond 1997:118
July 1848	Maya abandon Sotuta and Yaxcabá, retaken by Creoles	Reed 1964:101
Aug. 24, 1848	Maya attack Yaxcabá, Colonel Pasos retreats to Sotuta; Creole forces reoccupy Yaxcabá one day later	Reed 1964:104–5; Dumond 1997:143
Sept. 8, 1848	Rebel Maya attack Yaxcabá, breach government lines by Sept. 21; govt. troops withdraw to Sotuta from which they mount a counteroffensive and regain Yaxcabá	Dumond 1997:146–47
May 1851	Govt. troops mutiny in Yaxcabá over starvation rations	Reed 1964:141
Sept. 1853	Govt. troops from the Yaxcabá-Sotuta area called back to Mérida; many suffer from cholera; rebel Maya attack Yaxcabá, Santa María, Taccibichén, and Tixcacaltuyú, looting and burning; as govt. troops return, rebels withdraw to Tihosuco	Reed 1964:150, 152; Dumond 1997:202
June–Sept. 1854	Rebel Maya raid Sotuta area, as government troops retreat from Chan Santa Cruz; Maya raid garrisons at Yaxcabá and Tixcacaltuyú (4th attack)	Dumond 1997:205; Reed 1964:154
Apr. 1856	Rebel Maya attack and raze Yaxcabá, Tibolon, Tiholop, Hacienda Xul, and Kancabdzonot; more than 160 dead	Dumond 1997:207–8
Aug. 1857	Rebel Maya attack Chikindzonot, kill 61	Dumond 1997:208
Dec. 19, 1858	Rebel Maya attack Tiholop, Tixcacaltuyú, and Taccibichén; rebels assassinate 81 people (mostly Indian)	AGA 1850–61 Monforte
July 1859	Rebel Maya strike Yaxcabá, Tiholop, Ichmul, and Tihosuco, but are defeated in each case	Dumond 1997:232
1863	Rebel Maya engage in hit-and-run raiding, often burning towns and taking captives	Dumond 1997:253
July 1, 1869	José Antonio Munoz (El Chelo), previous leader of a mutiny in the Mérida citadel, joins the rebels in the Sotuta region; they issue an ultimatum to the government, burn Yaxcabá, and attack and burn Tzucacab	Dumond 1997:304
1906	Riots in Yaxcabá, Peto, and Temax over reelection of Porfirio Diaz; end with Madero revolution.	Reed 1964:248
1924	Liberals attack Yaxcabá, Kancabdzonot, Yaxuná, and Xkopteil in the liberalist-socialist disputes following the revolution.	Redfield and Villa Rojas 1934:25–27

Tzakum resigned after eight years of service, citing "considerable losses due to the invasions of the rebels to this unfortunate town as well as misery and sickness."[69] He was succeeded by Matias Chan and later in 1864 by Pascual Poot.

In 1864 the ayuntamiento passed a new schedule of arbitrios.[70] Unlike the previous tax plan developed in 1813, this schedule seldom mentions production of goods or taxation of commercial establishments and instead focuses on taxing specific items imported to and sold within the town. Vendors of cattle and pigs slaughtered for public sale, wax, soap, chocolate, wheat bread, beans, cucumbers, chilies, sugar, flour, jars, grinding stones (manos and metates), liquor, hammocks, mules (even nags), rice, salt, and smoked or salted fish (including shark) were taxed according to the amount of goods sold. Even peddlers and street sales of retail items were taxed. The schedule suggests that Yaxcabá's productive and commercial infrastructure was in shambles. Many basic goods and foodstuffs were imported from other areas of Yucatán.

The church maintained an extremely low profile throughout the Caste War era. Yaxcabá's designated curate during the Caste War was Eusebio Villamil, who stayed in Mérida with the bishop's permission. In 1850 Villamil's move was made permanent when he was made dean of the cathedral chapter. Routine parish business of recording baptisms, marriages, and deaths was left to interim priests in the nearby parishes of Tixcacaltuyú and Sotuta.[71]

The parish registers for the Sotuta-Yaxcabá region contain one book of burials for Tixcacaltuyú and its auxiliaries, dated 1850 to 1861.[72] These were recorded for Creoles and Indians alike by the curate of Tixcacaltuyú, José Antonio Monforte, who apparently remained in the region throughout the Caste War. In July 1856 he received an order from the bishop uniting the parishes of Tiholop and Yaxcabá to the jurisdiction of Tixcacaltuyú. The inhabitants of those communities had lacked observance of the sacraments for some time due to the rebel uprising. After the curate of Yaxcabá had been ordered to Mérida, Monforte became responsible for the spiritual health of a widely dispersed population. Typically the death records list the date, the name of the deceased, the place of interment, town of origin (if different from the place of burial), the name of the deceased's spouse (if married), the names of the deceased's parents (if a child), and sometimes age and cause of death. Some evidence from the register suggests that the Maya population moved fluidly between outlying settlements in the Yaxcabá-Sotuta region and the rebel Maya frontier. Several entries mention that the surviving male spouse was living among the rebels. A number of deaths for the years 1851–53 officially were recorded later in 1858 because of the difficulties posed by the uprising. Although the population of Monforte's communities had declined drastically, both Maya and Creole families continued to live in Tixcacaltuyú, Taccibichén, and Tiholop, away from the garrison's protection throughout the 1850s.

Although natural causes led to most deaths, two sets of entries stand out. First, a cholera epidemic claimed thirty-seven people between August and December 1853 and another seventeen in August and September 1854. In 1853 mortality was triple the parish average for other years. Second, in 1858 Monforte buried in mass graves in Tiholop, Tixcacaltuyú, and Taccibichén a total of eighty-one persons who had been murdered during the rebel Maya attack of December 19. The deceased included one family from Yaxcabá who had been in Tixcacaltuyú at the time of the assault.

By 1863 Manuel Vicente Hernández had been appointed interim priest for Yaxcabá and nearby towns. Although his entries seem more sporadic than Monforte's, Hernández paid

TABLE 3.8: Census of 1886

Settlement	Labrador	Albañil	Carpintero	Sastre	Barbero	Teladora	Alfarera	Comerciante	Total
Yaxcabá	275	1	1	1	1	4	2	3	288
Mopilá	44								44
Libre Unión	155								155
R. Acula	28								28
R. San José	28								28
R. Uidah	8								8
Total	538	1	1	1	1	4	2	3	551

greater attention to cause of death, often listing fever, measles, smallpox, typhus, miscarriage, pneumonia, pain in the side, and drowning. Later entries by José Inez Castro, curate from 1866–71, listed three deaths for 1870 in Rancho Cutu and one death near Rancho Tekom (both near Taccibichén) as "assassinations by barbarous Indians." The continued attacks in the Yaxcabá area no doubt provoked the comments made in the 1880 visita pastoral of Sotuta, "being on the frontier of the enemy camp of Indian rebels and thus constituting one of the military colonies of the State, as such, poverty is widespread and life violent and full of danger."[73]

By 1870 Yaxcabá had become a dependency of the Parish of Sotuta along with Tabi, Libre Unión, Tibolon, Zavala, Cantamayec, Rancho Cholul, Mopilá, Tixcacaltuyú, and Nenela. Population in Yaxcabá and Mopilá remained low through the 1880s to 1900 (see Figure 3.3). An 1886 census lists a total of 551 individuals living in Yaxcabá, Mopilá, Libre Unión, and three nearby ranchos (Table 3.8, see also Table 3.1).[74] The census-taker also recorded occupational information for both men and women. Yaxcabá had three merchants, one mason, a carpenter, a tailor, a barber, four weavers, and two potters. The weavers and potters were women. All other individuals listed for Yaxcabá and other settlements were farmers. The information suggests that 4.5 percent of Yaxcabá's population were specialists of some sort, a substantial decline from a population that supported 17 percent specialists in 1841.

Summary

The documentary evidence presented above suggests consistency in the long-term patterns of accommodation and resistance to state, church, and elite hegemonies in Yaxcabá. Avoidance was the predominant strategy used to retain production autonomy, whether it involved dispersal to independent ranchos (distancing produce and activities from the eyes of the authorities), establishment of sectarian communities such as estates of religious confraternities, flight to the forest, or playing one potential patron against another. Dispersal produced conflicts over land with neighboring indigenous communities. Formal recognition of legitimate land rights along the old provincial boundaries between Sotuta, Cupul, and Cochuah was attained through litigation (manipulating state authority) or later by attempting to co-opt new Creole patrons by selling disputed land to would-be hacienda owners. Independent rancho communities sometimes established land rights by inviting or accepting the ministrations of the church (patron swapping and manipulating ecclesiastical authority) in an effort to deny the claims of hacienda owners.

Soon after the conquest, native leaders and Maya elite contested the authority of the church and the state. Although the idolatry trials of the late 1500s hint at ecclesiastical contrivance, providing an excuse for heavy-handed interference in rural areas, the authority of the cacique over ritual matters clearly was lost at this juncture. Maya ritual expression within individual homes was also curtailed, such that it became compartmentalized. As a result, indigenous ritual was relocated to the milpa and the monte beyond the community and beyond the reach of priests, where it remained active to the present day. The state reduced the cacique's civil authority to the local level, as sanctioned in the activities of the república de indios. Their authority was further eroded in the late eighteenth century under the Bourbon intendancy when government officials were stationed in rural municipalities. Nevertheless, except for occasional flare-ups, as occurred in the Cisteil revolt, cacique resistance apparently was passive—consisting of "ineptitude" in collecting taxes.

The reduction of ecclesiastical authority in the early nineteenth century created a crisis of legitimacy among those who depended on church patronage in Yaxcabá. Increased flight to the forests, lack of attendance at mass, and nonpayment of obventions became common problems in the parish. The withdrawal of ecclesiastical protection for religious confraternities prompted a search for new patrons. The cofradías of Yaxcabá managed to hang on by convincing the curate to establish one community as a pueblo, and others persisted through the financial assistance of a female Creole benefactor. The structure of hegemony and rural patronage shifted radically after 1821, and Creoles assumed control of local civic affairs. During this period the documents suggest Maya switched backing among different patrons. For example, the officials of the república de indios and the cacique supported the town council against the curate. Disputes between the different Creole factions probably offered opportunities to some, especially considering the frequency with which the Creole-led town council elected and removed native officeholders.

Ultimately, however, the economic activities of the Creoles, based on cattle raising, were insufficient to propel the market transition. In the early nineteenth century, changes in tax policy created additional demands on Maya farm production, which in turn affected the household's life cycle by altering mobility, land tenure and inheritance, household fissioning, and the likelihood that farmers entered into shareholding arrangements. Maya smallholders sold land to Creoles for the development of estates when it was politically advantageous, and especially to resolve disputes with other Maya farmers who lived in different municipal jurisdictions to the east. Farmers who were partially or wholly disenfranchised from their land base and access to labor negotiated diverse sorts of share, land-rental, labor-rent, or wage-labor contracts with both Maya and Creoles to sustain their households. This process increased economic stratification

and diversity within the system, such that smallholders existed side by side with extensive agriculturalists, craft specialists, and landless laborers (see Netting 1993:214).

Nevertheless, many of the haciendas were mired in debt, and cattle raising became a losing venture after independence. Mixed agriculture and stockraising gave way to even more land-
extensive strategies, focused more exclusively on raising cattle, as Creoles claimed and purchased
large tracts of terrenos baldíos. Even this expansion, however, could not make the estates
profitable in the fierce competitive climate that pitted Yucatán against the cattle markets of
Veracruz and Havana. Furthermore, this process was not accompanied by the hiring of more
Maya workers or increasing rural proletarianization. In Yaxcabá, expansion of the estates did
not create a large class of landless agricultural workers, and the hacienda did not replace the
indigenous village as the principal community form in the region. Smallholding was a less risky
and more efficient productive strategy that provided the foundation for diverse commodity
production and craft specialization in the parish in the 1840s. The development of commercial agriculture and stockraising in Yaxcabá was a brief boom-and-bust cycle, plagued by
insufficient capital and market access, even before the Caste War rebels launched their attack.

## CHAPTER FOUR

Archaeological Settlement Patterns

T he analysis of settlement patterns, the ways in which humans dispose themselves over the landscape, is a mainstay of archaeological interpretation (Willey 1953). Archaeologists commonly approach questions about changing political and economic hierarchy, population density, land use, and subsistence stress by comparing the distributions of different kinds of sites to their ecological setting. When settlement pattern research is applied to historical periods, however, we frequently find that archaeology and history do not tell the same story. An examination of the archaeological settlement patterns of Yaxcabá parish from the time of the Spanish conquest to 1900 reveals major changes in the use of different places on the landscape over time. With respect to the development of an agrarian crisis before the Caste War, archaeological settlement patterns provide an important and independent source of evidence with which to assess these arguments. This chapter addresses three themes: (1) a description of the distribution of different kinds of sites in time and space, with particular attention to cultural ecology, economic and political functions, fluctuating occupational histories, population density, and architectural infrastructure; (2) an assessment of the similarities and differences between archaeological settlements and their characterization in documentary sources; and (3) an evaluation of the evidence for land pressure among various community types by examining how postindependence agrarian legislation was implemented in the region. Although historical records do not permit a complete reconstruction of landholding in Yaxcabá parish, the comparison of the locations of different communities, the amounts of land legally granted to them, and estimates of their populations offer evidence of tensions over land between some Maya agriculturalists and Creole cattle ranchers.[1]

The Lay of the Land

In both the pre-Columbian and Colonial periods on the Yucatán Peninsula, the most important factor affecting the choice of settlement location was the availability of water (Garza Tarzona de González and Kurjack 1980). The peninsula is a karst geological system formed by a recently emerged limestone platform whose northern third is composed of horizontal, Pliocene-era strata of limestone, marl, and gypsum (Isphording and Wilson 1973; West 1964). Surface streams and lakes are absent, and rainwater filters rapidly through the porous substrate to underground channels. Collapse of the surface rock above the subterranean channels creates dolines that expose the water table; these are known as cenotes. The karst plain is peppered with these features that constitute the most important water sources for humans and animals alike. In some cases the limestone parent rock collapses, but the base of the resulting sinkhole does not reach the water table. Soil accumulates and retains moisture in these depressions, known as *hoyas* or rejolladas, such that they become desirable locales for cultivation. Shallow depressions known as *aguadas* also provide water; the depressions form permanent ponds in situations where clay has sealed the fissures of the limestone substrate. Similarly, caves and fissures also provide fresh water. In the Colonial period, natural water sources were supplemented by digging wells through the limestone cap rock down to the water table.

The karst plain is the largest of three distinct ecological zones in northern Yucatán. The other two are the coast and the Puuc hills (see West 1964). The northern and western coasts of the peninsula are characterized by barrier beaches that delimit lagoons and tidal swamps that were used for salt collection since pre-Hispanic times. The east coast typically consists of low cliffs and headlands with a string of coral reefs offshore. In contrast to the coast and the interior, the Puuc hills, located in the southwestern part of the peninsula, rise some 50 m above the surrounding plain. This zone has the best and deepest soils for cultivation, and the area contains numerous caves, aguadas, and cenotes. To the south of the Puuc range, elevation rises, and the topography gives way to a hilly karst zone around the city of Campeche.

Yaxcabá is located in the interior karst plain, some 150 km from the north coast (see Figure 1.1 in Chapter 1). Variation in elevation is minimal across the surrounding area; the region as a whole lies about 25 m above sea level. Like most of northern Yucatán, the climate is classified as tropical wet and dry (Aw in the Koeppen system), with a pronounced rainy season from June to October and a long dry season from November to May. Rainfall varies across the peninsula such that the northwest corner is arid, whereas the southeast is humid. Vegetation follows the rainfall pattern, and the cover becomes denser and more verdant as one moves toward the southeast. Yaxcabá receives between 1,000 and 2,000 mm of precipitation annually. Wet-season rainfall averages between 100 and 200 mm per month, but dry-season precipitation is usually less than 25 mm per month (Vivó Escoto 1964). Vegetation is classified as a dry evergreen woodland, with the canopy at 30 m (Wagner 1964). The dense secondary growth is a product of long-term agricultural activity. Soils are not deep (0 to 30 cm), with the exception of those that accumulate in sinkholes. In many spots, large areas of limestone bedrock are exposed. The soils are calcimorphic "terra rossa" forms, which include the Rendzina group so favored by pre-Hispanic cultivators (Stevens 1964).

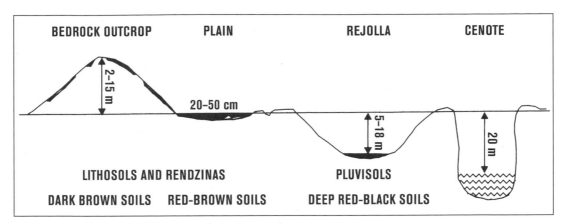

FIGURE 4.1. Geomorphology in the Yaxcabá Region (drawing by Rani Alexander and Mandi Martinez, after Pool Novelo 1980).

Although all of the settlements within the Yaxcabá region occur in the same ecological zone, inhabitants regularly exploited microenvironmental variability in topography, soils, and the locations of cenotes both in the pre-Hispanic and Colonial periods. The geomorphology of the region is characterized by four features: bedrock outcrops, plains, rejolladas, and cenotes (Figure 4.1) (Pool Novelo 1980). The bedrock outcrops rise 2 to 15 m above the surrounding plains. They are sparsely covered with soil, most of which is found in pockets within the limestone. Outcrops have been used since the pre-Hispanic period as ideal locations for residential structures, although the degree to which they were modified for construction varied. Pre-Hispanic builders frequently used the entire outcrop as a base over which a mound or platform was constructed. In all time periods, including the present, people have placed ephemeral foundation braces for perishable structures on top of outcrops, often filling uneven surfaces with *chich* (crushed limestone) and sascab (calcareous sand).

Plains and flat lands are located between outcrops and have more soil, although they are often rocky. These areas are desirable for use in milpa cultivation, especially if they are part of an archaeological site or abandoned settlement. Organic refuse deposited from previous habitation enriches the soil such that when these areas are cultivated, the farmer often achieves a better harvest.

Sinkholes, or rejolladas, vary in depth from 2 to 18 m below the surface and contain relatively deep soil with a high humus content. Because the rejolladas preserve moisture in the soil, even during the dry season, they are desirable features of any land parcel. Currently in Yaxcabá they are used for a variety of horticultural endeavors, especially for growing fruit trees. In the pre-Hispanic period rejolladas were used to grow cacao (Gómez-Pompa 1990; Kepecs and Boucher 1996; Schmidt 1980).

As in the rest of northern Yucatán, the cenotes constitute the principal water source in the Yaxcabá region. Today the freatic level is approximately 20 m below the surface. Cenotes are more numerous to the north and east of Yaxcabá and scarce in areas to the south. Pre-Hispanic and colonial settlements within the parish are almost always located near cenotes, and a number of norias (wells that pump water to the surface by means of wind power or animal traction) sometimes were constructed over small cenotes.

Settlement Survey

An archaeological settlement survey provides answers to several important questions relevant to an agrarian crisis in Yaxcabá. First, the distribution of sites of different sizes and configurations over the landscape and the changes in their distribution over time offer information about population density, land use, and site function. These variables permit us to assess the structure of agricultural production, stockraising, and the exploitation of natural resources in the region. Second, the location, size, configuration, and function of architecture within settlements allows one to assess changing political-economic structure within the region. Finally, the settlement survey provides the contextual basis for more intensive investigations of individual sites and house lots (see discussion of this in Chapter 5, below). It allows one to gauge the extent to which sites selected for further investigation are representative of those in the parish as a whole.

For the purposes of this study, the Yaxcabá region was arbitrarily defined as an area circumscribing all settlements pertaining to the parish in the eighteenth and early nineteenth centuries. A base map of the region was prepared using the quadrangle maps of the Instituto Nacional de Estadística, Geografía e Informatica (INEGI), specifically the Yaxcabá, Tixcacaltuyú, Chichén Itzá, and Chikindzonot quads at the scale of 1:50,000 (Figure 4.2). The *Atlas Arqueológico de Yucatán* (Garza Tarzona de González and Kurjack 1980) was also consulted for the locations of pre-Hispanic and modern settlements. The total area of the region is about 700 sq km, somewhat smaller than the 1,079 sq km encompassed by the modern municipality.

With the assistance of local farmers in Yaxcabá and surrounding communities and students from the Universidad Autónoma de Yucatán, I conducted an extensive archaeological survey in order to locate and describe the communities inhabited during the last five hundred years. Because the dense vegetation in the area does not permit unimpeded passage or ground visibility (even in the dry season), a full-coverage pedestrian survey was impractical. We therefore opted for an intensive reconnaissance strategy. Armed with a comprehensive list of settlement and place names gleaned from the documentary sources, we located, recorded, and partially mapped a total of thirty sites, twenty-nine of which were described by Granado Baeza in his visitas pastorales of 1784, 1804, and 1828.[2]

In the earliest stages of field research, we were forced to examine how our archaeological units of analysis—the region and the site—were related to places of cultural significance to the historical population—the parish and its communities. A site is defined as a localized area showing physical evidence of human alteration that ideally held some cultural significance for its inhabitants (Sanders et al. 1979:34). Sites in the Yaxcabá region could be as ephemeral as a scatter of artifacts near an isolated well or as substantial as a town of 4,000 people. Not all places named in the documents were sites, especially if the place-name referred to an agricultural parcel

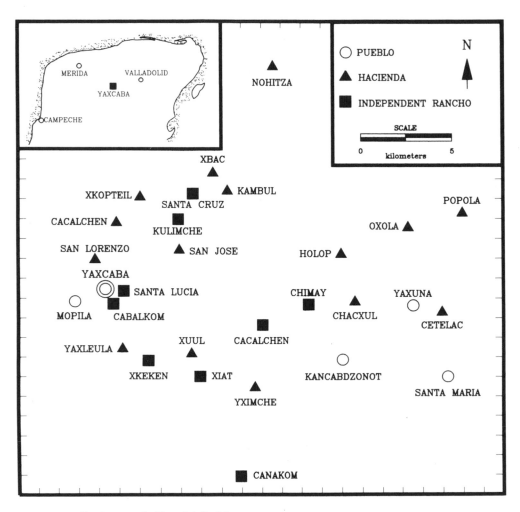

FIGURE 4.2. Settlements in Yaxcabá Parish.

lacking archaeological features. Similarly, we briefly noted several sites and archaeological features that were not recognized in historical documents as communities or places, such as roads and features located along roadways used as travelers' rest stops. To maximize the productivity of the survey, we allocated the most time to recording sites mentioned in documentary sources. Places known as sitios, unimproved agricultural parcels, established only a few years before the Caste War, were more problematic. Often owners would claim that these places were "haciendas," and some lay beyond the archaeologically defined region.

The degree to which the boundary of the archaeological region coincided with the boundary of the parish was another consideration. The archaeological region coincides with the parish as established for the late eighteenth and early nineteenth centuries before independence from Spain, when Yaxcabá was one of six parishes in the *subdelegación* of Beneficios Bajos. Political jurisdictions changed after independence such that Yaxcabá became a subordinate town within the Partido of Sotuta, Department of Tekax (see Güemez Pineda 1994). In the 1840s just before the Caste War, a number of Spanish Creoles in Yaxcabá had acquired property in the form of sitios and unimproved land parcels to the north, west, and southeast of the parish. Political and territorial jurisdictions between Yaxcabá and Sotuta were under negotiation, and a number of individuals argued that Yaxcabá should remain a separate partido.[3] In order to maintain consistency in the sampling universe, we retained the original parish boundaries during the survey and did not record all of the new sitios and land claims, even though some were named in the documents.[4]

Although incomplete coverage is always a problem using reconnaissance techniques, we were able to locate and describe even the most ephemeral settlements with the assistance of local consultants. All of the settlements listed in documentary sources retained their eighteenth- and nineteenth-century names and were well known to local farmers. In several cases, our consultants showed us places that did not appear in the nineteenth-century records. Some of these sites were modern ranchos, and others were subsequently identified on later censuses. Although it is always possible that the survey missed sites that did not appear in the documents at all, we did ask our consultants to show us places similar to the others that we had visited, no matter how small. As a result we located and visited many more sites and places—some pre-Hispanic, some modern farms, some twentieth-century ranchos. Those that were situated outside of the parish boundaries or pertaining to earlier and later settlement systems fall outside the scope of the present study and are not described here.

Site formation, visibility, and preservation were variable within the region. Six settlements, including Yaxcabá itself, are currently occupied and recognized as municipalities on the latest census. Several of these communities showed evidence of pre-Hispanic occupation, and mounds and platforms were still evident in the site center. These were the most visible and easiest to map. In many cases, the area of modern occupation was surrounded by unused house lots whose boundary walls were in disrepair and whose interiors were covered in dense secondary growth. In a few cases, we could determine that the orientation of streets and house lots had changed with the twentieth-century reoccupation. Although much of the nineteenth-century architecture in these communities was still standing and in use, other buildings had fallen into disrepair or parts were heavily reconstructed.

Although other settlements were abandoned and largely covered by dense tropical vegetation, local farmers still knew and used them as water sources, for milpa cultivation, apiculture, and small-scale livestock raising. The original roads and footpaths between them still see heavy foot and bicycle traffic. A patchwork of harvested milpas and dense secondary growth covered these places. Most of the archaeological remains consisted of fallen, dry-laid stone boundary walls that originally delimited house lots. Often, all that remained of the original house was a stone alignment or oval-shaped foundation brace. Small masonry shrines, wells, or the masonry platform and water tank surrounding a noria were still standing and sometimes used and refurbished. With a little work clearing the vegetation, it was usually easy to follow the stone walls that delimited streets. The presence of a cenote or other water source influenced the number and length of occupations and patterns of site reuse.

Most of the haciendas that were destroyed during the Caste War are in use today for mixed stockraising and agricultural activities, and a few are now privately owned. In some cases, the buildings of the main house were still standing and were occupied, but usually only the corrals and wells of the estate were in use or showed signs of refurbishment. Most masonry structures were partially collapsed. The remains of the house lots of estate workers were covered in tropical vegetation, and it was difficult to locate foundation braces or other features without extensive clearing.

Still other settlements, however, were completely abandoned. Except for people passing through on the roads who stopped to use the water source, all evidence of previous occupation was covered by dense tropical forest. Masonry shrines and wells were difficult to locate. These sites were quite inaccessible, and we only reached them after several hours of walking from Yaxcabá. According to local farmers, these sites served an important agricultural function and were sometimes used for milpa, but at the time of the survey they had been left fallow for many years, such that the vegetation resembled primary forest.

Settlement Typology

Typological classifications generalize variability in a range of attributes that are relevant to questions or problems of interest to the investigator (Hill and Evans 1972). For this study, I have constructed a settlement typology that reflects variation in political-economic function, population size, land use, and site function. Analysis of site size, the amount and characteristics of masonry architecture, and the spatial arrangement of the site center allowed me to classify the settlements into four discrete categories (Table 4.1). The archaeological typology also provides an independent framework for comparing sites' archaeological attributes to their historical classification—a typology developed by historians using different attributes to create generalizations relevant to a different range of questions.

Information collected for each site included its UTM coordinates, topographic and ecological setting, water sources, an estimate of site size, the amount and stylistic characteristics of standing architecture, evidence for specialized functions within sites, and presence or absence of pre-Hispanic occupation.[5] The central areas of each settlement were mapped either with compass and tape or with a laser theodolite. We located and mapped standing or ruined masonry buildings, norias, wells, corrals, stables, house-lot boundaries along streets, and other ancillary structures. We estimated site size by following one street from the site center to the perimeter. Mapping the vast network of corrals and/or house lots surrounding the site centers, however, was beyond the scope of the extensive survey.

Category I

Only one site in the region, Yaxcabá itself, is classified as a category I site (Table 4.2; Figure 4.3; see also Figure 1.2 in Chapter 1), and it is currently occupied. It shares a similar spatial arrangement with sites of categories II and IV. Residential house lots delimited by dry-laid stone walls (albarradas) are arranged along the street grid, centered on the church, the municipal building (audiencia of the ayuntamiento), and the main plaza. The cenote is located in a second

TABLE 4.1: Attributes of Archaeological Site Types in the Yaxcabá Region

Archaeological Category	Mean Size (ha)	Mean Maximum Population	Mean Masonry Construction (sq m)	Building Types
I (n=1)	100	3,292	10,711	Two churches, rectory, shrines, norias, municipal building, quintas, perishable pole-and-thatch houses
II (n=4)	47	1,327	1,661	Church, shrine, noria, one quinta, perishable pole-and-thatch houses
III (n=16)	0.84*	79	310	Main house, noria, water troughs, corrals, stables, perishable pole-and-thatch structures
IV (n=9)	27	295	55	Shrines, noria, perishable pole-and-thatch houses

*Area of core buildings and central corrals only.

plaza to the north of the church. Although the settlement focuses on a central water source, private wells and norias are found in house lots throughout the community. Site size measures 1 sq km, which, in addition to the larger scale and abundance of religious, public, and private masonry constructions, distinguishes category I from others in the classification system.

Yaxcabá has two colonial churches. The largest (San Francisco), completed around 1757, is located on the east side of the main plaza and is noted for its three towers and gilded retablo with salomonic columns (Bretos 1992). Adjacent to the northern and southern sides of the nave is an elaborate ossuary and rectory. The area to the back of the church and rectory is enclosed by a high masonry wall forming private space and gardens for the clergy. A large noria within this enclosure supplies water to the rectory and church. The smaller church is located on a bedrock outcrop to the north of the larger church; the keystone of the entrance bears a date of 1805. Civic buildings in Yaxcabá are also constructed of masonry. On the north side of the main plaza is the audiencia, also housing the *pósito* (granary), *cuartel* (militia barracks), and school, completed around 1829. The building is stylistically elaborate with a long series of arches defining the portico.

Residential masonry buildings, known as *quintas,* line the remaining sides of the main plaza. These are large, elaborate residences sometimes occupying an entire city block. The principal masonry structure/residence that faces the street typically exhibits decoration including scalloped doorways, embedded columns on sides of doors, and polychrome paint and *rajueleado* on exterior walls.[6] Areas behind these structures are enclosed by high masonry walls abutting

FIGURE 4.3. Features of Category I sites, San Francisco Yaxcabá (photo by Nigel Holman).

additional masonry structures and rooms used for sleeping quarters, food preparation, and stabling of livestock. The quinta once belonging to Claudio Padilla (the Huay Cote) is the largest example in Yaxcabá. It has its own noria, and a large masonry oven *(horno)* occupies most of one room. A niche on the exterior of the south wall, facing the street, served as a shrine. The architecture and facilities of the quintas in Yaxcabá recall the structures and facilities of the category III sites (haciendas) in the region.

As one moves away from the main plaza, the scale of residential architecture is reduced. Masonry constructions are much smaller and less common, rapidly giving way to the typical apsidal houses found throughout Yucatán. These consist of an elliptical ground plan, sometimes with a masonry foundation, walls constructed of wood poles chinked with daub and plastered, and a pitched roof covered with thatch. The remainder of the house lot is fenced not with masonry but with dry-laid, limestone block walls. Additional structures or features in the lot, such as pig sties, chicken coops, beehives, water storage *pilas,* and corn cribs, are made of unfaced limestone blocks or perishable materials.

Judging by size and permanence of the masonry buildings and facilities on the main plaza, the category I site is the top-ranking religious and civic center of the region. Residential

TABLE 4.2: Population, Age, and Architectural Features of Settlements in Yaxcabá Parish

Site	Archaeological Category	Maximum Population[a]	Size	Population Density	Age[b]	Municipal Building	Church	Rectory	Shrines & Chapels	Houses & Quintas	Noria	Total
Cabecera												
Yaxcabá	I	3,292c	100	32.9	313	1,500	4,578	1,024	9	3,600+		10,711
Pueblos												
Mopilá	II	1,028c	55	18.7	313		1,720			240d	100	2,060
Kancabdzonot	II	2,097	60	35	84		1,590		9	300		1,899
Yaxuná	II	896	30	29.9	78		894			300		1,194
Sta. María	II	1,290	43	30	78		1,492					1,492
Independent Ranchos												
Sta. Lucía	IV	151c	14	10.8	84							
Cabalkóm	IV	254c	17	14.9	78							
Canakóm	IV	560	20	28.0	78				+			+
Chimay	IV	178	21	8.5	78				+			+
Sta. Cruz	IV	380	43	8.8	34				9			9
Xkekén	IV	8c	1	8	78							
Cacalchén	IV	634	35	18.1	78				43	48		91
Cofradia Estates												
Xiat	IV	167	30	5.6	78				120	24	100	244
Kulimché	IV	322	61	5.3	78						100	100

Note: Architecture is measured in square meters; foundation braces of destroyed architectural features are indicated by +. Site size is measured in hectares.

a. Maximum population is from the 1828 Visitas Pastorales unless otherwise noted (AME, 1828, 1829).

b. Age of the settlement in 1862, date of the first census following the Caste War.

c. Yaxcabá's population in 1804 (UP Berendt 1837); Mopilá's population in 1600 (García Bernal 1978); population for Sta. Lucía, Cabalkóm, and Xkekén in 1784 (AME, 1784).

d. A colonial masonry platform is likely the remains of a quinta in Mopilá; the walls of the building no longer remain.

FIGURE 4.4a. Features of Category II sites: The church at Kancabdzonot (photo by Jeanne Randall).

architecture also demonstrates a range of quality, size, and permanence suggesting visible and obvious social stratification, as well as vast differences in household production, organization, and consumption. Yaxcabá has been occupied continuously since the Spanish conquest.

Category II

Four sites in the region—Mopilá, Kancabdzonot, Yaxuná, and Santa María—are classified in category II (see Table 4.2; Figure 4.4a–c). All except Mopilá are currently occupied. The center of these sites have the same spatial arrangement as the category I site. Administrative buildings are perishable. House lots bounded by albarradas are arranged along a grid and centered on the church and main plaza. The streets widen at intervals creating small public spaces. All of the category II settlements have either a cenote or a noria located in or next to the main plaza, and additional wells are located in house lots or in public spaces along the streets throughout each community. At Mopilá the noria is located on a large raised masonry platform and water could be stored in adjacent reservoirs.

Compared to Yaxcabá, however, these sites are smaller and the amount and diversity of masonry architecture is vastly reduced (see Table 4.1). Mopilá, Kancabdzonot, Yaxuná, and Santa María measure 55 ha, 60 ha, 30 ha, and 43 ha respectively. Each site has a church with an adjacent ossuary and an additional cemetery at the edge of town. Although the churches' T-shaped plans are similar to the church in Yaxcabá, they are much smaller in size and lack separate residences for clergy. In both Mopilá and Santa María the churches are elevated above the level

FIGURE 4.4b. Features of Category II sites: The church at Mopilá, east side (photo by Jeanne Randall).

FIGURE 4.4c. Features of Category II sites: House lots at Mopilá (photo by Rani Alexander).

FIGURE 4.5. Retablo of the Iglesia de San Mateo, Mopilá (photo by Jeanne Randall).

of the plaza on what likely are pre-Hispanic platforms. The church in Mopilá, dedicated to San Mateo, has very thick walls (80–100 cm) and probably dates to the seventeenth or early eighteenth century, contemporary with the church in Yaxcabá.[7] Although one document describes this church as roofed with thatch, a small corner of the nave retains a fragment of a wood beam and masonry roof. The church also has an elaborately carved wooden retablo with a free-standing figure of San Mateo on the main altar (Figure 4.5). In contrast, the masonry construction of the churches in the other three sites is less massive, even though the floor area of the structures approaches that of Mopilá. Church doorways in Yaxuná, Kancabdzonot, and Santa María bear the dates of 1817, 1813, and 1816 respectively, and the cemetery in Kancabdzonot is dated 1808. These construction dates correspond roughly to the dates of the visitas pastorales when these communities were named as pueblos instead of ranchos. Kancabdzonot also has a shrine containing a *huipil*-draped cross within a circular enclosure *(alameda)* at the easternmost entrance to the community. Today crosses made of stone or wood commonly demarcate town boundaries, roads, and travelers' rest stops in rural Yucatán.

Residential architecture in category II sites is also reduced in size, compared to the category I site. Yaxuná and Kancabdzonot each have one standing quinta, but the small size and limited decoration of these buildings bear little resemblance to the most elaborate examples in Yaxcabá. At Mopilá one house lot contained a colonial masonry platform constructed over a small pre-Hispanic mound. The platform likely is the foundation of a small quinta although the walls of the structure no longer remain. All other residential architecture in category II settlements consists of house lots containing small apsidal structures with perishable roofs and walls.

Category II sites are auxiliary towns of the municipal seat, Yaxcabá. The smaller religious architecture and lack of substantial housing for clergy indicates their subordinate relationship with the category I site. The absence of masonry civil architecture suggests a similar subordinate position with respect to state authority. The church likely invested greater resources within these communities than did the state. Residential architecture in Mopilá, Kancabdzonot, Yaxuná, and Santa María indicates less intracommunity social stratification but suggests severe class divisions between Yaxcabá and its auxiliaries within the region. For the most part, category II sites served as permanent residential locations for groups of farmers subject to taxation by both the church and state.

Mopilá was occupied before the Spanish conquest and abandoned in the early twentieth century in the wake of the Caste War. Now it is used as part of the ejido of Yaxcabá for agriculture and growing citrus. The other three settlements have had more sporadic histories, but are currently occupied, having been reestablished in the 1920s. Before 1750, however, these three sites were used for extensive agricultural activities. Population growth in the late eighteenth century prompted farmers to establish permanent communities in these places, and by the early nineteenth century Kancabdzonot, Yaxuná, and Santa María were recognized as pueblos de visita by the church.

Category III

Sixteen settlements are classified as category III sites. They comprise the most variable settlement class in the Yaxcabá region (Table 4.3; Figure 4.6a–c). Although all have facilities and infrastructure for raising livestock, their size and architectural investment varied considerably. Architecturally elaborate sites, such as Xbac, San José Yaxleulá, Kambul, Popolá, Cetelac, Chacxul, Holop, Nohitzá, Xuul, and Cacalchén, generally have a main house *(casa principal),* sometimes two-storied; a noria with its tank or reservoir; water troughs for livestock; two to four central corrals, often with decorative arches over corral entrances; and sometimes a small stable or *casa de burros.* Surrounding many of the larger settlements is an extensive network of walls that delimited corrals for livestock and streets and house lots for the resident population. Some also possess small water tanks (pilas), irrigation berms *(eras),* dovecotes *(palomares),* stone berms *(arriates;* these surround and protect trees, often in orchards), ovens, an altar or shrine within one room of the main house, apsidal masonry structures, and wells. The largest category III site in the region, Nohitzá, has a separate standing chapel and a separate building used to house machinery *(casa de máquinas)* (Roys 1939). Several of the smallest category III settlements (San Lorenzo, Oxolá, Santa Cruz, and Yximché), however, consist of little more than a noria or a

TABLE 4.3: Population, Age, and Architectural Features of Category III Sites (Haciendas) in Yaxcabá Parish

Hacienda	Maximum Population[a]	Age in years[b]	Area of Masonry Buildings (sq m)	Architectural Features
Nohitzá	220	148	650	two-story main house, chapel, noria, corral with arched gates, casa de máquinas, apsidal house, arriates
Cetelac	51	87	415	two-story main house, noria, corral with arched gates, apsidal house, arriates
Kambul	169	78	361	single-story main house, noria, corral, stable
Popolá	138	76	694	two-story main house, noria, corral with one arched gate, stable with dovecote, pyramidal monument
Chacxul	125	76	403	two-story main house, noria, pilas, eras, corral, arriate
Xbac	206	76	608	single-story main house, two norias, cistern, corrals, large stable with dovecote
Holop	107	56	226	single-story main house, noria, corral, stable, arriates
San José	58	45	350	single-story main house, noria, pilas, corral with arched gates, oven, arriate
Xkopteil	13	32	284	house platform, noria, corral
Xuul	39	32	352	two-story main house, noria, corral, pilas, arriates
Yaxleulá	27	32	240	house platform, noria, corral, stable, arriate
Cacalchén	20	32	145	single-story main house, noria, corral, apsidal house, arriates
Yximché	16	32	105	noria, corral, arriates
San Lorenzo	23	32	84	well and pila, corral, apsidal house, arriates
Oxolá	37	32	14	well, stable, corral, arriate
Santa Cruz	14	19	24	well, corral, apsidal house

a. From AME, Visitas Pastorales, 1828, 1829.
b. From AME, Visitas Pastorales, 1784, 1804, 1828; and ANEY Notarías, 1800–1850. Age is measured in reference to 1860.

FIGURE 4.6a. Features of Category III sites: The casa principal at Cetelac, west side (photo by Rani Alexander).

FIGURE 4.6b. Features of Category III sites: The casa principal at Cetelac, east side (photo by Rani Alexander).

FIGURE 4.6c. Features of Category III sites: Corral gate at Cetelac (photo by Rani Alexander).

well, a water trough, and a large masonry corral. Main houses are absent. Two other sites, Xkopteil and San Antonio Yaxleulá, have only masonry platforms that once supported presumably less substantial main houses. Networks of masonry walls linking the norias to water troughs and corrals are the principal features of these sites.

Category III settlements exhibit two basic patterns in the arrangement of structures at the site center. The noria may be located immediately adjacent to the main house, or it may be separated from the main house and connected to water troughs via a masonry wall and channel. Nohitzá, Cetelac, Chacxul, Xbac, Xuul, San José Yaxleulá, San Antonio Yaxleulá, and Yximché conform to the first arrangement. The noria platform and its water-storage tank are rectangular and abut the main house. Water troughs usually run in front of the house and are supplied with water via relatively short stone channels. Kambul, Popolá, Xkopteil, Cacalchén, and Holop exemplify the second pattern. In these cases the noria platform may be either round or square, and water troughs may be located either in front of the main house or on the sides of corrals. At Xkopteil, Cacalchén, and Kambul the channels that conduct water to the troughs are situated on top of an aqueduct constructed of thick masonry, often more than 1 m high. At Xkopteil, Popolá, and Holop, the noria provides water for troughs located in subsidiary corrals in addition to the main corral. These two patterns are not temporally distinct, because both are represented among the six oldest category III sites in the region. Three sites lacking norias, San Lorenzo, Oxolá, and Santa Cruz, do not conform to either arrangement. These sites have small apsidal or rectangular masonry structures and wells that deliver water to troughs within a masonry corral. They appear "unfinished" and are among the youngest category III sites in the region.

The buildings and facilities of these settlements indicate specialized production of livestock. Residential architecture within category III settlements also reflects the organization of labor and social stratification within the communities. All but three sites have one main house, likely the residence of the estate owner, similar in size and architectural style to quintas in Yaxcabá. A number of settlements also have a smaller residential masonry structure located near the main house, usually just outside of the main corral. These structures probably housed salaried foremen. In the outlying house lots, however, apsidal houses with perishable walls and roofs are the norm. The resident workers of the community, farmers or cowboys, lived further away from the casa principal.

The differences in the amount of masonry construction and in the spatial arrangement of buildings and facilities in category III sites also lend support to Pedro Bracamonte's (1990; see also Alexander 1997b; D. Jones 1980; Millet Cámara 1985) suggestion that the age of the settlement affected its form. Yucatecan haciendas underwent a growth cycle. As the estate developed over time, increased investment in the buildings and facilities on an estate and additional workers were necessary to maintain and increase production. Logically, the first buildings constructed were those for acquiring and controlling water and penning livestock. Housing for salaried workers and the owner was the next priority. Perishable constructions were gradually replaced with masonry. The size and elaboration of the hacienda's infrastructure, particularly the casa principal, reflected the success of the enterprise, the owner's social status, and attempts to ensure intergenerational transmission of wealth (Alexander 2003; Bracamonte y Sosa 1993, 1990:53; Brading 1977).

All of the category III sites were founded in the late eighteenth and early nineteenth centuries, and ten are as recent as the postindependence era. These cattle-raising estates interchangeably are called haciendas, estancias, ranchos, and sitios in the documents. With the exceptions of Nohitzá and San José Yaxleulá, all were pillaged and abandoned during the Caste War. Currently several of these sites remain the private property of individuals living in Yaxcabá or Mérida. They are used for agriculture, apiculture, and small-scale livestock raising. Others have been absorbed as parts of the ejidos of Yaxuná, Santa María, and Kancabdzonot where they are used for similar purposes. Only two sites, Nohitzá and Xuul, are still used for commercial cattle raising.[8]

Category IV

A total of nine settlements (Kulimché, Santa Cruz, Cacalchén, Xiat, Chimay, Canakóm, Cabalkóm, Santa Lucía, and Xkekén) were classified as category IV sites (Figure 4.7a–c).[9] Their spatial arrangement and size are similar to category II settlements. They range in size from 1 to 61 ha, with an average size of 27 ha. House lots are aligned along streets, but generally the grid pattern is slightly less formal than in category II and category I sites. Unlike category II sites, these settlements lack churches and quintas. All have a centrally located well, noria, or cenote in or near a central plaza. The streets of category IV sites also widen at intervals, creating small *plazuelas;*

FIGURE 4.7a.
Features of Category IV sites:
A chapel at Cacalchén
(photo by Jeanne Randall).

FIGURE 4.7b. Features of
Category IV sites: Masonry
house at Cacalchén
(photo by Rani Alexander).

FIGURE 4.7c. Features of Category IV sites: House-lot corner at Cacalchén
(photo by Rani Alexander).

additional wells are situated in individual house lots within the settlements. Masonry shrines
and small chapels *(adoratorios)* are common, as are cemeteries located at the edges of the settlements. Residential architecture consists of house lots containing apsidal structures with perishable roofs and walls. Like all other sites in the region, the house lots often contained features
such as pig sties, water storage pilas, and other agricultural infrastructure made of local limestone or perishable materials.

The development of facilities and infrastructure in category IV sites is variable (see Table
4.2). Cacalchén, for example, measures 35 ha in size and has three adoratorios, a cemetery, a
large cenote, and six additional wells located in house lots throughout the community. Xiat
and Santa Cruz each have one chapel and a cemetery. Xiat and Kulimché have norias as their
central water sources. Nevertheless, the smallest of these sites, exemplified by Xkekén and Santa
Lucía, consisted of little more than a well and small plaza surrounded by a few house lots.

Generally the size and population of category IV sites overlap the same figures for the category II sites (see Table 4.2). The principal difference is the scale of religious architecture, suggesting that the category IV sites were subordinate to both Yaxcabá and the auxiliary towns

and subject to minimal ecclesiastical and civil supervision. Residential patterns indicate little or no specialization among households, and stratification within the communities was not marked architecturally. These settlements were used as permanent residential locations for groups of farmers who wished to distance themselves from civil and ecclesiastical regulation.

Category IV sites also have sporadic occupational histories. Three of these sites, Canakóm, Chimay, and Cacalchén, were occupied before the Spanish conquest. After the policy of congregación was implemented, most category IV sites were abandoned and used for milpa cultivation. As the population grew in the eighteenth century, they again became permanent settlements, known as ranchos and haciendas de cofradía in historical documents. Xkekén was abandoned by 1800, as were Cabalkóm and Santa Lucía, both on the outskirts of Yaxcabá. The rest of the category IV sites saw impressive growth during the early nineteenth century but were abandoned during the Caste War. Chimay, Cacalchén, and Canakóm were reoccupied as permanent settlements in the 1920s, but Cacalchén was abandoned again in the 1950s when the road between Yaxcabá and Libre Unión was paved. The twentieth-century inhabitants severely modified existing house lots and street orientations to suit the activities and smaller scale of their communities. Recent refurbishment of wells and water troughs at Santa Cruz, Kulimché, and Cacalchén indicate they were used for small-scale livestock raising and apiculture in the twentieth century. The shrine at Santa Cruz is covered in candle wax and still in use. A number of families from Yaxcabá cultivate milpa, raise pigs, and keep bees at Xiat, Cacalchén, and Xkekén.

Distribution in Time and Space

To describe the distribution of different kinds of sites over time, archaeologists normally rely on established regional chronologies that divide time into periods and phases based on changes in ceramic and architectural styles (Sanders et al. 1979:93–94). Major changes in settlement pattern and material culture reflect changes in culture process and behavioral organization. Regional archaeological surveys in Mesoamerica generally place sites in chronological phases spanning 150 to 200 years, based on the assessment of ceramic material collected from the surface. When the site's chronology is based on excavated materials, however, a more refined interpretation of its occupational history results, often with phases of less than 50 years' duration. In Yaxcabá, the periods of occupation of most communities are documented historically and provide a much more refined chronology than that attainable from ceramic surface collections.[10] In many cases, additional physical evidence, such as dates inscribed on masonry buildings, confirmed the dates indicated in documentary sources. I have divided the postconquest chronology of Yucatán into seven phases corresponding to periods of significant historical change. By comparing the distribution of different archaeological settlement categories among these periods, one can examine changes in settlement patterns and the effects of political-economic processes on the archaeological record of Yaxcabá parish. Sites in each of the four categories discussed above are differentially distributed over time (Figure 4.8a–g, pp 90–93; Table 4.4).

text continues page 93.

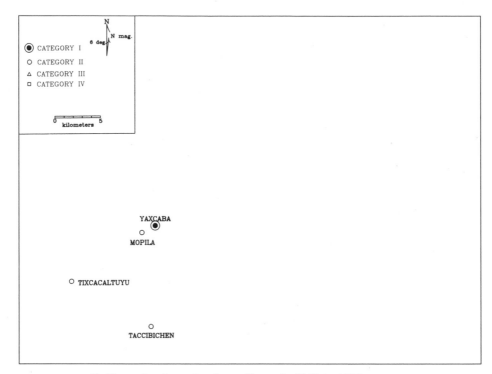

FIGURE 4.8a. Settlement patterns by phase: Phase 1, 1547 to 1600.

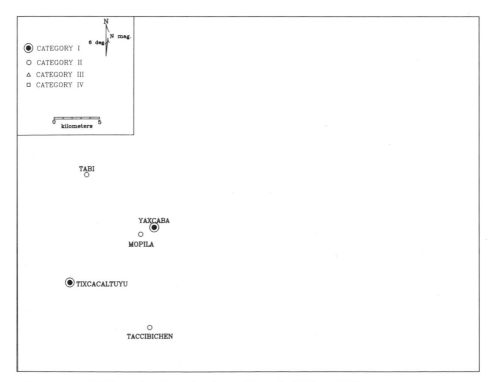

FIGURE 4.8b. Settlement patterns by phase: Phase 2, 1600 to 1750.

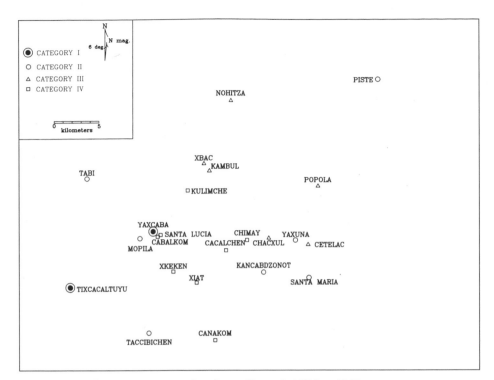

FIGURE 4.8c. Settlement patterns by phase: Phase 3, 1750 to 1800.

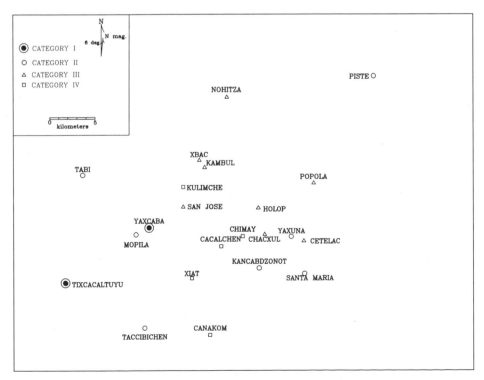

FIGURE 4.8d. Settlement patterns by phase: Phase 4, 1800 to 1821.

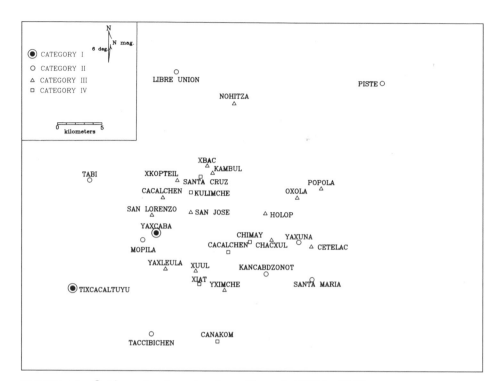

FIGURE 4.8e. Settlement patterns by phase: Phase 5, 1821 to 1847.

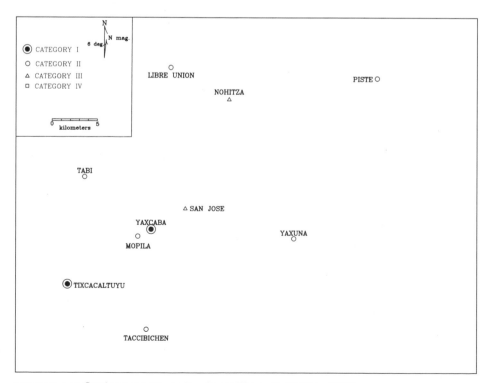

FIGURE 4.8f. Settlement patterns by phase: Phase 6, 1847 to 1862.

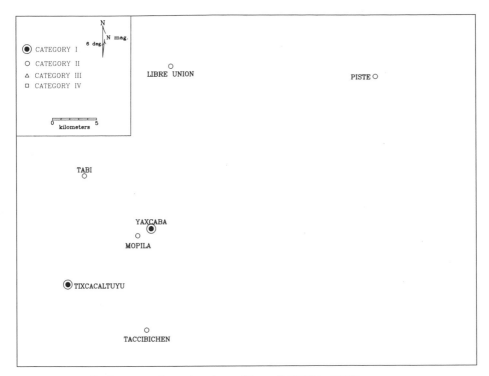

FIGURE 4.8g. Settlement patterns by phase: Phase 7, 1862 to 1900.

Phase I (1547–1600) begins with the suppression of the great revolt and the pacification of the native province of Sotuta. Crown representatives implemented the policy of congregación in the Yaxcabá region, and the secular clergy established a benefice there. As the population underwent drastic decline from pre-Hispanic levels, people were resettled in discrete aggregated towns. Within the region, the category I site (Yaxcabá) and one category II site (Mopilá) were inhabited at this time. Tixcacaltuyú and Taccibichén, category II sites located outside the survey boundary, were auxiliaries of Yaxcabá during this period.

A renewed demographic decline (due to yellow fever and famine) and administrative division characterize Phase II (1600–1750). Tixcacaltuyú and Taccibichén were separated administratively from the parish of Yaxcabá following an idolatry trial in 1688. Population reached its nadir around 1700. Some of the worst abuses of church and civil taxation occurred during this era. Only Yaxcabá and Mopilá, one category I site and one category II site, were inhabited at this time. Although the parish population remained aggregated within these two settlements, population size was significantly smaller than during the preceding phase.

Phase III (1750–1800) witnessed rapid and sustained population growth coinciding with the implementation of the Bourbon political reforms. Immigration to the Yaxcabá region from the northwestern part of the peninsula was heavy. The church was completed in Yaxcabá. Settlement patterns changed noticeably during this period; the population was more dispersed. Many new category IV settlements were colonized as farmers improved their access to and

TABLE 4.4: Distribution of Sites and Their Population over Time

Period	Cat. I #	Cat. I Pop.	Cat. I %	Cat. II #	Cat. II Pop.	Cat. II %	Cat. III #	Cat. III Pop.	Cat. III %	Cat. IV #	Cat. IV Pop.	Cat. IV %
1547–1600	1	1,336	69	1	617	31						
1600–1750	1	425	49	1	438	51						
1750–1800	1	1,491	34	1	155	3	6	343	8	11	2,413	55
1800–1821	1	3,292	45	4	876	12	8	632	9	5	2,522	34
1821–1847	1	3,128	28	4	4,625	42	16	1072	10	6	2,241	20
1847–1862	1	478	70	2	117	17	2	87	13			
1862–1900	1	288	87	1	44	13						

intensified their use of primary forest land. Spanish Creoles began to develop stockraising, establishing the first category III sites. Yaxcabá and Mopilá grew appreciably in size, and an additional eleven category IV sites and six category III sites appeared in the region.

Continued population growth, the development of livestock raising, and political instability under the Constitution of Cadiz mark Phase IV (1800–1821). Spanish Creoles began to dominate the ayuntamiento in Yaxcabá. Civil and ecclesiastical jurisdiction centered in Yaxcabá was extended farther into the hinterland. New churches were completed in Kancabdzonot, Santa María, Yaxuná, and Yaxcabá. The first quintas also appeared in Yaxcabá at this time. Their massive masonry construction resembles the core constructions of category III sites and contrasts with the perishable pole-and-thatch house construction found in most house lots. Differences in the cost of residential construction within Yaxcabá suggest increased social stratification. During this period the region contained one category I site (Yaxcabá), four category II sites, eight category III sites, and five category IV sites. A major shift in the political hierarchy is indicated in that three distant settlements (Kancabdzonot, Santa María, and Yaxuná) acquired the religious architectural attributes of category II sites. One category IV settlement, Xkekén, was abandoned, and all other sites showed an increase in population size. The tendency for farmers to disperse and create new category IV settlements decreased, and population continued to pack into existing communities. Two new category III settlements, both stockraising enterprises, were established, and additional masonry buildings were constructed on the older category III sites.

Phase V (1821–1847) begins with Yucatán's independence from Spain. Continued population growth, the proliferation of Spanish Creole–owned haciendas, the alienation of terrenos baldíos (especially into Creole hands), political instability in Maya leadership, a decline in the influence of the church, and political factionalism in Yaxcabá characterize this phase. The regional population reached its maximum accompanied by another significant change in settlement pattern. During this period the region contained one category I site, four category II sites, sixteen category III sites, and six category IV sites. A new municipal building, a cemetery, and several quintas were constructed in Yaxcabá, and shrines were built in a number of category IV sites. Although livestock-raising establishments (category III) virtually exploded throughout the parish, they tended to have small populations and lacked architectural elaboration. Although the numbers of category III sites increased, they did not support a corresponding proportion of the region's burgeoning population. The majority of the population growth occurred in Yaxcabá and existing category II and IV sites. The pattern indicates dispersal of specialized stockraising activities and nucleation of agriculturalists. It also suggests that more land and water within the parish were dedicated to stockraising and less to farming.

Phase VI (1847–1862) begins with the onset of the Caste War. During this era, the parish population declined by nearly 90 percent. Yaxcabá was attacked, pillaged, and burned as many as nine times when the rebel Maya and Creole militia fought over territory. Many settlements were abandoned, especially category III sites, and the remaining communities were reduced drastically in size. The settlement pattern indicates radical change in political and economic organization. Population was concentrated in Yaxcabá, which retained nominal control over two farming settlements and two cattle estates. During this phase, one category I site, Yaxcabá, and two category II sites, Mopilá and Yaxuná, retained reduced populations; two category III sites, Nohitzá and San José Yaxleulá, remained in operation.

Economic devastation marks Phase VII (1862–1900). The development of henequen in other parts of the peninsula, prompting emigration from the areas most affected by the Caste War, retarded population recovery in Yaxcabá. Haciendas and other stockraising enterprises in central Yucatán failed to recover. One category I site, Yaxcabá, and one category II site, Mopilá, were the only two settlements occupied during this time. The region's population fell below the level of Phase II.

Historical Community Classification

Throughout many decades of research, historians have assembled a well-known series of community classes, most often used to reconstruct local variation in the political economy. These descriptions are generalized, and although they provide some idea of variability in social organization and production between different kinds of communities, the distinctions between various type-classes depend largely on the context in which the term is used in documentary sources. Comparison of the archaeological settlement typology with the historical classes used in Yaxcabá enhances understanding of the parish's economy, the organization of particular settlements, and change over time. Archaeological evidence helps to specify just how "typical" a particular settlement may have been compared to others of the same historical class in Yucatán. During the nineteenth century, seven different kinds of communities are described in the historical literature for the Yaxcabá region: cabecera, pueblos, haciendas, privately owned ranchos, independent ranchos, cofradía estates, and sitios.

The *cabecera* is the administrative seat of a parish. It usually had a large, socially stratified, and ethnically diverse population, its own ayuntamiento and/or república de indios, a church, and a resident curate. Maya residents of Yaxcabá practiced subsistence agriculture, but they also produced cotton cloth, maize, beans, poultry, honey, and wax to pay civil and religious taxes. They also paid a tithe on raising minor livestock and were subject to repartimiento and labor drafts. Opportunities for wage labor were relatively common, and by the 1840s, some 17 percent of the population were occupational specialists.[11] Spanish Creoles living in the cabecera were merchants and hacienda owners who maintained elaborate residences in town. Other non-Maya residents were craft specialists and farmers who were responsible for paying tithes to the church, as well as fulfilling payment of miscellaneous taxes imposed by the ayuntamiento. The cabecera corresponds to the category I site of the archaeological classification.

A *pueblo* is a town, smaller and politically subordinate to the cabecera, also known a visita or an auxiliary. In some cases an assistant priest *(teniente de cura)* resided in the community. For the most part, inhabitants were maize farmers subject to civil and ecclesiastical supervision and taxation, and craft specialization was minimal. Inhabitants of the oldest pueblo in the parish, Mopilá, provided personal-service labor and produced a surplus in order to make tribute and obvention payments in cotton cloth, maize, beans, poultry, honey, and wax. By the early nineteenth century, an additional three pueblos (formerly independent ranchos) each elected their own local officials, paid civil and religious taxes, and supported small enclaves of Spanish Creoles who came to reside in these towns. Limited opportunities for wage labor were probably available, especially in Mopilá, which is located within easy walking distance of Yaxcabá. Pueblos correspond to category II sites in the archaeological classification.

A *hacienda* is a landed estate characterized by mixed agricultural and livestock production, permanent infrastructure, and employing large numbers of resident laborers who were often bound to the estate by debt (Wolf and Mintz 1957). Haciendas constitute a self-contained social unit as well as an economic unit (Patch 1985, 1979, 1991, 1993; Wolf and Mintz 1957). Tithes and tribute payments were made by the hacienda's owner on behalf of his laborers. Because these amounts were usually credited to the workers' accounts, they became indebted and thus bound to the hacienda. Haciendas in Yaxcabá parish produced agricultural products and cattle. Consequently they usually did not attract a large and indebted resident labor force, because cattle raising was not a labor-intensive activity (Bracamonte y Sosa 1993; Patch 1993:149; Strickon 1965). Instead, semipermanent workers, or luneros, cultivated lands of the estate in exchange for labor rent one day per week, or for agricultural produce harvested from additional parcels. The permanent labor force usually included a foreman and a few cowboys and horse-wranglers. Owners of haciendas in Yaxcabá parish did make tithe and tribute payments for their resident laborers, but payments for luneros were debated.[12] In general, luneros were not bound to the estates as debt peons. The hacienda owner's only leverage over a lunero was to deny him the use of the land and water of the estate (Patch 1993:149). Haciendas correspond to category III sites in the archaeological classification.

A *privately owned rancho* is a small agricultural estate, usually smaller than a hacienda, used for livestock raising or agricultural pursuits but not characterized by large numbers of resident laborers. Bracamonte (1984) suggests that the major difference between the privately owned rancho and the hacienda is that the total value of the buildings and facilities on the estate is much smaller in the former than in the latter.[13] Presumably, permanent laborers and luneros would have worked on privately owned ranchos under conditions similar to hacienda residents. In Yaxcabá parish and other areas of Yucatán, the term "rancho" was used interchangeably with the term "hacienda," which ultimately replaced it. The two estates called ranchos in the late eighteenth century, Chacxul and Xbac, were designated haciendas later in the nineteenth century. These communities were just as large and had as many resident laborers as any other hacienda in the region. Privately owned ranchos correspond to category III sites in the archaeological classification.

An *independent rancho* is a settlement of maize farmers situated on open or vacant land apart from other recognized communities (Thompson 2000:439). To judge from documentary sources, these communities generally were small, ephemeral, and often mobile (Dumond and Dumond 1982). Collection of tribute and obventions did not occur with regularity, and the church or state did not officially sanction independent ranchos. They likely functioned as safety valves, providing access to land needed by an expanding population, and people often migrated to ranchos to escape the social and economic exigencies of pueblos and haciendas. Opportunities for wage labor or occupational specialization were extremely limited, and forms of credit were not readily available. Although their economic organization is the least well known of all settlement types in the Yaxcabá region, historical population figures suggest that independent ranchos in Beneficios Bajos, and especially in Yaxcabá, were significantly larger than in other regions. Although Thompson (2000: 401–2) suggests that a lack of available land prompted the greater degree of aggregation in ranchos in this region, his suggestion rests only on the assumption that Maya farmers would have continued to disperse themselves among many small rancho settlements if land were available. The historical evidence from Yaxcabá indicates that these communities were always recognized as part of the parish, if somewhat clandestine in the eyes of the church, and by the 1840s exercised legitimate claims to surrounding lands. Their inhabitants also were occasionally tapped for contributions of supplies. Independent ranchos correspond to category IV sites in the archaeological classification.

A *cofradía estate* is the property of a religious confraternity whose produce was used to support the annual celebration of the cofradía's patron saint (Farriss 1984:266–68). Maya elite created these estates through endowments, and they consequently exercised considerable control over the confraternity's activities (Farriss 1984:267). Cline (1947) refers to them as "church haciendas," which has led many historians to suggest that they were managed like privately owned ranchos and haciendas. No less than five cofradías were active within Yaxcabá parish during the late eighteenth and early nineteenth centuries: Cofradía Kancabdzonot, Cofradía Xiat, Cofradía Nuestra Señora del Rosario, Cofradía Sohiste, and Cofradía Animas. Of these, three sites can be linked as estates of these organizations: Kancabdzonot, Xiat, and Kulimché.[14] Cofradía estates specialized in producing cattle and agricultural resources, but in Yaxcabá approximately 85 percent of their production was agricultural (Patch 1993:183, 187, 189). Although cofradías paid a tithe on their produce to the church, these estates were frequently used to hide elite Maya wealth from ecclesiastical and civil authorities. The extent to which residents of cofradía estates actually labored on behalf of Maya elites, were remunerated for their labor, or were disenfranchised from access to land in other communities is unclear. Kancabdzonot, a category II site, became a pueblo after the cofradía's "hacienda" was sold in 1782 (Farriss 1984:537 n. 582).[15] Xiat and Kulimché are category IV sites.

A *sitio* is a privately owned parcel used for apiculture and raising livestock, whose owner (often a Maya) did not have an official license to raise cattle. Infrastructure for production was minimal and usually consisted of a well, a corral, and occasionally a small resident labor force (Patch 1993:117, 183; Thompson 2000:439). Documentary sources in the Yaxcabá region do not mention the presence of sitios until 1841, at a time when Spanish Creoles were expanding their landholdings. A few of the sitios are later called haciendas.[16] Although at least two of these places were Maya-owned, it is more likely that establishing a sitio was a Spanish-Creole tactic for laying claim to land and accumulating the capital necessary to purchase a license for livestock raising, thus founding a hacienda. Of the four sitios (Santa Cruz, Chenche, Kancabchen, and Kuxubche) listed on the 1841 census, population ranged from twenty-three to six persons (see Tables 3.1 and 3.4, in Chapter 3 above). Three of the settlements had a foreman and cowboys, and two supported luneros in addition to farmers (labradores). The documentary evidence suggests they are similar to small haciendas in terms of population and occupational specialization. Sitios Santa Cruz and Chenche, located within the archaeological survey region, are category III sites in the archaeological classification.

Comparison of Historical and Archaeological Typologies

An important advantage to comparing archaeological and historical systems of classification is that it allows us to remove the ambiguity that surrounds particular kinds of settlements mentioned in historical documents. The archaeological survey data from the Yaxcabá region departs from the historical classification on three major points. First, the independent ranchos are larger and more carefully planned than previously suspected. The category IV communities of the survey are neither ephemeral nor haphazardly organized. Except for the absence of a church, these settlements closely resemble pueblos in terms of their residential architecture, layout, and community infrastructure. Religious architecture (chapels and cemeteries) is not absent at independent ranchos, merely reduced in scale. The gridlike arrangement of the house lots also conforms to that mandated for other authorized settlements. Independent rancho inhabitants in the Yaxcabá region were not unruly apostates fleeing to the forest. Although the political and administrative functions of pueblos were more integrated within colonial civil and ecclesiastical systems, and pueblo households consequently had to produce a surplus in order to meet tax obligations, population is not significantly different statistically between pueblos and independent ranchos in the Yaxcabá region (Alexander 1993, 1997b). Archaeological evidence for production, the degree of social stratification, and the religious practices of category IV inhabitants indicates that these were similar to those of people living in category II sites.

Second, cofradía estates do not physically resemble haciendas (category III sites); instead, they are indistinguishable from independent rancho settlements (category IV sites).[17] Xiat and

Kulimché are category IV sites, measuring 30 ha and 61 ha respectively, with sizeable populations.[18] Although settlement patterns at these sites refute the historical interpretation that cofradía estates were run like private haciendas, they do support Robert Patch's (1993:184) suggestion that Yaxcabá's cofradías emphasized agricultural production over livestock raising. The sites are composed of house lots fenced by albarradas and containing foundations for perishable buildings, the archetypical residences of Maya agriculturalists. Furthermore, at Xiat and Kulimché the central water source is a noria that pumped water into an adjacent water-storage tank, and at Kulimché additional water troughs were located on one side of the noria. The norias may constitute archaeological evidence of intensified production. A noria differs from an ordinary well because its operation is mechanized, such that wind or animal traction replaces human labor for drawing water to the surface. The presence of norias at haciendas and a few other settlements tentatively suggests that the activity of pumping water was intensified in contexts such as livestock raising, where water was required in greater quantities than that needed for daily household activities.[19] Other evidence for specialized production and storage facilities, however, is lacking at the cofradía estates, indicating low-level production. Similarly, the absence of variability in the size and location of residential architecture at cofradía estates does not attest to the severe social stratification or labor organization characteristic of haciendas.

Finally, variation in site size and the amount and elaboration of masonry architecture among haciendas and privately owned ranchos (category III sites) is much greater than suggested by historical sources (see Table 4.3). Although each of the category III sites was described as a hacienda at some point in its history, the estates demonstrate an architectural poverty that casts doubt on their role in producing significant amounts of agricultural products and cattle for local and regional markets. Although several of the estates are well appointed architecturally, Yaxcabá's haciendas do not begin to compare with the scale, architectural elaboration, and grandeur of the mid- to late-nineteenth-century henequen and sugar estates in other areas of Yucatán. To name many of these sites "haciendas" seems a gross exaggeration, especially when, based on the scale of the site's infrastructure, one would suspect that at most they should be classified as privately owned ranchos or sitios. Nevertheless, the estates described in documentary sources as privately owned ranchos, Chacxul and Xbac, are two of the largest category III sites in the region. On the basis of their archaeological characteristics, the privately owned ranchos are indistinguishable from estates historically classified as haciendas. Similarly, one site of the archaeological survey classified historically as a sitio, Santa Cruz, has equal or more substantial infrastructure than a couple of sites consistently classified as haciendas.

Explaining Variation among Haciendas

In a previous analysis, I suggested that the variability in the amount of masonry architecture at category III sites could be attributed to two processes: the development of production over time, and the entrepreneurial strategy pursued by the hacienda's owner (Alexander 1997a, 2003). The purpose of elaborate architectural construction on haciendas is debated. Many scholars logically assume the buildings functioned to provide the necessary infrastructure to intensify production. In such cases, variation in the size, arrangement, and facilities reflected the production and labor requirements of the specific goods produced (Bracamonte y Sosa 1988, 1990; Millet Cámara 1984, 1985). Others have argued that grandiose architecture was a form of consumption designed to enhance the prestige of the estate's owner, particularly in areas where local and regional markets were highly unstable and haciendas were relatively unprofitable (Brading 1977; Florescano 1977). Although the size and elaboration of masonry buildings at the core of an estate is usually considered a measure of wealth, especially in terms of production, other factors affect the development of buildings and facilities over time. These include family size, motivation to create an inheritance for sons and daughters, and the desire to create endowments for descendants or relatives entering religious life. All of these additional factors, including strategies that enhance prestige, also are closely related to wealth.

Investment in architecture is one of several tactics in a strategy that manipulates labor and resources to exploit temporal and spatial disparities in the values of goods (Barth 1966, 1967; Wolf 1982:79–88). In the late eighteenth and early nineteenth centuries, architecturally elaborate properties functioned to store capital. As the economy became increasingly market based, however, some hacienda owners focused on commodity production, and new architectural construction prioritized production infrastructure over ostentation. Nevertheless, not all hacienda owners adjusted to economic change in the same way, and evidence from Yaxcabá suggests that different families followed diverse strategies for capital accumulation.

Would-be entrepreneurs in Yaxcabá used a wide range of tactics to manipulate flows of agricultural produce, livestock, labor, and private property in order to generate wealth. Surpluses were used for a variety of purposes—to buy houses or solares, to purchase more land or additional ranchos and haciendas, to acquire more cattle, or to invest in property outside of the parish. Elaboration of the buildings and facilities of a hacienda or a quinta was another way of investing surplus. Houses, house lots, quintas, and haciendas could be mortgaged for cash (the capital of the estate was put at interest, usually 5 percent) based on the value and size of the facilities (Bracamonte y Sosa 1993:105; Brading 1977; Florescano 1987; Hunt 1974; Patch 1993:117). The church acted as the bank; mortgages secured on rural property provided a crucial source of credit extended to elite families. Entrepreneurs used architecturally elaborate properties as mortgage collateral, providing themselves with more liquid revenue for further entrepreneurial or political ventures or to establish endowments for relatives managed through religious institutions.

In the absence of detailed historical information regarding the value and production for most of Yaxcabá's haciendas, I constructed a relative measure of the differential wealth expended in architecture by estimating the total floor areas enclosed by masonry walls (see Abrams 1994; Turner et al. 1981). These figures include the sum of all floor areas in square meters for all structures (both stories), norias, and in any stables or outbuildings. The measure does not include masonry corral walls, nor does it take into account the effort and expense of architectural decoration, because the cost of constructing these features probably was variable.

The hacienda's amount of production was estimated by the number of resident laborers on the estate. Population is widely regarded as a measure of productive capacity, because in most cases it is highly correlated with the labor requirements and intensity of the crops produced

(Bracamonte y Sosa 1988, 1990; Farriss 1984:383; Patch 1985; Strickon 1965). In Yaxcabá, all estates were engaged in mixed agricultural and livestock production. As mentioned previously, the age of the settlement is also an important variable that affects its form.

Using multiple regression analysis, one can determine what percentage of the variation in the hacienda's architectural form, measured by the area of masonry buildings, is attributable to its productive capacity, estimated from the estate's number of residents. The analysis revealed that 61 percent of variability in architectural form is accounted for by the estate's population (Alexander 1997a). When the estate's age was added to the multiple regression model, no additional variation in estate architecture was accounted for, indicating an extremely close relationship between the hacienda's resident worker population and its age. This analysis confirms that as population and production increased on a hacienda over time, the owner invested greater resources in architecture and facilities to enhance production infrastructure (Bracamonte y Sosa 1990). Thirty-nine percent of the variability in architectural investment, however, remains unexplained by the regression model, indicating that additional variables conditioned the construction and elaboration of architecture on haciendas.

A qualitative analysis of additional historical information can assist in explaining the residual variability—the strategies used by Yaxcabá's hacienda owners for generating wealth. Table 4.5 summarizes the patterns of elite investment in Yaxcabá parish between 1780 and 1847. Three trends occurred during this period. First, individuals and families became owners of multiple estates, and the haciendas became concentrated in fewer hands over time. By 1845 four families controlled the largest haciendas and a significant proportion of the real estate in the parish. Second, while investment in new estates increased, investment in architecture decreased. Haciendas founded between 1815 and 1828 showed little architectural elaboration and had smaller resident worker populations compared to older estates (see Table 4.3). This suggests that using architecture as a form of collateral decreased relative to other forms of investment. Third, purchases of terrenos baldíos to enlarge the holdings of existing estates became more common in the 1840s. New mortgages became less common, and old debts were paid off or transferred to other individuals.

Differences in entrepreneurial strategies can be traced to specific individuals in Yaxcabá (Table 4.5). The Días family owned several of the older estates of the parish. The family was heavily invested in real estate, and much of its wealth was tied up in hacienda architecture. Investment and speculation in town real estate also provided the Días family with a source of liquid revenue. They owned houses and solares in Mérida, Yaxcabá, and Kancabdzonot, and one house was mortgaged. They owned four of the largest and most elaborate haciendas in the parish (totaling 2,162 sq m of masonry architecture), and two of their estates, particularly Nohitzá, were heavily mortgaged. In 1846, José Tiburcio Días sold Nohitzá with its mortgage to Pascual Espejo. As a result of the sale, Días was able to claim and purchase 5.25 leagues of terreno baldío (much of it outside the parish in neighboring Chikindzonot) and to win the mayoral elections. Overall, however, the Días family attempted to enlarge landholdings only around hacienda Popolá. Most of their land claims were distant from existing properties. Of all the hacienda owners in Yaxcabá parish, the Díases had the largest extended family and actively sought to develop and maintain property in the hands of family members or close friends and associates.

TABLE 4.5: Property Ownership and Investments of Spanish Creoles in Yaxcabá Parish

Owner	Houses, Solares, Quintas	Haciendas	Claims of Terreno Baldío
Claudio Padilla	1 quinta in Yaxcabá	Holop Kambul (600 p) Xbac Yximché Other lands	1 league, 402 p[a] 1 league, 65 p 1.5 leagues, 40 p 1.5 leagues
Sebastian, Francisco Antonio, José Tiburcio, and Benito Días	1 house in Mérida (600 p) 1/4 solar in Mérida 2 houses in Yaxcabá 1 house in Kancabdzonot	Popolá Cetelac (300 p) Chacxul Nohitzá[b] (2136 p) Other lands	2 leagues 5.25 leagues
Pascual Espejo		Xuul Nohitzá[b]	 0.5 leagues
José Francisco del Castillo, Florencia del Castillo	1 house in Yaxcabá (250 p) 4 solares in Yaxcabá 1 house in Tixcacaltuyú	San José Yaxleulá (600 p)	
Unknown		San Antonio Yaxleulá	
Unknown		Xkopteil	
Unknown		San Lorenzo	
Unknown		Oxolá	
Unknown		Cacalchén	

Note: Mortgages appear in parenthesis next to the corresponding property.
a. p = pesos.
b. In 1846 José Tiburcio Días sold Nohitzá to Pascual Espejo for 1,862 pesos plus assumption of the 2,136-peso mortgage.

The del Castillo family engaged in a similar strategy that used masonry architecture as a form of collateral. Although they owned only one hacienda, San José, the del Castillo family bought, sold, and mortgaged houses and house lots in Yaxcabá and Tixcacaltuyú. Some of this money was then lent to merchants, used for additional speculation in real estate, or used as endowments for cofradías.[20] Florencia del Castillo, in particular, pursued a strategy of using property to secure endowments for family and through which she could exercise patronage (especially to cofradías).

In contrast, Claudio Padilla's investment in architecture was relatively modest. He owned four haciendas and one quinta in Yaxcabá. The amount of wealth that he had invested in the architecture of his haciendas (totaling 1,300 sq m of masonry) was considerably less than that of the Días family, and he did not engage in real estate speculation. The average number of resident workers on his estates was higher. He took out only one mortgage on hacienda Kambul and made several claims of terreno baldío to enlarge his existing estates. Padilla apparently followed a more land-extensive strategy and was more intent on producing and marketing cattle and agricultural products. Although he had a large family and numerous descendents in Yaxcabá, his relatives do not appear frequently in documentary sources and probably did not engage in the scale of cooperative commercial or political activity as did members of the Días family. Ownership of his many estates was not partitioned among family members.

The amount and distribution of masonry architecture in Yaxcabá parish therefore is in part explained by differences in economic strategies pursued by Yaxcabá's elite. Before 1821 production centered around mixed agriculture and stockraising, and investment in architecture became a means of storing productive capital. Families with the largest investments in estate architecture also engaged in the transfer and mortgage of houses and solares. Mortgages of haciendas and speculation in the purchase of houses and solares were methods of assisting cash flow and convertibility of goods within a region that was gradually becoming integrated with the regional market economy. After 1821, the number of new haciendas in the parish increased dramatically, yet these estates demonstrated little investment in architecture. Acquisition of new land became the preferred form of investment. Spanish-Creole strategies shifted toward a land-extensive and labor-extensive productive strategy centered more strictly on stockraising.

The Question of Land Stress

The movement of Creoles to the countryside and the expansion of cattle haciendas drastically altered the distribution of land and population in the Yaxcabá region. Whereas elsewhere in Mexico these developments continued up to the 1910 revolution, in Yucatán the process was arrested and reversed by the Caste War. The disposition of land between agriculturalists and cattle ranchers consequently has become a critical question for assessing the origins of the conflict. In general, historians view the postindependence legislation permitting alienation of terrenos baldíos and the claims and purchases of these parcels by individuals, many of whom were hacienda owners, as evidence that Maya agriculturalists were under increasing land stress (see, for example, Cline 1947; Patch 1985). Seldom, however, has this proposition been carefully evaluated from the perspective of the Maya farmer.[21] Fortunately, data from the archaeological survey permit a more detailed analysis of changes in landholding in the Yaxcabá region. When combined with historical census figures, it is possible to consider whether alienation of land for cattle ranching and changes in land jurisdiction adversely affected Yaxcabá's agriculturalists.

Land stress is not a condition adequately described as present or absent. Agriculturalists constantly adjust cultivation intensity, plot size, labor investment, and scheduling in order to produce sufficient resources to sustain the household. Farmers adjust household strategies so that they intensify production among different parts of the agricultural system. At one end is the house-lot garden, under permanent cultivation, whereas at the other end is the milpa cultivated with extensive slash-and-burn techniques. Also, not all land is the same. Soil quality, water, drainage, geomorphological features, distance from the residence, and other variables all affect the farmer's choice of cultivation techniques. Limitation of land used for milpa prompts the agriculturalist to compensate by shortening fallow or by changing plot size, labor investment, or plot location among different components of the agricultural system. Above all, land ownership affects the pattern of intensification.

Consequently, the traditional calculations of carrying capacity and land stress for extensive swidden cultivators in the Maya Lowlands make numerous assumptions that do not adequately characterize the flexibility and intensity of smallholding cultivation systems (see Dewar 1984; Thompson 2000). Smallholders who experience land pressure usually do not revert to extensive swidden techniques as a default (Netting 1993:311–12). Farmers who lose ownership of land, however, often resort to extensive cultivation of rented plots. These problems aside, it is nevertheless possible to quantify the balance of population to land in Yaxcabá parish assuming swidden cultivation. These calculations demonstrate one extreme (and largely hypothetical) case that assumes a land-extensive cultivation system on plots of uniform agricultural suitability.

Could all Yaxcabá's agriculturalists have practiced extensive shifting cultivation before the Caste War? To answer this question, one needs several pieces of information, including the number of farmers residing in each settlement, the amount and locations of land available for cultivation, amount and locations of land alienated as baldíos, the number of cattle, milpa size, and length of fallow. Although calculations vary depending on the assumptions and conventions used, it is possible to estimate each of the variables listed above for the Yaxcabá region using independent lines of historical, ethnographic, and archaeological evidence. So long as the assumptions are reasonable and clearly stated, the results of the analysis are replicable.

Farming Population

The 1841 census breaks down Yaxcabá's population by community, age, sex, and male occupation such that it is possible not only to count the number of taxpayers in each settlement (including ranchos) but also to estimate the numbers of farmers (see Tables 3.4, 3.5, and 3.6 in Chapter 3, above).[22] Males are grouped into three categories: age fifteen and under; age sixteen to forty; and over forty. Women of all ages are listed separately. The demographic profile of the census is accurate; females outnumber males as is common in most populations. Adult males (over sixteen) also average 23 percent of the population, a figure comparable to population structure for other Latin American agrarian communities (Coale and Demeny 1966) where adult males comprise about 25 percent of the population. Here, I have assumed that all males over sixteen listed as farmers would have made milpa. Although some of the over-forty males may have been dependents of larger households, I regard them as able-bodied and assume that most individuals would have worked until they dropped. If all males over sixteen are considered heads of families, average family size in Yaxcabá parish is 5.22, a figure that accords well with twentieth-century Maya ethnography.[23] The population of the pueblo Yaxuná and its surrounding haciendas Nohitzá, Popolá, Oxolá, Holop, Chacxul, and Cetelac, are not included on the 1841 census. I have estimated the numbers of farmers in Yaxuná by multiplying the total population recorded for 1828 by 23 percent. When this method is applied to all settlements on the 1828 visita pastoral, a consistent pattern emerges. Slight population decline between 1828 and 1841 is indicated (Tables 4.6 and 4.7).

TABLE 4.6: Numbers of Farmers and Village Ejido Sizes in the Yaxcabá Region

Settlement	# of Farmers 1841	Estimated # of Farmers 1828	Legal Size of Ejido Grant (sq km)	Size of Ejido in Practice (sq km)
Yaxcabá	643	597	69.4	69.4
Mopilá	74	79	69.4	20.8
Kancabdzonot	421	482	69.4	49.7
Santa María	279	297	69.4	49.7
Yaxuná		206	69.4	49.7
Cacalchén	149	146	17.4	10.5
Canakóm	105	129	17.4	17.4
Chimay	63	41	2.81	0.43
Kulimché	42	74	2.81	2.33
Santa Cruz	77	87	2.81	2.81
Xiat	59	38	2.81	2.81
Total	2,118[a]	2,176	392.8	275.6

Note: Regarding the overlap of ejidos between Yaxcabá and Mopilá, I have assumed that the significantly larger population of farmers in Yaxcabá would have asserted its rights over the use of the ejidos, leaving only Mopilá's nonoverlapping ejido for use by its farmers. Regarding the overlap between Kancabdzonot, Santa María, and Yaxuná, I have assumed that the total area was divided proportionally among communities. Likewise it is unlikely that farmers in Cacalchén and Chimay would have asserted usufruct over the portions of their ejidos that overlapped with Kancabdzonot. a. Includes estimate fo Yaxuná.

To estimate the numbers of farmers on haciendas, I first calculated the average number of nonfarmers (cowboys and foremen) for haciendas listed on the 1841 census. On average, hacienda owners employed four nonfarmers to handle estate operations. If 23 percent of a hacienda's population were adult males, then it is likely that all but four of these individuals were farmers. When this method is applied to all haciendas in the parish, again there is a reasonable correspondence between the numbers of agriculturalists estimated for 1828 and the number of luneros or farmers recorded in 1841.[24] I have used the maximum estimate of farmers from each community recorded on either the 1828 or 1841 censuses. In total, 2,481 agriculturalists inhabited Yaxcabá parish. Of these, 1,707 resided in the cabecera and pueblos, and 561 lived in independent ranchos. The remaining 213 comprised part of the resident workforce on haciendas.[25]

Cattle

Haciendas also harbored cattle. Nohitzá had 379 animals, and San José Yaxleulá had 152 (Bracamonte y Sosa 1993:anexo 5, 6).[26] According to Robert Patch (1993:144), the mean number of cattle for

TABLE 4.7: Numbers of Farmers and Livestock for Haciendas in the Yaxcabá Region

Settlement	# of Non-farmers 1841	# of Farmers 1841	Estimated # of Farmers 1828	# of Livestock
Nohitzá			47	379
Popolá			28	129
Cetelac			8	129
Chacxul			24	129
Xbac	5	8	0	129
Kambul	6	28	35	129
Holop			14	129
San José Yaxleulá	4	0	11	152
Yximché	5	3	0	129
Xuul	2	10	5	129
San Antonio Yaxleulá	2	1	2	129
Xkopteil	2	4	0	129
Cacalchén	2	1	1	129
San Lorenzo			1	129
Oxolá			5	129
Santa Cruz		2		
Kuxubche		4		
Kancabchen		2		
Chenche		4		

estates whose tithes were recorded in the late eighteenth and early nineteenth centuries was 163, with a median of 129 animals.[27] If the remaining thirteen estates in Yaxcabá parish were average compared to other cattle haciendas in Yucatán, the region may have supported between 2,200 and 2,700 head of cattle before the Caste War.

Village Ejidos

The historical documentation does not yield a complete reconstruction of the pattern of land-holding in the parish; rather, it reveals the state's or the Spanish Creole's perspective of different land classes. Howard Cline (1947:572–92) has discussed the complicated changes of postindependence agrarian legislation in depth, such that these regulations can be used in the calculations presented below. For the purposes of this analysis, it is most practical to use the statutes implemented after 1840 as a guide for the distribution of land in the Yaxcabá region before the Caste War. At that time village ejidos (common lands) were limited to an area of 4 sq leagues (69.4 sq km), measured in each cardinal direction from the church door. In situations where the distance between

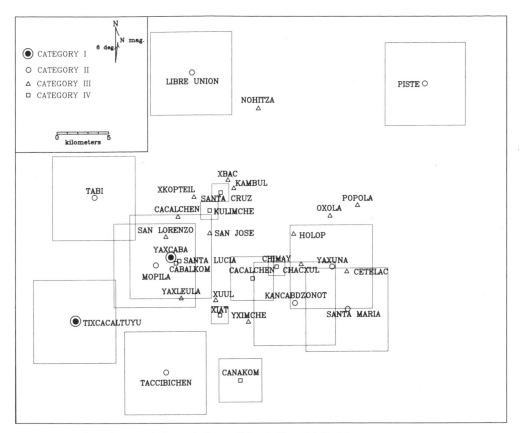

FIGURE. 4.9. Locations and sizes of village ejidos in Yaxcabá Parish.

communities did not permit each to have a full ejido allowance, land was divided proportionally between settlements (Cline 1947:577). Community lands held by the república de indios through title, purchase, or royal grant were declared inalienable, except in exchange for land needed to complete an ejido or for other lands needed by the inhabitants. These community or town lands were held or managed through usufruct as private property. Although independent ranchos and other settlements lacking municipal status originally were not given ejidos, the law was revised in 1844 such that ranchos with more than 150 taxpayers (adult males) were entitled to the standard-size ejidos, settlements of less than 150 taxpayers were permitted 1 sq league (17.4 sq km), and settlements with 60 taxpayers were allotted the area within 1,000 *varas* of the site center (2.81 sq km).[28]

When the extent of village ejidos is plotted on a map, the differences between legislation and practice become quite clear (Figure 4.9). The map demonstrates that most settlements did not have exclusive access to a standard allotment of ejido land. The problem of overlapping ejidos between neighboring communities was hardly negligible. Also haciendas ringed the edges of the ejidos to the north and south of Yaxcabá, to the north of Yaxuná, and to the southwest of Kancabdzonot. A number of estates also were located within ejido boundaries proper, as a result of the sale of land originally held by the república de indios to Creole entrepreneurs.

The smaller ejidos granted to independent ranchos overlapped the ejidos of pueblos, particularly for Cacalchén, Chimay, and Kulimché. Others, such as Santa Cruz and Xiat, likely had access to their entire ejido, but these communities were ringed by haciendas and baldío claims. Only one rancho, Canakóm, had unrestricted access to its ejido land.

The sizes of ejidos granted to the independent ranchos Cacalchén and Santa Cruz is not entirely clear. Although the number of taxpayers is 149 for Cacalchén and 77 for Santa Cruz, grounds for allocating ejidos of 4 sq leagues and 1 sq league to each rancho respectively, the map suggests that this was unlikely. If Cacalchén were granted standard-size ejidos, the area would have overlapped significantly with Kancabdzonot, completely enclosed Chimay, Xiat, and Xuul, and left no reasonable space for Juan Pablo Aranjo's baldío claim between the ejidos of Yaxcabá and Cacalchén. Similarly if Santa Cruz were granted ejidos measuring 1 sq league, the area would have surrounded haciendas Kambul, Xbac, and Xkopteil and enclosed nearby rancho Kulimché. I have assumed that for these "borderline cases" ejidos would have been scaled down to 1 sq league for Cacalchén and a 1,000-vara radius for Santa Cruz. Officials in Cacalchén and Chimay would have had to come to some agreement with those of Kancabdzonot.

To determine how much land was available for cultivation by farmers in each community, it is necessary to make a series of assumptions about the partitioning of overlapping ejido lands. First, it is reasonable to suppose that the tracts of town lands legislatively subsumed under the term village ejido would have been clearly demarcated, and each community would have defended its boundaries. I have assumed that the strength and effectiveness of each settlement's defense of these lands was related to its status in the municipal hierarchy. Thus, Yaxcabá probably would have laid claim to most of its ejido allotment to the detriment of its auxiliary, Mopilá. Therefore, I have divided the ejido area of Yaxcabá and Mopilá such that Yaxcabá retained its full entitlement, and Mopilá made due with the remainder. Likewise, I have allocated one-third of the combined ejidos of Kancabdzonot, Santa María, and Yaxuná to each community, even though in practice the division of town lands among these settlements was undoubtedly more complicated. I assume that independent ranchos would have made due with the portions of their ejido allotments that did not overlap the cabecera or pueblos.

Second, I have assumed that farmers in most communities except Yaxcabá would have had access only to ejido lands. Private land held by Maya elites doubtlessly was a significant component of the land tenure system, but in the absence of direct historical evidence of the numbers, sizes, and locations of these parcels, I can only suppose that private ownership would be concentrated in the cabecera and perhaps Mopilá, where land rights could be defended by the república de indios. Any private lands outside of the ejido boundaries, however, are subsumed in the "other land" category defined below. Since there are no less than sixteen haciendas and two sitios located on these lands, the amount of private land held by Mayas (other than Vicente Pech and Alejo Poot) or by the república was probably small.

Ejido area for the cabecera and the pueblos totaled 239.4 sq km. For independent ranchos, ejidos amounted to 36.2 sq km. Whereas according to the legislation Yaxcabá's communities should have had a total of 392.8 sq km of ejido land, the proximity of settlements and negotiation of proportional use reduced this amount to 275.6 sq km, or 70 percent of the legal entitlement (see Table 4.6).

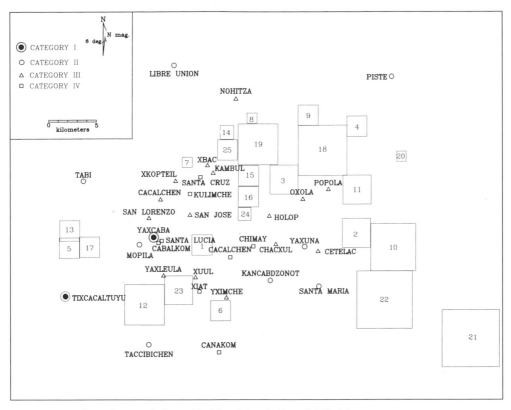

FIGURE 4.10. Locations and sizes of baldío claims in Yaxcabá Parish.

Claims of Terreno Baldío

Any land that was not part of village ejidos, community lands, or private property became identified as baldiós. Previously they were known as crown lands (tierras realengas), or the king's forest (monte del rey), and open to all for use. Theoretically, grants of terreno baldío were restricted to two claims, each measuring a maximum of 1 sq league, as a means of preventing the creation of large landed estates. Contemporary use of baldíos by farmers for milpa, cattle raising, or other activities were not impediments for a claim, but the purchaser was supposed to compensate those evicted for any improvements they had made. By providing Maya villages with ejidos and by permitting the privatization of baldíos, the government effectively limited cultivators' use of public land.

Claims of terreno baldío in Yaxcabá parish were listed in the 1845 Registro de las denuncias de terrenos baldíos, and purchases of some of the claims were recorded in the notary records.[29] These sources specify the numbers of claims in the region, the size of the claim, the individual making the claim, and the ownership and status of lands bordering the claim (Table 4.8).[30] The information about the status of lands bordering the baldíos is sufficient to plot the approximate location of each claim on a map (Figure 4.10). Although I have drawn the claims as square, they need not be, which would resolve most cases in which the baldíos overlapped village ejidos. Most baldío claims were located in the northeastern and eastern parts of the parish, along the old Cupul

TABLE 4.8: Claims of Terreno Baldío in Yaxcabá Parish

Map No.	Person Making Claim	Size of Claim (ha)	Neighboring Haciendas	Neighboring Ejidos
1	Juan Pablo Aranjo	434		Cacalchén
2	Doña Andrea Martinez	868	Cetelac	
3	Julian Espinoza	868	Popolá	
4	Juan Pio Cupul	434		Piste
5	Baltazar Baeza	434	Santa Rosa	
6	Alejo Poot	434	Sitio San Miguel	Canakóm
7	Claudio Padilla	interstice	Xbac	
8	Pascual Espejo	217	Nohitzá	
9	José Tiburcio Días	434	Nohitzá	
10	Marcelino Paz	2,345		Santa María
11	Francisco Antonio Días	868	Popolá	
12	José María Esquivel	1,736		Yaxcabá and Taccibichén
13	José Dolores Días	434		Tabi
14	Claudio Padilla	206	Xbac and Nohitzá	
15	Vicente Pech	434	Sitio Chenche	
16	Claudio Padilla	1,788	Holop	
17	José Clemente Padilla	434		Mopilá and Tixcacaltuyú
18	Francisco Antonio Días	2,604	Popolá	Piste
19	Ceferino Días	1,736	Nohitzá and Chenche	
20	José María Esquivel	217		Cenote Cohodzil
21	José Tiburcio Días	3,472		
22	Sebastian Rubio	3,472		Santa María
23	Claudio Padilla	868	Xuul	
24	Claudio Padilla	174	Holop	Yaxuná
25	Claudio Padilla	434	Kambul	

Note: The size of claims is described in square leagues and varas. One sq league equals 1,736 ha. The size of claim #7 is included with claim #14. Claim #8 is described as "un intersticio," which I have estimated at 1/8th sq league, or 217 ha. Claim #15 is described as "un terreno," which I have estimated at 1/4 sq league, or 434 ha. Modal claim size is 1/4 league. Claims #20 and #21 are outside of the defined region, in the jurisdictions of Piste and Chikindzonot respectively.

and Cochuah borders (Roys 1939). Individuals who acquired the land for the most part were Creole males from Yaxcabá; however, there were four exceptions: three Maya, Vicente Pech (a former cacique of Yaxcabá), Alejo Poot, and Juan Pío Cupul (from Piste) made baldío claims. Vicente Pech and Alejo Poot owned sitios, and the claims enlarged their property. One claim was also made by a woman, Doña Andrea Martínez, bordering hacienda Cetelac. In all, a total of 210 sq km of vacant land was claimed as private property between 1845 and 1847.

Cultivable Land

Based on the information presented above, land jurisdiction within the Yaxcabá region can be divided into three classes. The total area of the region is 700 sq km. Village ejidos measure 275.6 sq km, or 39.4 percent of land in the region. Terrenos baldíos amount to 210 sq km, or 30 percent of land in the region. All other land including haciendas, sitios, privately held parcels, and community lands purchased by or granted to the república de indios measures 214 sq km, or 30.6 percent of the land in the region. These land classes obviously bear little relation to categories of land tenure recognized by the indigenous inhabitants of the parish. The postindependence legislation imposed a "communal" status on Indian land that grossly oversimplified rights of access, usufruct, inheritance, and private ownership maintained under the república de indios. Village ejidos and community lands clearly were not "commons" or open access systems for cultivation, even though the Creole government regarded their management as such (see McCay and Acheson 1987). Although there is no direct historical evidence from Yaxcabá that describes Maya land tenure systems, evidence from other communities indicates the system included substantial private lands held by Maya, community lands available to commoners for cultivation (for which they provided one day of labor per week to the town), haciendas belonging to the town and administered by the república de indios, and haciendas de cofradía administered by the corresponding religious confraternity (Thompson 2000:125–30).

Rural towns were economically stratified, to the extent that Maya elites often hired luneros and wage laborers to work their privately held lands and sitios. Inheritance was similarly complicated, and private land, usufruct rights to community lands, animals, house lots, and other resources could be partitioned in fair shares among offspring, left in common for a group of kin, or given as gifts to nonkin (Restall 1997:207; Thompson 2000:106–24). It is reasonable to assume that similar conventions would have prevailed in Yaxcabá. With the fragmentation of Maya leadership and the decline in the power of the república de indios, however, the alienation of land from Maya to non-Maya hands likely was severe.

Calculations

Would the village ejidos be sufficient to sustain extensive swidden production, given the numbers of farmers in each community? To answer this question, it is necessary to estimate how much land each swidden farmer normally would require, for a specified plot size and length of fallow. Fortunately we have several sources for these estimates: E. Hernández's (1980) studies of farming in Yaxcabá in the late 1970s; Steggerda's (1941) ethnography of Piste and nearby communities and Redfield and Villa Rojas's (1934) study of Chan Kom for the early twentieth century; Granado Baeza's (1845) description of cultivation in Yaxcabá in the early 1800s; and Thompson's (2000) analysis of land tenure in late eighteenth-century Tekanto.[31] These sources clearly demonstrate that farmers adjust fallow length and the area of cultivation sizes from year to year as necessary.

Cultivated area or plot size varies depending on the needs of the household and on whether the farmer is cultivating primary forest land (milpa roza), secondary forest land (milpa de caña), or a combination of both. Arias Reyes's (1980) study in Yaxcabá records plot sizes varying from 30 to 300 mecates (1 ha = 25 mecates), with a mean of 83.4 mecates for milpa roza and 124.3 mecates for a mix of primary and secondary forest cultivation. The overall mean for plot size is 103.8 mecates with median and modal plot sizes for both kinds of cultivation at 100 mecates. Fallow periods are seven years.

Steggerda indicates that average milpa size in Piste, Xocenpich, and Chan Kom was 99.23 mecates (1932–36) with a range of 46 to 152 mecates, whereas Redfield and Villa Rojas documented a mean milpa size of 72 mecates in Chan Kom in 1930 and 62 mecates in the following year. Steggerda indicates that plots are cultivated for two years and left fallow for ten. Redfield and Villa Rojas report that milpa is cultivated for two consecutive years and left fallow for seven years.

On the basis of Steggerda's figures and the frequency of bequests of forest land measuring 100 mecates in the Tekanto wills, Thompson (2000:135) suggests that a standard milpa size was 100 mecates. The recent data from Yaxcabá also support this figure (Arias Reyes 1980; Arias Reyes et al. 1998). The other possible convention for milpa plot size is 60 mecates. In the 1840s, farmers were required to plant at least 60 mecates per year (Cline 1947:562–79; Farriss 1984:127). At this time, milpa was also taxed at 1 real per mecate, with the proceeds accruing to the municipal or state treasury. Earlier in 1815, however, the governor decreed that each farmer should cultivate 125 mecates. In all likelihood, the 60-mecate milpa standard was less a validation of existing farming practices and more a means of ensuring a steady flow of tax revenue.

Calculation of the amount of land needed per farmer is straightforward. Plot size is multiplied by the ratio of number of years required before returning to the same plot to the number of years of cultivation.[32] For example, a farmer who normally cultivates a 100-mecate plot for two years and leaves it fallow for 10 requires 600 mecates of land (100 new mecates every two years for twelve years, or 100 x 12/2). The farmer who uses the same size plot but under a seven-year fallow period requires 450 mecates of land (100 x 9/2). If the farmer cultivates his land for three years instead of two, with the same seven-year fallow period, he requires 330 mecates of land (100 new mecates every three years for ten years, 100 x 10/3).

Haciendas and sitios also supported farmers, a total of 213 divided among fifteen haciendas and four sitios. In addition to the produce needed to sustain their households, luneros and hacienda residents commonly cultivated an extra 20 mecates of milpa (instead of labor rent) in return for the use of water and lands of the estate (Granado Baeza 1845). To practice extensive swidden on 100-mecate plots plus an additional 20 mecates with ten-year fallow periods would require 28.8 ha (720 mecates) per farmer. In total, luneros and resident farmers on haciendas would need 61 sq km of land. This leaves 153 sq km of land in the "other" category plus

210 sq km of baldíos (a total of 363 sq km) for all other private agricultural and stockraising activities, including the support of between 2,200 to 2,700 head of cattle.

Table 4.9 presents the results of this analysis for all communities in Yaxcabá parish except private estates. Figures in the body of the table indicate the total amount of land in square kilometers needed by the number of farmers in each community, given a range of options for fallow length and plot size. When compared to the amount of available village ejido land in the first column, one can distinguish which communities had adequate ejidos for their farmers to practice extensive slash-and-burn agriculture and which did not. For example, it would require 86.8 sq km of land for all farmers in Kancabdzonot to practice extensive swidden on plots of 100 mecates with 7-year fallow periods. When one compares this figure to the 49.7 sq km of available ejido land in Kancabdzonot, it is apparent that ejido land was insufficient for all farmers to use this cultivation method.

The degree of "sufficiency" among settlements was variable. Independent ranchos were the hardest hit by the legislation limiting the size of town lands. Others were under varying degrees of "pressure" to adjust plot size and fallow periods. For example, farmers in Mopilá and Yaxuná could practice extensive swidden comfortably, even though their share of legally allotted ejido land was significantly reduced. The amount of land required for all their farmers to cultivate 100-mecate plots with ten-year fallow periods is actually less than the amount of land likely allocated as ejido. Farmers in Santa María may have been pressed to reduce plot size or fallow length, whereas those in Yaxcabá and Kancabdzonot would have had considerable difficulty making due with just the ejido lands. The data for Yaxcabá, Kancabdzonot, and Cacalchén show that farmers could not have compensated for a lack of land simply by shortening fallow; they likely would have adjusted plot size as well.

These data also indicate that the 1,000-vara (2.81 sq km) ejidos allocated to communities of roughly sixty taxpayers were inadequate to support extensive swidden cultivation. If the legislature had not revised the statute or if ranchos had ignored the revision and retained ejidos of 1 sq league (17.4 sq km), however, the village lands would have been sufficient to maintain the population of swidden farmers. The spatial information presented on the map nevertheless shows that this alternative is improbable. For most of the small independent ranchos, there is simply not enough surrounding unoccupied land.

Discussion

The figures presented in Table 4.9 do not flag land stress per se. Instead they simply suggest whether reduction of average plot size or length of fallow could have accommodated all cultivators or whether these conditions would have encouraged individuals to seek other lands for cultivation—those under private ownership or on unclaimed baldíos. Most likely the pressure to reduce plot size and/or the length of fallow in Yaxcabá was alleviated by the availability of privately owned Indian land and smallholder cultivation strategies. The Maya community in the cabecera was highly stratified, to the extent that some Maya elites held sitios and made baldío claims. In other towns, however, wage labor and cultivation of private land was prob-

TABLE 4.9: Amount of Land Needed by Farmers for Each Settlement in Yaxcabá Parish

Settlement	Ejido Size (sq km)	# of Farmers	Plot Size (mec.)	Years Fallow					
				10	8	7	6	5	4
Yaxcabá	69.4	643	100	154.3	128.6	115.7	102.9	90.0	77.2
			60	92.6	77.2	**69.4**	61.7	54.0	46.3
Mopilá	20.8	79	100	**18.9**	15.8	14.2	12.6	11.1	9.5
			60	11.3	9.5	8.5	7.6	6.6	5.7
Kancabdzonot	49.7	482	100	115.7	96.4	86.8	77.1	67.5	57.8
			60	69.4	57.8	52.1	**46.3**	40.5	34.7
Santa María	49.7	297	100	71.3	59.4	53.5	**47.5**	41.6	35.6
			60	**42.8**	35.6	32.1	28.5	24.9	21.4
Yaxuná	49.7	206	100	**49.4**	41.2	37.1	32.9	28.8	27.7
			60	29.7	24.7	22.2	19.8	17.3	14.8
Cacalchén	10.5 (17.4)	149	100	35.8	29.8	26.8	23.8	20.8	**17.8**
			60	21.5	**17.8**	16.1	14.3	12.5	10.7
Canakóm	17.4	129	100	30.9	25.8	23.2	20.6	18.1	**15.5**
			60	18.5	**15.5**	13.9	12.4	10.8	9.3
Chimay	0.43 (2.81)	63	100	15.1	12.6	11.3	10.8	8.8	7.6
			60	9.1	7.6	6.8	6.0	5.3	4.5
Xiat	2.81	59	100	14.2	11.8	10.6	9.4	8.3	7.1
			60	8.5	7.1	6.4	5.7	5.0	4.2
Kulimché	2.33	74	100	17.8	14.8	13.3	11.8	10.4	8.9
			60	10.6	8.9	8.0	7.1	6.2	5.3
Santa Cruz	2.81	87	100	20.9	17.4	15.7	13.9	12.2	10.4
			60	12.5	10.4	9.4	8.4	7.3	6.3

Note: Ejido size and amount of land needed for each fallow period and plot size are expressed in square kilometers. Plot size is expressed in mecates; 25 mecates = 1 hectare or 0.01 sq km. The number of farmers is the maximum estimate drawn from the 1828 and 1841 censuses. All calculations assume two consecutive years of cultivation. Numbers marked in bold indicate plot size and fallow conditions that could be accommodated by the specified ejido size. Numbers in parentheses indicate the legally allocated sizes of ejidos for Cacalchén and Chimay, and to which the inhabitants may have had access. For communities with approximately sixty taxpayers, the ejido allocations legislated by the Yucatecan government were too small.

ably less of an option. Nevertheless, to the south lay a sizeable stretch of open land, unclaimed as baldío, which farmers may have exploited.

The calculations presented here illustrate that land pressure (as traditionally conceived for swidden cultivation) was not necessarily an overarching condition in the Yaxcabá region. Its severity depended largely on the location of the settlement relative to others and the degree of legitimacy accorded the community within the civil hierarchy. Agriculturalists living in small independent ranchos who had long maintained their "unofficial" status were not provided for under the postindependence legislation and experienced the greatest difficulty. Many would have had little choice but to become shareholders or to cultivate unclaimed baldío lands far from their residences. Farmers in some pueblos, particularly those that had seen rapid population growth in the early nineteenth century, also encountered difficulty to reduce plot size and/or shorten fallow.

Nevertheless, in most legally sanctioned settlements of the parish, as well as on haciendas, the land pressure on extensive swidden techniques was not strong. The numbers of farmers working on haciendas, sitios, and other private parcels was small. Among estate residents, pressure to reduce plot size or shorten fallow was probably negligible, even though they shared the hacienda's lands with the livestock. Also, because hacienda residents did not own land, they had little incentive to intensify cultivation or to invest in land improvements.

Smallholders and intensive cultivators, who use less land than extensive cultivators, certainly would have had sufficient land to make ends meet. Under these conditions, any subculture of resistance related to lack of farmland likely would have arisen in the independent rancho settlements. It is more likely that resistance arose in response to limitations of private land ownership, rather than access. Maya officials and inhabitants of legitimate settlements would have preoccupied themselves with maintaining private holdings and use rights over ejido lands that were contested as a result of overlap with neighboring communities. Consequently, acts of defiance would have been directed not solely at Spanish-Creole property owners whose enterprises circumscribed the settlements, but also toward the town councils of pueblos whose ejidos abutted and overlapped those of other communities.

Summary

The review of archaeological settlement patterns presented here indicates that the process of agrarian change accelerated after 1821 in Yaxcabá parish. Population recovery after 1750 spurred agricultural expansion and intensification. Maya households dispersed to outlying independent rancho communities. During the late eighteenth and early nineteenth centuries, rural production became increasingly diverse as haciendas devoted to cattle ranching were established in the region. Rural communities also became more ethnically diverse, as Spanish Creoles migrated to the countryside. The development of Creole cattle ranching in Yaxcabá transformed patterns of settlement and architecture across the landscape. Special function sites dotted the region. No longer were elaborate masonry buildings the exclusive province of the state or church. The haciendas and quintas in Yaxcabá parish formed part of a larger pattern in which storage of capital in the form of architecture became an important component of elite strategies. The decision to deploy resources by investing in architecture was related to the processes by which elites converted surplus to capital. Improving the infrastructure of production in rural areas was the first step in a move toward an integrated market economy.

During the early nineteenth century, economic stratification in Yaxcabá parish became marked. Class divisions took on a "castelike" quality because they tended to break along the rigid and ascribed ethnic lines separating Indians from non-Indians.[33] The widening economic gulf between Creoles and Maya is marked archaeologically by the distribution of masonry architecture (both residential and institutional) and spatial patterning within Yaxcabá itself and between settlements within the region.

After 1821, however, Yucatán's position relative to the macroregional economy worsened. The bottom fell out of the cattle market. Consequently, the proliferation of haciendas in Yaxcabá parish was ill timed, and very few became profitable. Architectural elaboration of rural properties declined. Estate owners turned to a land-extensive, monocrop (cattle) strategy that absorbed available land. Further dispersal among the growing population of Maya agriculturalists was curtailed as more land was used for cattle production rather than maize cultivation. The market transition in Yaxcabá was unsuccessful and never completed—arrested by the advent of the Caste War in 1847.

Did this process aggravate land pressure for Maya agriculturalists by the mid-nineteenth century? Certainly some communities, especially those whose legitimacy in the eyes of the state was questionable, were denied access to sufficient land necessary to support their populations by extensive swidden cultivation. Farmers' options for coping with restricted access to land, however, were widely divergent. Those living in Yaxcabá or nearby legitimate communities engaged in wage labor or agricultural share contracts with Maya and Spanish-Creole elites. Inhabitants of independent ranchos, however, tended to diversify and intensify agricultural production and animal husbandry. The uneven quality of "agrarian pressures" across different settlements within the parish produced varied responses among different groups of rural inhabitants.

CHAPTER FIVE

Archaeological Site Structure before the Caste War

Ethnoarchaeological investigations in the humid tropics of Mesoamerica suggest that differences in household production, labor organization, land use, and the household's domestic cycle affect the spatial organization of residential units, their surroundings, and the long-term formation processes of household series (Arnold 1990; Deal 1985, 1998; Hayden and Cannon 1983, 1984; Hirth 1993; Killion 1990, 1992; Santley and Hirth 1993; M. Smith 1992; Smyth 1990). The redundant sets of activities regularly performed by household members in the course of their daily work leave a mark in the archaeological record, such that they can be detected through site structural analysis. Site structure refers to the study of spatial patterns among artifacts, ecofacts, features, and structures on archaeological sites (Binford 1987, 2001; Clarke 1977). Residential site structure, however, reflects the activities of a household series, the sequence of households that successively inhabit a given structure or house over a span of more than one generation (M. Smith 1992:30). In situations where household activities can be securely linked to a focal point where they were performed, site structural analysis permits the archaeologist to identify specific past behaviors and practices and to suggest how they were organized.

Members of different communities in the Yaxcabá region experienced varying land pressures, changes in ownership status, levels of taxation, and rates of population growth. Nevertheless, the idea that these conditions created pressure for change must remain a supposition unless one can show how Maya agriculturalists responded to them. Nineteenth-century

Maya farmers situated their household activities within house lots. Long after the lots were abandoned, archaeologists still can locate the boundary walls and find parts of dwelling foundations, gardening features, wells and water-storage tanks, and animal pens. The house lots constitute archaeologically visible loci for the performance of past household activities, including intensive gardening and animal husbandry. If land used for milpa cultivation in some nineteenth-century communities was restricted, to the extent that farmers altered agricultural tactics, then the resulting changes in the organization of household production should be visible in the archaeological patterns of the house lot.

Below I compare internal spatial patterns and house-lot site structure among three settlements: the pueblo Mopilá, the hacienda Cetelac, and the independent rancho Cacalchén. Population density, land use, taxation, labor organization, and social stratification differed appreciably among these three communities. To determine how the inhabitants responded to these conditions, I first describe and analyze the settlement pattern within each community, paying particular attention to the configurations of house lots. Next, I examine the evidence that these residential units were configured along the lines of the house-lot model (Killion 1990), with dwellings surrounded by a patio and a garden. Variation in house-lot size, the numbers and kinds of dwellings and features, and the sizes of garden and patio areas suggest differences in agricultural production and labor organization. Maya householders living in Mopilá, Cetelac, and Cacalchén employed notably different production strategies on the lot to cope with the political and economic changes of the first half of the nineteenth century. Their choices of agrarian-based survival strategies were linked to their community's political situation, level of integration with the regional economy, and legitimacy in the eyes of the church and state.

House-Lot Composition in Yaxcabá Parish

Households are social units that serve as interfaces that link the everyday practices of members with larger-scale ecological and political-economic processes (Small and Tannenbaum 1999; Wilk 1991; Wilk and Netting 1984; Wilk and Rathje 1982). Consequently, archaeologists do not study households directly; they study material correlates of the household—the spatial patterns of settlement that include dwellings, compounds, and house lots. Here I compare the archaeological patterns within the house lots of Mopilá, Cetelac, and Cacalchén to a general house-lot model that relates the behavior of household members to material patterns to ascertain whether nineteenth-century household strategies at Mopilá, Cetelac, and Cacalchén were similar or different (see related discussion above in Chapter 2). Using results from ethnoarchaeological studies in tropical Mesoamerica, Maya ethnography, detailed historical information about Yaxcabá parish, and modern observations of house lots in Yaxcabá itself, I modify the house-lot model so that it is an appropriate frame of reference for interpreting nineteenth-century spatial patterns for sites in the Yaxcabá region.

Archaeological households usually are identified by isolating the smallest, redundantly occurring, modular unit of settlement, which in the Yaxcabá region is the house lot (Alexander 1998; Ashmore 1981; Ashmore and Wilk 1988; Clarke 1972). The spatial patterns of these units result from the accumulation of production, consumption, deposition, reuse, abandonment, and postabandonment activities of a sequence of households that successively inhabited a given space for more than one generation (Hirth 1993; M. Smith 1992:30). Therefore, the archaeological remains do not simply mirror the synchronic behavior of the house lot's last inhabitants. Instead spatial patterns are created by long-term series of natural and cultural processes envisioned as palimpsests or "life histories," inscribed by the addition, removal, and rearrangement of archaeological materials over time (Binford 1968:21–22; Deal 1985, 1998; La Motta and Schiffer 1999; Schiffer 1976, 1987). Life histories of house lots generally unfold in several stages known as habitation, abandonment, reoccupation, and postabandonment.

Habitation

Like most agriculturalists in tropical Mesoamerica, Yaxcabá's householders inhabit lots composed of a dwelling area or structural core, a swept patio, and a garden (Arnold 1990; Deal 1985, 1998; Hayden and Cannon 1983, 1984; Killion 1987, 1990; Manzanilla and Barba 1990; Santley and Hirth 1993; Smyth 1990). In the present as in the past, houses and house lots are privately owned. Today when a family moves to a new community and establishes residence in a house lot for the first time, the household head usually pays a fee to the town council for usufruct rights to the *fundo legal* of the town. The family may purchase an existing vacant lot, or its members may develop a solar "from scratch," extending the area of settlement. The first tasks involve building or repairing the boundary wall, or albarrada, and clearing a space to construct a dwelling. Patios and garden zones are established during the course of daily activities, the most common of which is sweeping the patio. Sweeping produces a ring of midden at the edge of the patio. Refuse is also dumped beyond the edge of the patio, distributed through the garden (especially organic debris that augments and maintains soil fertility), and occasionally collected against the albarrada and burned. Hazardous waste, such as glass shards, may be deposited in special areas of the lot, away from traffic, and large refuse fragments also end up near boundary walls. Patio maintenance produces a pattern whereby inorganic material of low weight and small piece size remains in the clear area surrounding the residence, and items of higher weight and larger size are deposited in the toft zone.

The intensity and scheduling of household activities may further affect the organization of the house lot. Items that could potentially be reused or recycled, such as large pieces of broken pottery, plastic containers, or glass bottles, are provisionally discarded or stored along the outside walls of houses and ancillary structures. When the lot is abandoned, these items are often left behind (Deal 1985). Discrete maize-washing areas are usually placed at the edge of the patio where mud and water will not hinder other activities (Smyth 1990). Storage structures, especially corn cribs, are located either within the patio or within the dwelling. Although pigs and poultry normally wander loose, animal-penning structures are situated in the garden zone if the movement of too many animals through the house lot becomes disruptive. Beehive-logs harboring the stingless American honeybee usually are stacked under a perishable shade structure out in the garden zone.[1] Latrine areas also are located toward the back of the house lot, where they are not visible from the street. Cultivation of herbs, seedlings, or decorative plants occurs in segregated spaces, sometimes protected by stone surrounds, or arriates. Soil is some-times imported to the lot for this purpose if the existing substrate needs improvement.[2]

Ethnoarchaeological research in the Mesoamerican tropics indicates that variation in the relative sizes of patios and garden zones is sensitive to the kinds and intensity of agricultural activities conducted both within and outside of the house lot. Large patios and more formal-ized refuse disposal result from the need for ample staging areas for agricultural or other production activities occurring near the community or within the house lot itself (Arnold 1987, 1991; Killion 1990). In southern Veracruz, for example, large patios are prevalent for households that intensify agricultural production on infields near the settlement, whereas households that intensify agricultural production on monocropped outfields have smaller patios and larger gar-dens within the lot. Similarly, smaller available work space correlates with the more formal-ized arrangement, scheduling, and segregation of activity areas (Arnold 1991; Hayden and Cannon 1983). Arnold (1990) demonstrates that potters engaged in intensive craft production segre-gate areas of their house compounds such that other household activities conducted simulta-neously do not interfere with the production process. The more itinerant potters, however, use compound space sequentially, scheduling ceramic production within the same space used for other activities.

The repertoire of household activities shifts seasonally, from year to year, and as house-hold composition changes over time. Specific activities may be added or dropped, or the pro-portions and intensity of different practices may change relative to others. For example, during November through May of 1988 and 1989, when we were conducting archaeological fieldwork in Yaxcabá, farmers were preoccupied with providing enough food for their families and secur-ing seed for the next planting season at a time when the previous year's harvest should have been sufficient. In August 1988, however, hurricane Gilbert struck the peninsula, effectively wip-ing out crops that were almost ready for harvest. Many farmers in Yaxcabá immediately sowed a second corn crop in their solares, hand irrigating it over the dry season, and harvesting by February (see Re-Cruz 1996). Farmers also salvaged seed from devastated milpas. Coping with the emergency entailed changes in both the spatial organization of the house lots and the labor organization of the household.

Archaeological remains in house lots also reflect the course of the family or domestic cycle (Fortes 1958:2–5; Goody 1958) in which households undergo a regular sequence of change as members are added or lost, until the original household is dissolved and replaced by one or more similar units. This process produces archaeological remains known as the household series. Today in Yaxcabá nuclear families generally build two structures on the house lot—a house facing the street used for most domestic activities, as well as receiving visitors, and a kitchen located behind or sometimes adjacent to the back of the principal dwelling. If married chil-dren continue to reside in the house lot of their parents, additional buildings will be constructed as needed. Seldom do these extended-family or multifamily households surpass three gener-ations, however.

A series of domestic cycles occurring within a single house lot often may result in patterns of serial reuse of dwellings (see Moore and Gasco 1990). In Yaxcabá, however, such activity is coupled with limited intracommunity mobility, thorough scavenging, and reuse of construction materials in other buildings. Dissolution or fissioning of the household can cause periods where the house lot is unoccupied, especially if there is some dispute over lot ownership or inheritance. In some cases, married children have established residence elsewhere in town, and those that inherit a solar upon the death of a parent may use the lot and its existing dwellings for storage. If the house lot is not sold or otherwise reoccupied, the dwellings and furnishings eventually may be dismantled over time for reuse elsewhere.

In another case in Yaxcabá, the death of a family patriarch spawned a dispute over house-lot usufruct within a group of half brothers. The youngest son had been living with his wife and children in a separate dwelling on the house lot of his father, and some of his brothers wanted him and his family to vacate the lot. A lawsuit followed, which the youngest son lost, and the family was forced to move to a new house lot. They did not go quietly. Instead the family called on kin and neighbors to help them literally "move house." The dwelling was tightly bound with rope, uprooted from its foundations, and carried by a large group of helpers two blocks down the street to the new house lot. A new sascab floor was prepared for the structure, and its walls were refilled with mud daub covered with white plaster. The family also transplanted all their useful plants and herbs from the old house lot to the new. The old house lot remained unoccupied, the patriarch's dwelling padlocked, and after four months one could hardly distinguish the spot on which the youngest son's house had once stood.

At Mopilá, Cetelac, and Cacalchén the length of the habitation stage of each site's life history varies considerably in length. Household series at Mopilá span more than four hundred years, whereas at Cetelac and Cacalchén habitation stages are much shorter—seventy-five and one hundred years respectively.

Abandonment and Reoccupation

The process by which a community is abandoned also affects archaeological house-lot assemblages. Fortunately in the Yaxcabá region we have historical information about the likely course of abandonment in Mopilá, Cetelac, and Cacalchén. "Abandonment" in this discussion refers to abandonment of the community, not temporary abandonment of individual lots within communities. Similarly, the term "reoccupation" refers to the reuse of an abandoned settlement for residence—the reestablishment of a community as opposed to the postabandonment use of settlements for extensive activities such as farming or animal husbandry.

Michael Deal's (1985, 1998:126–28; see also Schiffer 1976) ethnoarchaeological studies in the Maya Highlands supply a useful framework for examining how abandonment affects archaeological patterns within house lots. He demonstrates that two principal variables—the rapidity of departure and the anticipation of return to the site at a future date—affect the size, condition, value, and location of archaeological materials left in house lots. In cases where abandonment is gradual or planned and in which return is not anticipated, very few useable or valuable items are left in the dwelling or on the lot, including items in provisional discard. During a planned abandonment, refuse that would normally be disposed of properly sometimes accumulates in dwellings and outbuildings. Where return is anticipated, useable items more often are left on site, and storage of functional artifacts is common. In situations where abandonment is rapid, for example in cases of attack, epidemic, or natural disasters, many more complete, useable, and valuable items will be left in place, especially if return is anticipated. Where return is not anticipated, items of value are removed from the site. Other variables that affect what material is left on the lot include the portability of material culture, the means of transportation, distance to the new residence, the season of movement, and the utility of the item (Deal 1998:270).

Deal (1985:274, 1998:130–32) presents six hypothetical models that describe the ways that abandonment and postabandonment activities combine to produce specific archaeological patterns within house lots. The house lots in Mopilá, Cetelac, and Cacalchén closely conform to his "model 6" in which patios and pathways are blurred, no provisional discard or whole vessels are present, and the entire lot is characterized by high ceramic sherd densities. Deal suggests that the model 6 pattern refers to situations where postabandonment gardening is extensive, abandonment processes are unclear, and the site has been occupied for successive generations.

Rapid and repeated abandonments in the face of multiple attacks best characterize the Caste War years and are likely to have affected the archaeological assemblages at Mopilá, Cetelac, and Cacalchén (see Table 3.7 in Chapter 3, above). Repeated episodes of scavenging by both the rebel Maya and Creole militia in the wake of the attacks and raids also took a cumulative toll. Although most residents anticipated return to their communities once it was safe to do so, in the end many did not come back. Epidemics, especially cholera (see discussion above in Chapter 3), often carried off whole families and no doubt affected the abandonment process. In one sense, the desertion of individual communities in Yaxcabá parish is symptomatic of a broader-scale, regional abandonment, in which flight and loss of life during the Caste War years resulted in a demographic decline of nearly 90 percent.

Cetelac most likely represents a case of rapid, one-time abandonment. The hacienda was burned and pillaged in 1848 during the initial rebel offensive. No historical evidence from censuses or other documents indicates that it was subsequently reoccupied. Most contemporary residents of the area believe that the hacienda's owner anticipated returning and hid his valuables on the site; consequently, subsequent scavenging has been thorough.

Likewise, Cacalchén was abandoned during the first years of the Caste War. Although burning was one of the rebel Maya's favorite methods of attack, it is difficult to discern whether burning was involved at Cacalchén (or Mopilá), because current use of these areas for slash-and-burn cultivation obscures previous episodes. Archaeological evidence of breastworks in the streets of the settlement suggest that the community was attacked at least once, although oral histories suggest that it was more common for the population to flee into the forest before an impending attack (Bricker 1981:255).

Similarly, at Mopilá breastworks indicate an actual attack on the community. After a number of episodes of rapid evacuation and return, however, final abandonment of this community was planned. The forty-four people residing at Mopilá in 1900 were gradually attracted to Yaxcabá. The inhabitants' proximity to their new location also suggests that such a move would have left few materials at Mopilá.

Cacalchén, as well as a number of other communities in the parish, was reoccupied in the early and mid-twentieth century. Reoccupation is a complementary process to planned, gradual abandonment of portions of communities spurred by a need to be closer to one's milpa, to acquire new land, and to avoid village factionalism and land disputes. This classical process is described in Redfield and Villa Rojas's (1934:24–30) ethnography of Chan Kom. At Chan Kom, a new town was created in response to the need for agricultural land, factionalism in the parent community of Ebtun, difficulties in implementing the new agrarian laws governing the distribution of ejido, revolutionary turbulence in nearby communities (resulting in massacres in Yaxcabá, Kancabdzonot, Yaxuná, Xkopteil, and Piste in 1924), and the presence of a strong leader. A similar process occurred in Yaxcabá. A number of related families from the parent community reestablished themselves at Cacalchén so that they could reside closer to their milpas and gain access to new lands. In the twentieth century, inhabitants situated their houses near the existing water sources (a well and the cenote), modified and realigned existing house-lot boundary walls, and accumulated twentieth-century refuse, left behind when the site was abandoned again in the 1950s.

Postabandonment

Postabandonment processes also drastically affect archaeological assemblages and settlement patterns. Modification of archaeological patterns occurs as both natural and cultural processes impinge on the site. Soil erosion and deposition, vegetation growth and succession, rodent activity and other bioturbation, as well as the decay of perishable remains and ecofacts all impact the distribution and condition of archaeological remains on the site (see Schiffer 1987; Wood and Johnson 1978).

In the Yaxcabá region farmers who cultivate milpas far from their residences commonly make use of the facilities and infrastructure (especially water) offered in abandoned settlements. Production activities such as slash-and-burn cultivation of agricultural plots, collection of firewood, small-scale animal husbandry, beekeeping, harvesting fodder (particularly *ramón* leaves) for animals, collecting fruit or other wild resources, and hunting occur at historic-period sites in Yaxcabá parish. Scavenging of useable materials is widespread. Other, more passive behaviors also modify the archaeological record, including vacant-lot activities and shortcutting or creating new pathways across a site (see Deal 1998:128; Wilk and Schiffer 1979). In some cases, particularly if the site is close to a modern community, farmers situate specialized and cooperative agrarian activities within an abandoned settlement. For example, farmers recently located a citrus cooperative, a pig- and cattle-raising endeavor, and a grain storage facility at Mopilá.

Archaeological Site Structure

We chose Mopilá, Cacalchén, and Cetelac for intensive investigation because each represents one discrete site category in the Yaxcabá region. These places were unoccupied at the time we conducted fieldwork, and specific historical information about each community also was available to complement the archaeological study. Although all three sites were abandoned in the aftermath of the Caste War, occupational sequences varied. Mopilá was occupied the longest, from before 1581 to 1900, with only a brief period of abandonment during the war. Cetelac, the hacienda, was the shortest, from 1773 to 1848. Cacalchén was occupied from about 1750 to 1848, but ten to fifteen families resettled the site in the 1920s. They subsequently returned to live in Yaxcabá in the 1950s.

Each of the sites also contained pre-Hispanic components. Mopilá showed evidence of Post-classic period (A.D. 1250–1545) settlement, while Cetelac and Cacalchén contained structures and artifactual material dating to the Classic period (A.D. 250–600). Currently farmers use Mopilá, Cetelac, and Cacalchén for extensive milpa cultivation, beekeeping, citrus cultivation, and occasionally for grazing and watering livestock.

Today, dense tropical secondary vegetation has overgrown the house lots in Mopilá, Cetelac, and Cacalchén. Only where farmers continue to use wells, shrines, or roads is previous habitation apparent. Sometimes clearing and burning the vegetation in preparation for planting milpa will expose boundary walls, house foundations, or old animal pens. House lots in these abandoned communities look like the unoccupied, overgrown lots used for harvesting firewood that commonly ring contemporary communities. Although stripped of their structures and facilities, they could be made suitable for habitation simply by clearing and repairing the boundary walls and by building a new house. Mopilá, Cetelac, and Cacalchén are "abandoned" but not forgotten. Whereas previously farmers staged the entire gamut of coresidential practices in these places, they now are used less intensively for specific cultivation activities. The communities and their constituent features are part of the cultural and historical geography of Yaxcabá's current inhabitants, whose practices constitute the most recent postabandonment processes to modify the archaeological record.

Mopilá

The pueblo Mopilá is located 1.5 km southwest of Yaxcabá and covers an area of 55 ha (Figure 5.1). Gently rolling terrain consisting of bedrock outcrops interspersed with more level areas characterizes the site. Vegetation consists of secondary forest in various stages of regeneration and one area of primary forest surrounding the church and main plaza. Scattered throughout the area are a number of large fruit trees, including cocoyol and zapote. One unpaved road suitable for vehicles runs from the southwest limit of Yaxcabá through Mopilá's main plaza and to the back of the church. Two other roads currently used for foot, horse, and bicycle traffic also pass through the site. One extends west to Sotuta, and the other runs southwest to Tixcacaltuyú.

Mopilá is centered around its noria, the seventeenth-century church dedicated to San Mateo, and the main plaza. Six major arteries lead away from the plaza into the remainder of the settlement, and house lots are aligned along streets according to the Spanish colonial grid plan (see Figure 4.4b–c of related category II sites in Chapter 4, above). The intersections of the main streets had been blocked with additional albarradas, and a trench and small parapet were constructed on the road leading southwest toward Tixcacaltuyú. Both Reed (1964) and Dumond (1997) mention blockades and construction of breastworks in the streets used by defenders and assailants during the Caste War.

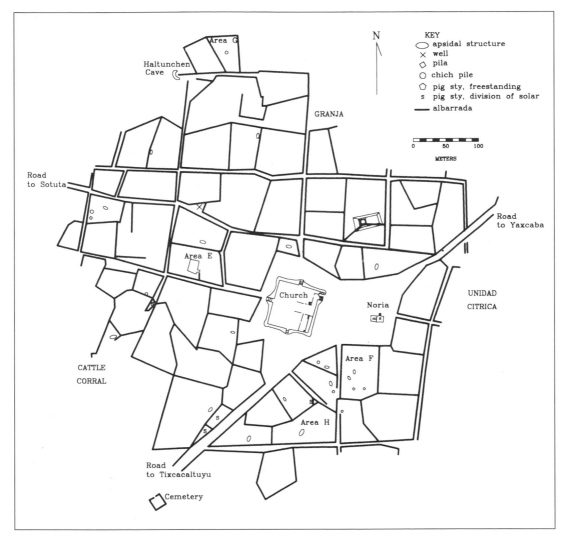

FIGURE 5.1. Site plan of Mopilá.

The church conforms to a regular cruciform plan oriented east-west and is constructed atop a square, 5-meter-high platform that is probably pre-Hispanic. Four stairways, one on each side, provide access to the platform. We found a baptismal font near the top of the west stairway. The roof of the church as well as the main entrance to the nave have collapsed, but remnants of a wood-beam-and-mortar roof remain in the southeastern corner of the sanctuary. An ornate wood retablo adorns the main altar, and an ossuary (cemetery) is located adjacent to the south side of the nave (see Figure 4.5 in Chapter 4, above, that details this retablo). A narrow stairway located along the east wall of the ossuary leads to the roof. Adjacent to the north side of the sanctuary are four rooms arranged linearly. The church is still used for the annual cofradía ceremonies from Yaxcabá in early July. Aside from the church, the only other standing architecture at Mopilá is a rectangular colonial platform located within a house lot near the center of the site. Two stone alignments remain on top of the platform, and access is provided by a stairway on the east side.

Another feature located within the settlement consists of a large circular pit, 6 m in diameter and 1.5 m deep, lined with heavy masonry and dug into the top of a pre-Hispanic platform. Similar features have been found in other early colonial settlements, and some scholars suggest the pits may have been used to produce indigo dye (Hanson et al. 1994; Ruz 1979).

Besides the noria, three other water sources were available to Mopilá's inhabitants. A limestone cave *(haltunchen)* located in the northwest of the settlement contains water year round. Two additional wells also presently contain water. One is situated in a small plazuela northwest of the church; the other is located in the southeastern part of the site now used as the citrus cooperative.

The main cemetery at Mopilá is located on the southwestern edge of the settlement along the road leading to Tixcacaltuyú. It measures some 400 sq m and is surrounded by a wide albarrada, nearly 1 m wide and 1 m high. Two massive limestone blocks mark the entrance facing the street. No monuments, mausoleums, or headstones were present, as they are in modern Yucatecan cemeteries.

Several areas of the site have been modified by the agrarian activities of Yaxcabá's modern inhabitants. When the site was mapped, the most notable were the citrus cooperative on the east side and the grain storage cooperative to the north. These activities all but obliterated the original house-lot boundaries in these areas. Many other parts of the site are cultivated for milpa. Although some portions have been repeatedly cleared, burned, and planted, cultivation has not severely disturbed the original locations of house-lot walls and features.

Cetelac

The hacienda is located 1 km east of the pueblo Yaxuná and extends over an area of 35 ha (Figure 5.2). The site is centered around the main buildings of the estate, including a two-story masonry house and adjacent noria. The house consists of four second-story rooms level with the noria platform, arranged in a linear fashion, that open to the west along an open corridor. One room contains a niche, possibly to accommodate a household altar. The ground-floor rooms are accessed via wide archways opening to the east and were probably used for storage (see Figure 4.6a–c in Chapter 4).

The noria is adjacent to the north side of the house, accessed by a ramp off the east side. Water troughs run along the west side of the house below the corridor and under a narrow stairway that permitted passage from the house to the main corral. Outbuildings include a perishable apsidal structure to the south and east of the noria's ramp, which likely served as a kitchen. A group of nine arriates, probably infrastructure for starting an orchard, are situated off the southeast corner of the main house. To the south and east of the house is a large rejollada. A masonry apsidal structure is also located on a platform to the north and west of the main house, outside the main corral. This structure may have served as a residence for the mayoral or foreman. A second well is located to the north of this house. The

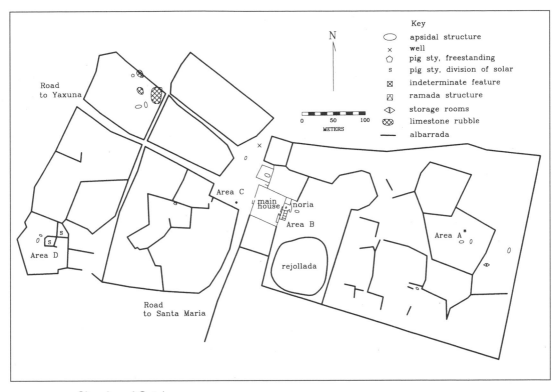

FIGURE 5.2. Site plan of Cetelac.

walls of the main corral are constructed of masonry, and elaborate gateways adorn its three entrances (see Figure 4.6a–c, in Chapter 4, above). Additional corrals are constructed of dry-laid stone walls, and the house lots of the resident population are situated farther away from the central buildings and corrals. These house lots are aligned along streets only in the north-west part of the settlement.

Although the roof and walls of the main house have collapsed inward, the rubble is pitted with secondary excavations. Local farmers believe that hacienda owners, expecting that their estates would be plundered during the Caste War, hid their wealth in secret places—sometimes down the well or in a cenote or within subterranean chambers under the house or outbuildings. The itinerant excavations common at most haciendas in the Yaxcabá region represent a search for the lost treasure.[3]

Pre-Hispanic remains within the hacienda are substantial and include both platform mounds and albarradas. Cetelac is situated just over 1 km from the center of the Yaxuná archaeological zone. In many cases the layout of the house lots at Cetelac follows or only slightly modifies the alignment of pre-Hispanic walls. Many pre-Hispanic structures were robbed for building stone during the historic period.

Currently Cetelac is part of the ejido of Yaxuná and is used for milpa cultivation, apiculture, and harvesting fodder (zacate) for livestock. Consultants from Yaxuná readily identified modern constructions, most used to support apiculture. Some of the old corrals are still used to confine cattle and horses, and the noria, well, and water troughs are used in conjunction with these activities.

Cacalchén

Cacalchén is located 7.5 km east of Yaxcabá and extends over an area of 35 ha (Figure 5.3). Its rolling terrain is covered with dense, high secondary growth that remains verdant throughout the dry season. At the time the site was mapped only two small areas in the northern and southwestern sections were burned in preparation for sowing milpa.

The site is centered on a plaza containing a large cenote and a platform supporting a large masonry altar with a niche that in the past accommodated a small statue and religious figure. The platform and altar together likely formed a ramada-style church (Andrews 1991) in which the nave was constructed of perishable materials. It is probably the chapel referred to by Eusebio Villamil in 1842 (see related discussion in Chapter 3). Two additional shrines occur at Cacalchén. The largest, a small chapel, is located in a house lot west of the site center (see Figure 4.7a in Chapter 4, above), and the other is located in the extreme southeast part of the site, adjacent to the cemetery. Like the cemetery in Mopilá, it was enclosed by a 1-meter-wide albarrada, and no monuments or headstones were present. Aside from the altar and shrines, architecture at Cacalchén consists only of two large masonry apsidal structures in one house lot in the northeastern part of the site (Area K) (see Figure 4.7b in Chapter 4, above). The buildings measure 4 by 6 m in area and lack roofs; one structure has a niche at the north end of the building, probably for a household altar.[4]

Streets and house lots at Cacalchén are laid out on a grid pattern along eight major arteries extending outward from the main plaza. Most of the streets widen at intervals forming small plazuelas or public spaces. Street intersections were blocked by hastily constructed walls, as noted at Mopilá, which likely were used by the community's defenders during the Caste War. Overall, the streets at Cacalchén are narrower than those at Mopilá or Cetelac. In addition to the cenote, six other wells are located within the settlement. One is next to a shrine, and the other five are in house lots. Only three of the wells contained water at the time of the survey.

Structures and features pertaining to the twentieth-century occupation at Cacalchén were readily identified with the assistance of a consultant, Agustino Ku, who was born in the settlement and lived there to early adulthood. The Ku family and their relatives, who had lived at Cacalchén in the mid-twentieth century, today use the settlement for farming and beekeeping. In most cases, reoccupation was obvious. A water trough had been added adjacent to a well, albarradas were discontinuous and rearranged, and at least one house foundation brace still contained items discarded provisionally (a Pepsi bottle) along an inside wall. Construction of the paved highway also modified several house-lot boundaries along the main plaza, and modern artifactual material was encountered along the verges. In one spot a soft-drink distributing truck had overturned, leaving a dense patch of shattered glass. Albarradas bounding streets would terminate at the highway, only to resume on the other side.

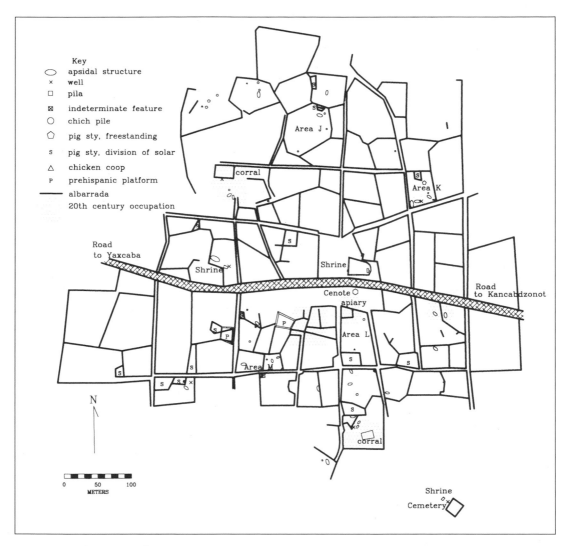

FIGURE 5.3. Site plan of Cacalchén.

The House Lots and their Features

In each of the three sites, house lots were delimited by dry-laid stone walls called albarradas. These boundary walls had collapsed such that they measured only 50 cm high and 30–40 cm wide and obscured the original points of entrance and egress. The house lots themselves were large, irregularly shaped spaces, averaging 4,110 sq m, although there is substantial variation in house-lot size within and among the three sites. Once cleared of vegetation, we frequently found the remains of foundation braces for perishable houses, animal pens, wells, water-storage tanks, irrigation berms, arriates (protective surrounds for seedlings and trees), and chich (crushed rock) piles, all constructed of local limestone (Figure 5.4a–g). The most common structure encountered within the lots was the foundation brace for an apsidal house that once had a perishable superstructure. Although

FIGURE 5.4a. House-lot features: House foundation, Cetelac
(all photos this chapter by Rani Alexander).

the surface of each house lot was inspected by means of 100-percent pedestrian coverage, the majority of the house lots contained no features or structures at all. Table 5.1 presents an inventory of the various house-lot configurations for Mopilá, Cetelac, and Cacalchén.

The functions of structures and features were identified on the basis of modern analogy. Maya householders today construct houses, pig sties, chicken coops, beehive stacks, arriates, pilas, and the like out of local limestone, wood, and thatch that are practically identical to the remains of the historical examples recorded during archaeological survey. The functions of chich piles, however, are more problematic. They are commonly found in pre-Hispanic sites as well as in historical and modern settlements. Functions attributed to chich piles in Yucatán include foundations for small structures or for storage facilities (Killion et al. 1989; Ringle and Andrews 1988; Smyth 1990) and stone mulch for protecting tree roots from soil erosion and moisture loss (Kepecs and Boucher 1996). The numbers and kinds of ancillary features are important clues for understanding strategies of diversification and production within the house lot.

Apsidal Structures

Apsidal structures consist of an elliptical alignment of irregularly shaped limestone blocks, never more than 1 course high (Figure 5.4a). In most cases only a portion of the alignment remains, and entrances and thresholds are seldom identifiable. They usually measure 4 by 6 m (24 sq m in area) but regularly vary between 15 and 40 sq m. Metate fragments were also

TABLE 5.1: House-Lot Configurations in Mopilá, Cetelac, and Cacalchén

Configuration	Mopilá	Cetelac	Cacalchén
Lacked any features whatsoever	40	20	48
Contained the foundation brace of one apsidal house	9	2	4
Contained the foundation brace of one apsidal house and one chich pile	2		
Contained the remains of one chich pile	2		1
Contained the remains of one animal pen	2		7
Contained the foundation brace of one apsidal house and one animal pen	1		2
Contained the foundation brace of one apsidal house, one chich pile, and one pila	1		
Contained the foundation brace of one apsidal house and two animal pens	1		
Contained the foundation braces of two apsidal houses and one animal pen		1	
Contained the foundation braces of two apsidal houses and two animal pens	1	1	1
Contained a raised masonry colonial platform	1		
Contained one animal pen and one indeterminate feature			1
Contained two animal pens and one chich pile			1
Contained the foundation brace of one apsidal house, one chich pile, one animal pen, and two indeterminate features			1
Contained two masonry apsidal houses, one work area, one well, one pila, one era, two animal pens, and two indeterminate features			1
Contained the foundation brace of two apsidal houses, one pila, and one animal pen			1
Contained the foundation brace of one apsidal house, one well, and one shrine			1
Contained one chich pile and three animal pens			1
Contained the foundation brace of one apsidal house and three animal pens			1
Contained the foundation brace of one apsidal house, one animal pen, and one indeterminate feature			1
Contained one chich pile and one pila			1
Contained the foundation brace of one apsidal house, one well, one pila, and two animal pens			1
Contained one pila			1
Contained one indeterminate feature			1
Contained the foundation brace of one apsidal house and underground storage rooms		1	
Contained foundation braces of two apsidal houses and one work area		1	
Total House Lots	**60**	**26**	**76**

FIGURE 5.4b. House-lot features: Pig sty, Cacalchén.

FIGURE 5.4c. House-lot features: Poultry coop, Cacalchén.

FIGURE 5.4d. House-lot features: Chich pile, Mopilá.

encountered adjacent to the outside of the foundation brace or nearby. Areas of crushed rock fill were used to level bedrock surfaces, and in some cases soil and rubble containing pre-Hispanic artifacts were used as floor fill. Only the kitchen at Cetelac had a definable sascab floor. For all other examples, the floors of the structures had been completely eroded.

Animal Pens

Four kinds of structures are identified as animal pens.[5] The first consists of a roughly circular or elliptical area, ranging in size from 6 to 8 sq m in area, enclosed by a dry-laid stone wall (Figure 5.4b). Unlike the apsidal structures, the volume of limestone blocks composing the wall indicates that it was originally several courses (up to 1 m) high. These pens usually have a single opening. Whereas these large circular pens were probably used for housing pigs, a second, smaller kind of pen, consisting of a circular arrangement of large limestone boulders, 1.5 to 2 m in diameter, also was common (Figure 5.4c). Usually the stone wall was only a single course high but composed of boulders in the 80-cm range. These pens also have a single opening. They were probably used for protecting chickens and turkeys. Today these small stone-ring pens often contain a pan of water where poultry congregate to drink (see also Redfield and Villa Rojas 1934:plate 4b). The third kind of pen consists of a quadrangular or triangular area partitioned from the rest of the house lot by an additional albarrada. Such pens are common in modern Maya lots. In many cases the partitioned area (as well as the circular features) are used as pig sties, but in other cases partitions may separate flower gardens from the activities occurring in the rest of the house lot. Finally, pens created by using collapsed areas of bedrock outcrops and sascaberas (caves or limestone overhangs) were also noted at the three sites. Usually an additional bit of albarrada closed off the entrance of the natural feature.

Chich Piles

These features consist of circular piles of limestone rubble, or chich, measuring roughly 3 m in diameter (Figure 5.4d). In some cases the rubble fragments (5 to 10 cm across) are mixed with larger, irregularly shaped limestone blocks located near the perimeter of the pile. The piles are about 20 cm high in the center and taper off to the level of the ground surface at the edges. Others lack perimeters defined by larger stone blocks. In one case at Mopilá, surface collection units associated with a chich pile contained noticeable lumps of *bajareque,* or daub, but no evidence of intense burning was present.

The chich piles have few strong analogs in modern Yucatecan house lots. As mentioned above, the current consensus is that chich piles may be foundations for small structures, storage facilities, or work areas. Another possibility is that they simply may be rock piles similar to ones found in the Maya Highlands (see Gasco 1987, 1992; Hayden and Cannon 1983). In Yucatán, house-lot walls and other constructions are fabricated of local limestone. Chich piles could be formed during routine lot maintenance. The crushed limestone might have been kept on hand and used for repairing and chinking albarradas and ancillary structures, resurfacing house floors, or repairing other masonry.

Arriates

These are circular stone enclosures of variable size used for starting seedlings, growing herbs and flowers, or protecting tree roots from livestock and foot traffic. They vary from the formally faced and carved stone surrounds in hacienda orchards, like the ones found at Cetelac, to roughly circular arrangements of unshaped limestone blocks. Yucatecan house lots contain many sorts of stone enclosures—the larger ones are used as animal pens, while others (arriates, lower in height and usually lacking an opening) are used for horticultural activities. In areas where soil is poor, stone mulch used to prevent moisture loss may resemble chich piles rather than the more formal arriates (Kepecs and Boucher 1996).

Wells and Water Storage

In addition to norias where the well opening is surrounded by square or round masonry platforms that support water-pumping mechanisms, a number of wells were found in public spaces and within house lots at Mopilá, Cetelac, and Cacalchén (Figure 5.4e). Usually the well openings were circular, measuring 90 to 120 cm in diameter. Several had protective masonry walls, about 1 m high, encircling the edge of the well. One had flat-faced limestone flagstones set along the opening, but others had no such barriers and were simply open. Several wells had handholds and footholds scored into the sides to permit access to the bottom.

A number of water-storage features, or pilas, were also encountered in the sites (Figure 5.4f). Although tanks and smaller pilas frequently were situated adjacent to noria platforms, a number of free-standing pilas were located within house lots. The most common type consists of a

FIGURE 5.4e. House-lot features: Well, Cacalchén.

FIGURE 5.4f. House-lot features: Pila, Cacalchén.

FIGURE 5.4g. House-lot features: Pila and era, Cacalchén.

rectangular open box, constructed of upright limestone slabs set in mortar. They range in size from 1 to 1.5 meters in area and measure 40 to 50 cm deep. A second kind of pila is cut into the surface of the limestone bedrock. Usually the opening is square, measuring 0.75 to 1 sq m in area and anywhere from 40 cm to 80 cm deep. One pila of this kind at Mopilá had a limestone slab that served to cover the opening.

Finally, irrigation berms or *eras* were associated with pilas at Cacalchén (Figure 5.4g). Eras consist of roughly faced limestone blocks, set in mortar adjacent to each other and forming an alignment. They serve to guide water from the pila to a specific area of the house lot. The longest era at Cacalchén measures 10 m.

Work Areas and Indeterminate Features

Some house lots contained patches of bedrock in which the uneven areas had been leveled with chich fill. Associated with the areas of filled bedrock were large stones, 20 to 30 cm across, poorly articulated but delimiting an alignment or perhaps part of an elliptically shaped foundation brace. In one case two to three large limestone blocks were located next to natural fissures in the bedrock, forming a square area measuring 4 by 4 m. Some of these features likely represent work areas for outdoor cooking and washing. Others may be the remains of shade structures—a thatched roof supported by four posts commonly used to shelter beehives—or raised maize storage cribs (Re-Cruz 1996:124; Redfield and Villa Rojas 1934:plates 9b and 9c; Smyth 1990). A few additional features of indeterminate function were located in Cetelac and Cacalchén.

They are small, low rectangular platforms, built of well-articulated, faced limestone blocks (sometimes set in mortar), measuring roughly 1.5 m long by 1 m wide and 30 to 60 cm in height. These constructions are never more than 1 course of masonry high. They may constitute infrastructure for work and activity areas.

Underground Storage

This feature was unique to Cetelac. A small cave or sascabera (limestone depression) in one of the house lots had a prepared floor and a masonry partition constructed from the floor to the top of the limestone overhang. The sascabera had been divided into two small rooms, possibly functioning as a storage facility. No artifactual material in primary context remained.

Surface Collections and House-Lot Patterning

Determining whether the house lots were arranged with a patio and a garden surrounding the residence required a more intensive survey strategy. Eleven house lots were selected by means of a stratified random sampling design for surface collection—four in Mopilá, five in Cacalchén, and two in Cetelac. At Cetelac, areas surrounding the main house, noria, and ancillary structures and the plazas also were collected. Within each house lot, surface collection transects, consisting of 3-by-3-m squares continuously laid end to end, were placed to crosscut structures, features, and different areas within the lot. The transects were cleared of all vegetation. The surface of each collection unit was scraped with a trowel, and the soil was screened through 6-mm mesh. Artifacts of ceramic, chert, obsidian, shell, metal, bone, and glass were recovered for subsequent analysis.

Surface collection transects were placed to crosscut different sectors of the house lots, running through house structures and ancillary features. Assuming that the clear area surrounded the dwelling core and was maintained by daily sweeping, it was possible to delimit the extent of patio and garden areas by measuring the density of inorganic refuse in different areas of the lot.[6] The house-lot maintenance activities structured the location and density of colonial refuse and altered the preexisting substrate of pre-Hispanic refuse at the same time. Ceramics, both pre-Hispanic and colonial, were the most common materials recovered from the surface collections. The locations and extent of patio and garden areas were estimated by examining the fall-off patterns of average sherd weight and other artifacts across the transects. Although exposed bedrock was common within the house lots, most areas were covered with a thin layer of soil. Modification of the existing pre-Hispanic substrate was also indicated. Not only was stone taken from nearby pre-Hispanic mounds, but dirt containing pre-Hispanic artifactual material was used for floor fill and added to garden areas.

The Structural Core

At Mopilá, Cacalchén, and Cetelac, the structural core was characterized by the presence of one or occasionally two semicircular, apsidal foundation braces (Figure 5.5). Within the area

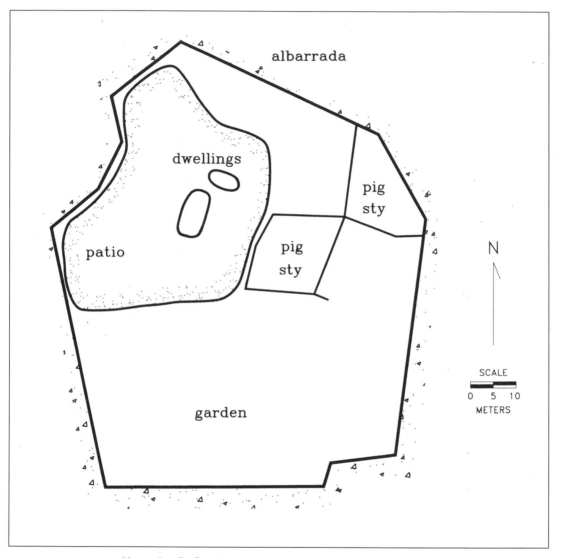

FIGURE 5.5. House Lot D, Cetelac.

of the foundation braces, fill of crushed limestone and/or dirt remained, but floors had eroded. Metate fragments were often located along the edges of the foundation braces, and sometimes fragments of metal nails, latches, and hinges were found. Large values for ceramic frequency, weight, and average sherd weight were common in surface collection units located on or near the foundations of dwellings. Erosion of floors and floor fill in the colonial settlements is principally responsible for the large values of ceramics, and decomposition of the structures likely accounts for the distribution of metal artifacts. The broken metate fragments, however, might also indicate provisional discard areas (Deal 1985; Hayden and Cannon 1983). Ethnoarchaeological studies show that most refuse generated in the dwelling is also swept out the door, dumped

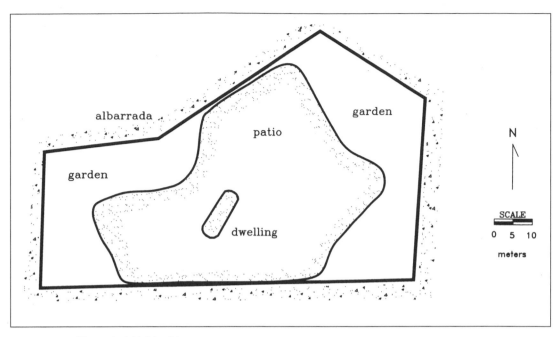

FIGURE 5.6. House Lot H, Mopilá.

next to the door, or thrown out the door into the patio or garden, and foot traffic near the dwelling tramples items into the underlying matrix (Arnold 1991:129). Frequency and weight of inorganic refuse in the patio decreases with distance from the dwelling.

The scarcity of dwelling remains at these sites is unusual considering the length of their occupation (Figure 5.6). Many house lots contained no structural remains at all. Normally, house lots containing multiple structures and occupied by large households are difficult to distinguish from the serial reuse of structures and the growth and decline of the domestic cycle over time (Moore and Gasco 1990). At Mopilá, Cacalchén, and Cetelac, however, indications of the serial use of structures are absent. Although this pattern could indicate a small house-lot population or the presence of nuclear families, the existence of completely perishable structures cannot be overlooked. On occasion, surface collection transects would cross portions of bedrock that had been filled or partially leveled, but where few foundation stones remained. Remaining foundation braces may represent cases where significant amounts of labor and materials were invested in house construction.

Contemporary Maya are also extremely thorough in collecting and reusing building materials from unoccupied structures, and the proximity of colonial and modern settlement in the Yaxcabá region may account for this pattern. If serial reuse of structures occurred, which is plausible especially at Mopilá, reuse of materials from previously occupied dwellings was complete. The structural core and ancillary features probably reflect the final configuration of structures within the house lot of the last occupants, as modified by postabandonment processes (Deal 1985).

The Patio and Garden Zones

Patios and garden areas within the house lots could be approximated by a fairly marked change in the size and density of ceramic remains, usually at the point where average sherd weight rose sharply, around 3.5 to 4.0 grams per sherd. A principal-components analysis was conducted using ceramic frequency, ceramic weight, mean sherd weight, bone frequency, lithic frequency, metal frequency, and frequency of glazed ceramics. The principal components most useful for distinguishing the patio from the garden and structural core usually displayed high loadings for mean sherd weight, metal, and frequency of special artifacts. When the value of the principal component was plotted for each unit across individual transects, it was possible to distinguish the structural core from the patio from the garden zone. Patios contained relatively small and light sherds as well as small bone fragments, whereas garden areas contained dense amounts of refuse resembling sheet midden. No intermediate refuse zones, such as those that accumulate at patio edges, could be distinguished in this analysis (see Killion 1990). Raw values for ceramic frequency and weight were less useful in this analysis. They proved somewhat more sensitive to topographic conditions, especially the degree of slope and amount of exposed bedrock. Rodent and other biological activity also affected the size of ceramic and lithic variables for some units given the thin soil conditions.

The karst geological conditions suggest that the hindrance potential of large sherds in the cultivation process was probably less of a consideration in colonial settlements than retaining and augmenting soil within the lot (cf. Deal 1985; Hayden and Cannon 1983). Ancillary features, particularly pig sties and chicken coops, were located in garden areas and associated with very high densities of inorganic debris. Pilas and wells were often situated near patio edges (Figure 5.7). Among the Maya living in the Puuc region of Yucatán, maize washing areas are located near wells and pilas. Smyth (1988, 1990) suggests that because maize washing creates muddy areas and requires the undivided attention of the participant, these activities frequently take place at patio peripheries or in intermediate refuse disposal zones away from traffic.

Unlike the structural core, the sizes of the patio and garden areas, as determined archaeologically, probably do not represent the final abandonment phase of the lot. Because the boundaries of the patio and garden expand or shrink over time according to the population of the house lot and in response to the different space needs of activities that take place in the lot, the relative sizes of these areas probably represent a mosaic of overlapping patios whose location and size has shifted over time. Given the karst conditions, the patio area defined archaeologically probably represents the maximum combined extent of all patio areas over the life of the house lot, and the percentage of patio area within the house lot in this case is correlated with the length of household series.

Site Structural Variation among Settlements

Analysis of site structural patterns in house lots among Mopilá, Cetelac, and Cacalchén revealed distinct differences in use of space. House-lot size, the numbers of ancillary features within house lots, patio size, and consumption of nonlocal items vary among the three sites. Together,

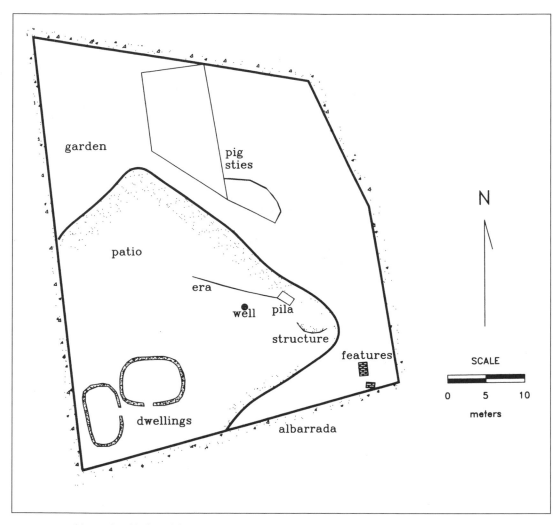

FIGURE 5.7. House Lot K, Cacalchén.

these analyses suggest that different communities in the parish employed different strategies for coping with the changes in agrarian legislation after 1821. Table 5.2 summarizes the site structural variation and historical information for each settlement.

Mean house-lot size at Cetelac is larger than mean house-lot size at Mopilá, which in turn is larger than at Cacalchén. The Kruskal Wallis test, a nonparametric statistical comparison procedure, indicates that mean house-lot size is significantly different ($p < 0.002$; $\alpha = 0.05$) among the sites, and nonparametric pairwise comparisons (Wilcoxon tests) show significant differences among all three sites ($p < 0.004$ between Mopilá and Cacalchén; $p < 0.0001$ between Cacalchén and Cetelac; $p < 0.0001$ between Mopilá and Cetelac; $\alpha = 0.05$).[7]

Conversely, the mean number of ancillary features per house lot is much higher at Cacalchén than at Mopilá or Cetelac. A Kruskal Wallis test performed for this variable indicates a significant

TABLE 5.2: Comparison of Population, Land Pressure, House-Lot Size, Ancillary Features, and Size of House-Lot Components among Three Sites in Yaxcabá Parish

Variable	Mopilá	Cetelac	Cacalchén
Site size[a]	55	35	35
No. of house lots mapped	60	26	76
Mean house-lot size	3,451	6,110	2,770
Mean no. of ancillary features per lot	0.217	0.346	0.645
No. of house lots surface collected	4	2	5
Mean garden size	1,934.8	5,069.5	1,664.8
Percent garden area	50.9%	73.7%	61.8%
Mean patio size[b]	1,967.8	1,807.5	730.0
Percent patio area[b]	49.1%	26.3%	38.2%
Mean no. metal artifacts per lot	33.5	2.0	8.0
Mean no. glazed ceramics per lot	20.0	3.75	1.75
Length of occupation[c]	266	74	97
Population growth[d]	155 to 342	8 to 51	184 to 634
Population density	6.22	1.28	18.11
Land pressure	Moderate	Very low	Acute

a. Site size in hectares; all other measurements of area are in square meters.
b. Includes the area of the structural core.
c. In years.
d. During the period 1784 to 1828.

difference ($p < 0.027$; $\alpha = 0.05$) among the sites, and nonparametric pairwise comparisons show that the mean number of ancillary features per house lot at Cacalchén is significantly higher than at Mopilá ($p < 0.019$; $\alpha = 0.05$). The Wilcoxon tests found no significant differences between Mopilá and Cetelac ($p < 0.999$; $\alpha = 0.05$) or between Cetelac and Cacalchén ($p < 0.110$; $\alpha = 0.05$).

For the house lots that were surface collected, the proportions of patio to garden zones were not variable. Statistical analysis reveals no significant difference in the percentages of patio and garden areas among the three sites. Comparison of the absolute size of patio, however, revealed a statistically significant difference in the distribution ($p < 0.05$; $\alpha = 0.05$). The size of patios at Cacalchén is notably smaller than those at Mopilá and Cetelac and is largely a function of house-lot size. Although the sample of surface-collected house lots is small, the lack of variability in the proportions of patio and garden zones probably reflects a consistent agricultural strategy based on intensive use of gardens, cultivation of milpa plots at varying distances from the settlement, and the use of patios as agricultural staging areas.

House Lot Size and Ancillary Features

Comparison of the archaeological patterning with historical evidence and ethnoarchaeological models of the house lot suggest some possible explanations for the variability among sites.

Population size, density, and rate of population growth are much higher at Cacalchén than at Mopilá or Cetelac (Table 5.2). Therefore, the settlement containing the largest house lots (Cetelac) also had the lowest population density, the lowest rate of population growth, and the smallest population. In contrast, the settlement with the smallest house lots, Cacalchén, had the highest population density, the greatest rate of population growth, and the largest population. At Cacalchén, neighboring haciendas infringed on the land that the inhabitants were using for cultivation. Therefore, the problem of a rapidly growing population within a circumscribed community with limited arable land seems to have been dealt with by subdividing house lots when an additional residence was needed. At Mopilá house lots were not subdivided to the same extent. Because the pueblo inhabitants were not competing for land to the same degree as independent rancho dwellers, the increased population at Mopilá could be accommodated by expanding the area of settlement. At Cetelac, the population density was so low that there was never a shortage of residential space.

Killion (1987:364–67) has discussed the relationships among nucleation and dispersal of settlement, population density, house-lot size, and intensity of agricultural cultivation among the different segments of the settlement agriculture continuum in his ethnoarchaeological study in the Tuxtlas Mountains of Veracruz. He found that site aggregation and dispersal are correlated with the variable intensity of use of infields versus outfields surrounding the settlements. Areas with high population density are characterized by nucleated settlements and small house-lot size, and they occur where infield parcels are more intensively cultivated than outfields and where arable land circumscribes the settlement. Dispersed settlements with low population densities occur where outfield parcels are more intensively cultivated than infields, and in this situation the house lot itself serves as an infield agricultural plot.

In some respects, Killion's results are referable to Stone's (1996:42–50) arguments linking settlement dispersal, population density, and agricultural intensification for the Kofyar of Nigeria. Stone argues that under conditions of growing population density and increasing land pressure, the radius of intensive cultivation increases (toward outfields), and dispersal occurs as residences are pulled toward fields in order to reduce the distance between field and residence and minimize daily energy expenditures. Conversely, examples of the co-occurrence of aggregated settlements with agriculturally intensive strategies usually involve conditions that override the trend toward dispersal. This tendency for "settlement gravity" may be induced by the cultivation of widely dispersed agricultural parcels from a central location, the need for agricultural collaboration among households, or the location of other key resources or facilities such as water (Stone 1996:44). In the Tuxtlas Mountains, the impetus for dispersal with increasing intensification is overridden by the topographic circumscription of arable flat lands near areas of settlement.

Killion's ethnographic findings show some similarities to the Yaxcabá case. For both areas, population size and density of communities are inversely correlated with house-lot size. In terms of the degree of community aggregation, none of the three colonial settlements are "dispersed" to the same degree as communities in the Tuxtlas, but the least nucleated settlement, Cetelac, corresponds to large house-lot size and low population density. The historical data also suggest that the land surrounding the most nucleated settlement, Cacalchén, was circumscribed in some manner. Although no evidence specifically suggests that the inhabitants of Cacalchén intensified cultivation on plots nearer to the settlement, the scenarios in both the Tuxtlas and Cacalchén indicate some sort of restriction on access to land located at greater distances from the community. In the Tuxtlas the restriction is related to topography. The arable flat lands are located close to nucleated settlements, whereas outfields for these communities may be situated on steep slopes less advantageous for cultivation. For Cacalchén, the land located farther away from the settlement was limited by competition with neighboring communities.

Conversely, dispersed settlements with large house lots in the Tuxtlas are characterized by intensive cultivation of outfields, and access to land near the settlement is restricted in some manner. The historical data suggest that similar conditions were prevalent at Cetelac. The resident agriculturalists of the hacienda would not have had to compete with other agriculturalists for land in outlying areas, but land close to the hacienda's central water sources would have been shared with the cattle of the estate. Also, resident workers on the hacienda did not own the land they cultivated. Reliance on produce from agricultural plots located relatively near the area of settlement would have been risky, and substantial fencing to prevent damage to the crop by livestock would have been necessary. Building albarradas to protect one's crop is also a labor-intensive activity; it is unlikely that farmers would have invested large amounts of labor to fence plots they did not own. In the house lot itself, however, resident workers could exercise more secure rights of usufruct, even though their continued residence on the hacienda was at the estate owner's discretion. Under these conditions cultivation of areas located well away from the core of the hacienda may have been a reasonable strategy, and the large house lots within the settlement zone may have functioned as infield agricultural plots, as Killion suggests for the Tuxtlas.

The results from the Tuxtlas and Yaxcabá both suggest that house-lot size is conditioned by population size and density as well as the location and accessibility of arable land relative to the zone of settlement. The accessibility and ownership of land, however, may be determined by any number of systemic conditions. In Yaxcabá parish land use was restricted not by environmental variables but by political and economic conditions that sparked competition among communities for primary resources and created an imbalance between cattle raising and subsistence agriculture in the region.

With regard to the second pattern, the variation in the construction of ancillary features may indicate differences in strategies of intensification and risk reduction among the three communities. At Cacalchén the construction of permanent facilities for raising small livestock and for irrigation or water control in portions of the house lot suggests an intensification and diversification of house-lot use that is less evident at Mopilá and Cetelac. Among the twentieth-century Maya, raising small livestock, especially pigs, is often used as a source of emergency cash (Hayden and Gargett 1990; Wilk 1991). Intensive gardening or irrigation of a crop within the house lot during the dry season may also be used to hedge against a bad harvest. Intensified house-lot production seems to have occurred in the independent rancho, the community whose claim to surrounding land was least legitimate in the eyes of civil authorities. By contrast, at the pueblo and the hacienda house-lot production was not as intensive or diversified.

In Yaxcabá parish, Maya who raised small livestock paid religious taxes in the form of diezmos. In communities such as Mopilá, which fell under parochial jurisdiction, livestock raising was common. Because intensively raising small livestock would have been noticed and taxed, however, it was a less attractive method of supplementing one's income or hedging against unforeseen risks. At Cetelac the diezmo on small livestock was paid by the hacienda owner on behalf of his workers. Furthermore, because Mopilá and Cetelac were more closely integrated with the colonial economy, the inhabitants probably had access to some forms of credit and opportunities for wage labor; also see discussion above in Chapter 3).

Independent rancho communities such as Cacalchén, by contrast, were much less subject to parochial and civil supervision, and sources of credit would have been unavailable to the inhabitants. Changes in the legal status of lands near Cacalchén meant that Maya farmers faced increased competition with neighboring communities and the threat that their plots were no longer treated as private property. Under these conditions, intensification and diversification of production within privately owned house lots was an appropriate smallholder strategy that reduced risk of subsistence shortage due to a diminishing land base. Intensive gardening and raising small livestock, as evidenced by the construction of permanent facilities for these activities, was perhaps one of the few options available to the inhabitants. Other tactics used in times of shortage, such as wage labor or borrowing, were dependent on the community's or household's links to the broader economy and likely were not practicable in Cacalchén.

Ethnoarchaeological studies indicate that smaller available work space correlates with the formalized arrangement of activity areas in scheduling and segregation of space (Arnold 1990; Hayden and Cannon 1983). The presence of numerous permanent constructions for penning livestock therefore might be expected in the smaller house lots, because the animals must be prevented from interfering with other activities occurring in the lot. This relationship, however, is not borne out for the Yaxcabá settlements. House-lot size demonstrates no correlation with the numbers of ancillary features per lot either within individual settlements or for all house lots among all three sites. The lack of correlation suggests that the greater numbers of ancillary features within some house lots, and particularly at Cacalchén, are not strictly a function of restricted residential space at the site. They likely indicate an actual difference in the household production strategy.

Wilk (1983, 1984, 1991) has discussed the relationship between the availability of land, the scheduling and organization of household labor, and strategies such as cash cropping, wage labor, and diversification among the Kekchi Maya of Belize. The households and communities of his study are peripheral to the capitalist economic system and were undergoing a transition from a subsistence to a mixed economy, not unlike the situation of smaller pueblos and independent ranchos in nineteenth-century Yaxcabá.

Wilk has demonstrated that a limited availability of primary forest land corresponds to the development of intermediate-sized labor groups and greater complexity in scheduling of subsistence production within households. Settlements with plentiful amounts of primary forest are characterized by relatively greater numbers of independent households, whereas settlements experiencing a shortage of primary forest tend to organize as household clusters, a tactic that serves to improve the efficiency of access and scheduling of labor. A principal risk-reduction tactic in all communities of Wilk's study is diversification through raising small livestock, especially pigs. The pig herds are larger for settlements composed of household clusters that resort to cultivation of secondary forest. For these communities, intensive pig raising is a method of diversifying the subsistence base for which sufficient labor is co-opted through the household cluster. Kekchi communities with higher availability of primary forest also raise pigs, but it is not an intensive activity requiring labor rescheduling.

Although the archaeological evidence from the house lots of Mopilá, Cetelac, and Cacalchén is insufficient to characterize households as independent or clustered, the settlement containing the most substantial physical evidence of diverse sets of house-lot activities corresponds to the community with the lowest proportion of privately managed outlying milpa lands, Cacalchén. Presumably, household labor at Cacalchén would have been organized to accommodate the complex scheduling of subsistence activities on the house lot. Similarly, at Cetelac the house lot itself, with its large garden area, was the only component of the household's agricultural system that could be worked and managed more or less as a private plot. In contrast, the scheduling of labor between the house lot and milpas at Mopilá, where farmers exercised legitimate claims to private lands surrounding the community, was substantially different.

The archaeological site structure of the three settlements suggests that household-level production organization varies with land ownership. Subsistence and risk reduction strategies chosen by the inhabitants of Mopilá, Cacalchén, and Cetelac are strongly related to the legitimacy of land holding, nineteenth-century tax structure, and the availability of credit within the broader political economy.

Consumption of Nonlocal Items

The surface collections from house lots at Mopilá, Cacalchén, and Cetelac yielded two classes of nonlocal items, metal and glazed ceramics, that could be chronologically assigned to the late 1700s and early 1800s. Variation in the quantities and distribution of these items permits a consideration of consumption within house lots and between sites, as well as the relationship of household consumption to political-economic structure. The amount of nonlocal items recovered in the house lots actually refers to processes of discard, abandonment, and postabandonment deposition for these artifacts (Deal 1985; Hayden and Cannon 1983; Schiffer 1987). Although these processes cannot be directly equated with consumption, they are roughly related, and the frequencies of these items will be used as an approximate measure of household consumption of nonlocal material culture.

Table 5.2 lists the mean frequency of metal artifacts and the mean frequency of glazed ceramics per house lot for each of the three settlements. Differences in the sampling fractions of surface collection areas between house lots and between sites are minimal. For Cetelac, these figures include artifacts collected in areas that correspond respectively to the main residence and extramural areas of the hacienda's owner and the residence and extramural areas of the hacienda's mayoral. Both metal and glazed ceramics are present in significantly greater frequencies at house lots in Mopilá than at the other two sites (Kruskal Wallis tests, metal $p < 0.012$; glazed ceramics $p < 0.020$; $\alpha = 0.05$).

The presence of metal and glazed ceramics among individual lots in Mopilá also varies considerably. The maximum number of metal artifacts recovered from a single house lot is seventy-six, and the minimum number is eleven. For glazed ceramic fragments, the maximum is thirty-seven and the minimum is nine. House lots at Cacalchén generally demonstrate low frequencies of these nonlocal items, and variation among individual lots within the settlement is less than at Mopilá. At Cetelac, the low frequencies of metal and glazed ceramics recovered from some units inside the main house of the hacienda probably can be attributed to the depositional context of the collection units that were located on top of rooffall. The house lots of the hacienda's resident workers demonstrate the lowest frequencies of metal and glazed ceramics of any house lots of the three sites.

This admittedly rough archaeological measure tentatively suggests that the consumption of nonlocal manufactures in the parish corresponds to the inhabitants' access to basic resources and is related to each community's position in the political economic hierarchy. Historical information demonstrates that inhabitants of Mopilá were more active in the regional economy than those of Cacalchén (and for a much longer period of time); consequently, the archaeological evidence shows a greater presence of metal and glazed ceramics, along with variation in the amounts of those items among house lots, at Mopilá. House lots and residential areas of hacienda dwellers, however, indicate a reduced frequency of nonlocal items, even though the hacienda's connections to the broader economy should have facilitated access to such products for the owner and his workers. Nevertheless, the permanent residents of Cetelac apparently did not consume these items in significantly greater quantities than Cacalchén's inhabitants. These patterns suggest that households with less secure ownership of agricultural land, such as hacienda residents, consumed nonlocal utilitarian products in lesser amounts.

Occupational Longevity and Household Series

In colonial Yucatán, access to land was maintained by two forms of mobility known as dispersal and drift (Drennan 1988; Farriss 1978; see also Wilk 1991). Dispersal refers to the establishment of satellite settlements around the congregated towns and the gradual movement of population to those settlements (Farriss 1978:205). Drift is a process of intercommunity migration, usually in response to excessive labor drafts and civil and religious taxes (Farriss 1978:203). Restriction of access to community lands or alienation of private land in Yaxcabá parish directly affected subsistence productivity and the household's ability to pay civil and religious taxes. Dispersal to established satellite settlements was a response that avoided both problems: it conferred opportunities to acquire new lands while avoiding tribute. Over the long term, establishing independent rancho settlements was an effective tactic that placed produce out of reach of civil and ecclesiastical authorities and avoided the excessive demands of the church and state. Dispersal and drift also promote agricultural intensification by moving household labor closer to production locales, increasing crop oversight, and reducing travel time (see Stone 1996). Relocating one's household to an outlying milpa transforms an extensively cultivated parcel to an intensively cultivated house-lot garden and furthermore establishes a more secure claim to land ownership.

Comparison of specific life histories of Mopilá, Cetelac, and Cacalchén reveals differences in the ways Maya householders structured their use of the landscape over time. From an examination of the sequences of occupation at Mopilá, Cacalchén, and Cetelac from the pre-Hispanic period to the present, it appears that limited mobility and dispersal were fundamental ways of coping with short-term imbalances of population, land, and labor that affected agricultural production. Locations on the landscape may be classified according to their intensity of use. Yaxcabá's inhabitants intensively used the cabecera and the pueblos as permanent residential locations for house lots and kitchen gardening, whereas they used haciendas and independent ranchos sometimes for house-lot residences and at other times for extensive swidden agriculture, apiculture, or stockraising. Household series in the cabecera and pueblos consequently were long, broken only by the Caste War. Household series in haciendas and independent ranchos, however, were more attenuated.

Yaxcabá and Mopilá were occupied as permanent residential space from 1581 to the Caste War, whereas Cetelac and Cacalchén had more sporadic occupational histories. The length of household series, therefore, corresponds to the intensity of use of different places on the landscape and security of land tenure within a community. The length of household series also expresses a relationship to a cycle of limited residential mobility, longer than the domestic cycle, among agriculturalists in this region. This cycle produces a pattern whereby some sites are permanently occupied and manifest very long household series. Other sites with more sporadic occupational histories consist of multiple episodes of short residential series interspersed with periods of special function or extensive use activities.

Summary

A comparison of the site structural patterns in Yaxcabá's solares with a detailed model of settlement agriculture yields several conclusions. First, the components of the house-lot model—the dwelling, patio, and garden zones—could be distinguished on the basis of the distribution of inorganic artifacts within house lots in Yaxcabá parish. Mopilá, Cacalchén, and Cetelac also demonstrate variable lengths of occupation, yet even for Mopilá, whose occupation surpasses four hundred years, house-lot components were recognizable. Postdepositional noise in artifact distributions was present (see Deal 1985), but it did not completely obscure detection of patio and garden zones. Notably, length of occupation did not seem to affect detection of house-lot components. In some cases house-lot components in Mopilá were clearer than in Cetelac. The use of aggregate data from successive coresidential groups, even in karst central Yucatán, demonstrates distinct patterning in the use of space within the lots.

Second, the comparison of site structural patterns among different settlements suggests that variation in house-lot morphology is related to a community's or a coresidential group's ownership of basic resources. House-lot residents in Mopilá, Cacalchén, and Cetelac were agriculturalists who practiced cultivation under different conditions of land stress and tax structure. Land constituted the critical basic resource necessary for production. Population density and land ownership are reflected in several archaeological patterns that include (1) the length of household series; (2) the size of the house lot; (3) the numbers of ancillary features within house lots; and (4) consumption of nonlocally produced metal and glazed ceramics.

The size of the house lot is clearly related to population size and density. With the expansion of haciendas in Yaxcabá parish, communities were threatened with the loss of land used for milpa plots located at varying distances from the settlement. The size of the garden area is a measure of the intensity with which the settlement zone itself is used for agricultural production. For agriculturalists on the hacienda who did not own their milpa land, the garden area within the house lot was critical. Similarly at Cacalchén, where changes in legislation threatened private status of village land and competition with surrounding communities limited the use of other parcels, garden areas were used for intensive production not only of cultigens but also of pigs and poultry. At Mopilá where the town's long-term position as a community of taxpayers secured ownership of land, garden areas were substantial but used less intensively for other activities than at Cacalchén and Cetelac.

Measures of the intensity of use and maintenance within individual house lots in Yaxcabá parish are somewhat more problematic. The size of the patio area, the accumulation of refuse at patio edges, and the formalization of the use of activity areas are the ethnoarchaeological indicators that suggest intensive use of the house lot as a staging area for near-lot activities and production within the lot (Killion 1987, 1990). In Yaxcabá parish, however, variation in patio-edge refuse accumulation could not be distinguished in the distribution of nonorganic artifacts. Also, the construction of permanent features for penning livestock—a more formalized use of space—did not correlate with house-lot size. It is unclear how patio size relates to the use of the lot as a staging area. Generally, patio size seems to correspond to the site's length of occupation, which suggests that the patio area is related to the length of the household series.

Comparison of occupational sequences and the length of the household series among sites in Yaxcabá parish reveals differences in the intensity of use of specific places on the landscape. Yaxcabá and Mopilá were used as permanent residential locations. In contrast, Cetelac and Cacalchén demonstrate fluctuation in the intensity of use. In some periods the sites were used as permanent residential locations for intensive settlement agriculture, while at other times they were used for more extensive activities such as milpa cultivation, apiculture, and livestock raising.

Dispersal of settlement in Yaxcabá parish corresponded to episodes of population growth in situations where inhabitants needed to improve their access and ownership claims to land, intensify production, simplify labor organization, and maintain soil fertility (Drennan 1988; Stone 1996; Wilk 1991). After 1840, however, the historical evidence suggests that dispersal and drift of the population to independent ranchos ceased to be an effective means for coping with limited land. Continued dispersal did not occur. New farming communities were not established in the decades following independence from Spain, but new cattle-raising estates multiplied. Some farmers had to adopt alternate strategies for contending with the increasingly limited availability of land. Intensification of production within the settlement zone and house lot was the response at Cacalchén and Cetelac.

CHAPTER SIX

Yaxcabá and the Caste War in Archaeological Perspective

doubt anyone will ever have the final word on the Caste War of Yucatán. Notwithstanding the excellence of recent treatments of the conflict, all demonstrate its multifaceted complexity in the past and the diversity of meanings it holds in the present. Modern scholarship suggests the Caste War was not a unitary response to an imposed progressive agenda that drastically altered agricultural production, land use, and ethnic and class relations in the early nineteenth century. Nor was the conflict a grassroots phenomenon supported by all Maya. In northwestern Yucatán, workers on the henequen haciendas did not rise in rebellion. Similarly in southern Campeche, southern Quintana Roo, and Belize, some Maya negotiated uneasy truces with the Caste War rebels, Spanish Creoles, and the British. Even in the Yaxcabá region, the rebel advance probably owed more to the splintering of interests among Maya communities than to their wholehearted backing of the cause.

Assessing the role of the Caste War in the succeeding agrarian reform is equally complicated. Dumond (1997) is convincing when he argues that agrarian change was the unintended result of the war's disastrous demographic decline, contrary to the notion that agrarian pressure and a drive for reform resulted in the Caste War. Although the revolt resolved itself as a revitalization movement in the eastern forests, modern historiography reveals a devastating conflict with few redeeming values and no satisfactory conclusion to the dispute (see Sullivan 1989). The romance of Caste

151

War resistance consequently has been put to rest. In one sense this is a positive trend. It neither oversimplifies Maya struggle by ascribing some happy ending at the close of the nineteenth century, nor implies that further social change was unnecessary, once the Maya reasserted "traditional" cultural forms. It does not trivialize the efforts of today's Maya farmers as they pursue social justice, improved access to resources, and greater autonomy to shape fields of political and economic relations within an expanding global system.

By contrast, these newer assessments of the Caste War leave unanswered the larger question of how changes in state and rural relations affected (and were affected by) Maya household strategies and resistance. Dissatisfaction with relatively synchronic treatments of globalization, the Caste War, and Maya agriculture first prompted reexamination of these issues through the lens of household archaeology. This study demonstrates that in the end, the explanation for agrarian change in nineteenth-century Yaxcabá rests not with the rebellion itself but with long-term processes that link tactics of accommodation, survival, and resistance to political-economic structure. Maya farmers retained control over the allocation of land, labor, and resources despite the heavy-handed efforts of the Yucatecan government to harness the region to an expanding market economy increasingly dominated by capitalist relations of production. Although similar struggles among rural agriculturalists, state institutions, and non-Maya elites continue today, constantly revived through modern constructions of the Caste War, here I will try to draw the various strands of this investigation to a close.

Resistance and Agrarian Change in Yaxcabá

At the beginning of this book, I proposed that historical archaeological research could help answer two related questions: How was the process of agrarian change in nineteenth-century Yaxcabá related to expressions of Maya resistance? Were the Caste War and related forms of resistance responsible for restoring a more balanced agrarian pattern and traditional forms of land use? In keeping with an archaeological perspective, the investigation focused on describing the long-term cultural process by which rural communities of Yaxcabá parish developed systems of defense and accommodation to the intrusion of a colonial state. Methodologically, resistance was defined broadly, along the lines suggested by Stern (1987), as a long-term system of tactics and strategies practiced by rural inhabitants that presents obstacles to state intervention and the exercise of hegemony. Here, archaeological settlement and residential patterns in nineteenth-century Yaxcabá were compared with those of the present and the distant past to define a range of "traditional" variation in agricultural tactics and land use. Although this approach does not specify the origins of the Caste War itself, it contextualizes the progress and outcome of the rebellion in Yaxcabá with reference to variable configurations of coping and survival strategies among households and communities within the region.

The investigation shows that during the past five hundred years the principal arena of resistance concerned ownership and access to agricultural land.

The answers to these questions hold significant implications for the interpretation and explanation of the archaeological record. Today in Yaxcabá we see a settlement pattern dominated by few sizeable communities whose population operates dispersed smallholdings in maize agri-culture, apiculture, and livestock over a landscape littered with ruins of haciendas, quintas, churches, shrines, and abandoned settlements. Some of the colonial religious architecture in the largest communities is now being restored for tourism.

Modern scholarship presents competing ideas about the cultural processes that produced the archaeological pattern. On the surface, many observers attribute the archaeological record to a rather romantic idea about peasant revolt and end of the "time of slavery," coupled with an interpretation that the agrarian reform preserved Maya culture from the ravages of capi-talism. If one places Yucatán's nineteenth-century settlement pattern within a broader tem-poral and spatial context, however, one concludes that Mexico's economic development is variable (Alexander 2003; Charlton 1986, 2003). Regional variability in nineteenth-century settlement patterns is linked to uneven penetration of market economies, difficulties in rural develop-ment, and a rocky road of nation-state formation. Explaining the archaeological record of nine-teenth-century Yaxcabá demands a more nuanced view of the initial processes of globalization and the complexities of resistance.

The exchange of dissenting historical arguments about Caste War origins also presents con-tradictory implications for communities like Yaxcabá. For example, if one accepts the current argument that progressivism, hacienda expansion, and land pressure were not causally related to onset of the Caste War, it suggests that Yaxcabá was merely caught in the crossfire. The causes of violent resistance were located in the eastern forests of Quintana Roo, and the Maya of cen-tral Yucatán perhaps did little to resist the oppressive policies of the progressive agenda. Possibly their passive forms of resistance were ineffective, or more was to be gained by accommodat-ing Spanish-Creole interests. By contrast, previous scholarship indicates that the Caste War rebels would not have advanced their cause so successfully without the support they received in the Yaxcabá-Sotuta region (Dumond 1997; Reed 1964). Maya of this central zone were experienced in resisting incursions by the state and church. Even if Maya in Yaxcabá adopted the Caste War opportunistically, they must have done so because the rebel cause was consonant with their efforts to ameliorate the conditions of domination imposed under the progressive agenda.

Scholars are similarly undecided over the attribution of successful agrarian reform after the war. Current historical debate calls into question the idea that peasant agency and Caste War resistance restored traditional patterns of land use, especially considering that some parishes in the central region lost 90 percent of their populations (Dumond 1997). Many scholars sit-uate land reform and its concomitant developments not with the Caste War but with the 1910 Mexican Revolution, even though Maya oral histories conflate the two movements (see also Bricker 1981; Joseph 1985; Sullivan 1989; Wells and Joseph 1996).

A related point of deliberation concerns the issue of "restoration" and what constitutes "tra-ditional" land use for the Maya. One outcome of the Caste War was to delay or even reverse the intrusion of the market economy and transition to capitalist relations of production. The violence of the conflict induced Spanish Creoles to abandon their properties and drove many out of the region. Nevertheless, the idea that practicing extensive swidden agriculture on com-munal ejidos, as described by twentieth-century ethnographers, epitomizes traditional folk cul-ture has long been questioned in cultural anthropology (Castañeda 1996; Re-Cruz 1996; Strickon

1965). If anything the early-twentieth-century pattern is aberrant, initially a function of low population density that under population growth results in disputes over land rights (McCay and Acheson 1987; Netting 1993:325). Recent ethnographies are overwhelmingly concerned with the cultural contradictions, factionalism, increasing economic inequality, unsustainable resource extraction, and push for emigration inflicted by contemporary processes of globalization on rural Maya communities (Faust 1998; Re-Cruz 1996).

Here the value of long-term studies and the potential for historical archaeology to clarify these issues becomes apparent. Consider, for example, that Yaxcabá's settlement pattern in 1900 is nearly identical to its pattern in 1600, following the massive population decline of the Spanish conquest. This suggests that the configuration of land use seen in the early twentieth century is typical of situations where the state's forcible or heavy-handed efforts to incorporate the Yucatecan hinterland resulted in demographic disaster. Although this is hardly a traditional agrarian pattern, the Maya did experience a similar systems collapse before, in the ninth century A.D. In contrast, Yaxcabá's settlement pattern in 1986 looks like that of the mid-eighteenth century, when sizeable populations were found in only a few settlements and most agricultural activities (on privately owned parcels) were dispersed over the landscape. Parallels in the material record hint at comparable cultural processes and relationships among agriculturalists, the environment, and political-economic structure. For these reasons, any assessment of Maya resistance in Yaxcabá benefits from a systematic, long-term investigation into the variability and range of local subsistence, survival strategies, and agricultural structure among Maya households.

Specific Findings

To explain the transformation of settlement and agrarian structure in nineteenth-century Yaxcabá, I suggested that it is useful to understand how the actions, behavior, and organization of a key player, the Maya agriculturalist, inscribed the archaeological record. I have argued that understanding the role of resistance in this process requires knowledge not only of the political-economic pressures that were brought to bear on Maya cultivators but also of the ways in which farmers actively managed or coped with variable systems of domination and hegemony. Moreover, as Stern (1987) has suggested, this understanding is enhanced by examining the long-term patterns by which peasants politically engaged the state—for times of quiescence as well as rebellion. The preexisting structures of resistance and accommodation spanning centuries rather than decades are critical to developing adequate explanations for the course of agrarian change.

To determine how various productive activities were organized among settlements within the region and among households within communities, this study examined the archaeological variability in regional, community, and household-level spatial patterns in Yaxcabá parish during a span of five hundred years. Variability in rural settlement generally is a function of culture, history, and the ecological substrate on which strategies of production and consumption are based (Stone 1996:11). Consequently, interpretations of Maya behavioral organization rely on comparison of archaeological spatial variability against two independent frames of reference (sensu Binford 2001): (1) a general analogy developed from the study of settlement ecology for smallholders living in tropical settings, specifically a model called settlement agriculture (Killion 1992; Netting 1993; Stone 1996; Wilk 1991); and (2) detailed historical control, drawn from the analysis of documentary sources, over the structure of state and rural relations in Yucatán, especially those that had bearing on the inhabitants of Yaxcabá.

The results of the investigation indicate the following conclusions. First, the documentary evidence suggests that various forms of avoidance protest constituted the principal means of resistance from the sixteenth to the twentieth centuries. Direct confrontations between native Maya caciques and the state and clergy over civil and religious authority only occurred early after the Spanish conquest and were met with severe coercive repression. Maya leaders were removed from local government and/or prosecuted for idolatry. Disputes over land ownership following congregación were settled by imposing a process of litigation that established land treaties between contending native provinces.

Maya groups who were disadvantaged by these decisions subsequently resorted to more passive forms of resistance. Native religious practices were relocated away from towns to milpa plots and to the forests. Caciques responsible for tax collection proved "inept." Population dispersed away from Yaxcabá and Mopilá to reside in sectarian communities on cofradía estates or to establish independent rancho settlements. Although settlement dispersal fostered agricultural intensification, it also permitted Maya householders to avoid difficulties associated with local political factionalism, disenfranchisement due to uneven inheritance or population growth, and excessive taxation. Distancing household production from Spanish civil and ecclesiastical authority, in the absence of land pressure, constituted a form of resistance that had archaeological consequences. Moreover, maintaining ownership of uncultivated land, by renewing sixteenth-century land treaties in the late eighteenth century, can be seen as a defensive posture that secured options for the continued practice of avoidance protest and a smallholding agricultural strategy.

By the early nineteenth century, the system of hegemony had changed such that resistant and accommodative practices occurred within a broader social milieu that included Spanish Creoles, state officials, the clergy, the Maya elite, and Maya agriculturalists. Individuals within these groups had varying interests; seldom were members of one group consistently pitted against those of another. Before the Caste War, documentary evidence shows that the Maya avoided the exigencies of the progressive agenda through patron swapping, as well as through flight. Less than 10 percent of the population, however, became resident wage workers or shareholders on cattle haciendas. Not all Maya communities in the parish faced the same set of hegemonic pressures or options for resistance, nor did they present a unified response.

Second, analysis of archaeological settlement reveals an oscillating pattern of nucleation and dispersal that corresponds to demographic shifts in the region. In some respects this oscillation is part of a long-term pattern of political-economic fluctuation that has characterized the Maya Lowlands throughout the pre-Hispanic and Colonial periods (Freidel 1983; Marcus 1993). The two periods of severe settlement contraction and population decline (in 1600 and 1900), in which only Yaxcabá and Mopilá were occupied, followed instances of state expansion in the countryside that forcibly congregated agricultural populations, curtailed dispersal, forced changes in land-ownership status, and restricted use of nonresidential locations for specialized activities. Dispersal of settlement and the proliferation of other settlement types (independent ranchos and haciendas) corresponded to a period of demographic recovery, expanding agricultural activity, and regional market integration. Population growth also correlated with increasing production specialization and economic stratification. Yaxcabá parish shows a pattern of cyclical settlement change related to the expansion and contraction of the Yucatecan political economy.

Four types (categories I–IV) of archaeological settlements were present in the parish. These correspond to the historically known community types—cabeceras (I), pueblos (II), haciendas (III), and independent ranchos (IV). Several historically defined community classes did not show any distinctive physical characteristics that would set them apart from the four classes listed above. Privately owned ranchos and sitios proved indistinguishable from haciendas, and cofradía estates could not be differentiated from independent ranchos.

If one considers length of occupation and continuity of site function in relation to the archaeological classification, however, a clear distinction emerges between category I and II sites and category III and IV sites. Locations on the landscape may be classified according to their intensity of use. Yaxcabá's inhabitants intensively used the cabecera and the pueblos as permanent residential locations for house lots and gardening within the settlement zone. In contrast, they used haciendas and independent ranchos as special-purpose locations for practicing extensive swidden agriculture, apiculture, or stockraising. When agriculture or stockraising was intensified, ranchos and haciendas became residential locales. Category III and IV sites manifest short residential occupations interspersed with periods of varied extensive use.

A distinctive change in land use occurred between 1770 and 1821. As agricultural settlements expanded, architecture within the top-ranking sites of the political-economic hierarchy became increasingly differentiated. Large-scale civic and religious masonry buildings were constructed in Yaxcabá and its auxiliary towns. In the independent ranchos, however, religious architecture was minimized, and civic architecture apparently was perishable. By 1800, the region was peppered with haciendas, specialized for stockraising, which also contained substantial masonry construction. Both within settlements and between settlements in the region, masonry architecture marked increasing economic stratification. Variation in the amount of masonry construction on haciendas in Yaxcabá parish was related to the strategies by which Creole entrepreneurs accumulated capital in an expanding market economy. Furthermore, the hierarchical structure of labor organization on the cattle estates is reflected in the fall-off in masonry construction with distance from the hacienda's core. Within Yaxcabá itself variability in the size and construction of residential architecture clearly marked social differences between economically active elites who lived in quintas and agriculturalists who resided in house lots with perishable dwellings.

After 1821, however, the international cattle market soured, and entrepreneurs in Yaxcabá had difficulty turning a profit. Architectural elaboration of rural properties declined. Estate owners turned to a land-extensive, monocrop strategy that increased the size of cattle herds and absorbed available land. Further dispersal among the growing population of Maya agriculturalists was curtailed, and cultivators increasingly concentrated in the cabecera, pueblos, and independent ranchos.

Third, the movement of Creoles to the countryside, the expansion of cattle haciendas, and the privatization of terrenos baldíos after independence drastically altered the distribution of land and population in the Yaxcabá region. Although legislation enacted in the 1840s severely limited the amount of village lands available for cultivation in pueblos and independent ranchos, the renewed efforts to concentrate the Maya population in official settlements aggravated land pressure only in some settlements. As demonstrated in the analysis in Chapter 4, changes in legislation altered land-ownership status and community control of village land, such that independent ranchos of sixty inhabitants were denied sufficient land necessary to support their populations by extensive swidden cultivation. Similarly, farmers of larger independent ranchos whose village ejidos were limited by proximity to pueblos likely would have had to alter plot size, length of fallow, or other patterns of agricultural intensification to compensate for loss of plots distant from the settlement. Agriculturalists living in Yaxcabá itself probably engaged in wage-labor or agricultural share contracts with Maya and Spanish-Creole elites.

Nevertheless, calculations presented in Chapter 4 show that even when one assumes extensive swidden cultivation for all farmers (as a heuristic exercise), land stress was not an underlying condition for all agriculturalists in Yaxcabá parish. In the cabecera and the pueblos, farmers would have had to adjust plot size and/or fallow length in order to accommodate all agriculturalists under extensive swidden cultivation. Only in Kancabdzonot were these limitations truly severe. In Mopilá and Yaxuná, no land pressure is evident. Similarly, the land available to hacienda residents was ample, despite the need to share the lands of the estate with cattle. Nevertheless, all of the independent ranchos, with the exception of Canakóm, lacked sufficient land for all of their farmers to cultivate milpa by means of extensive swidden techniques. The disparate quality of agrarian pressures across different settlements within the parish produced varied responses among different groups of rural inhabitants.

Fourth, the variable impact of population growth, land ownership, tax status, and distance from authority prompted different responses among Maya householders in different settlements. Variability in household strategies in Mopilá, Cetelac, and Cacalchén was monitored by analyzing the spatial organization and site structure of residential house lots relative to a model of settlement agriculture (Killion 1990, 1992). As discussed in Chapters 2 and 5, agriculturalists regularly adjust cultivation intensity, plot size, crop diversity, labor investment, and scheduling in order to produce sufficient resources to sustain the household. The intensity of land use is a continuum that varies from a permanently tended house-lot garden to milpa plots located at varying distances from the settlement, cultivated with extensive slash-and-burn techniques. Potential for intensification among the different components of the land-use continuum is flexible, but it is most strongly affected by land ownership. House lots, except on haciendas, were privately owned, and therefore intensive production was most logically focused within the lots. Even on haciendas, however, the house lot was the parcel over which inhabitants had the most control and security. Farmers altered household strategies and patterns of intensification depending on whether ownership of outlying milpa plots was secure.

Variation in house-lot size, the numbers and kinds of dwellings and features, the sizes of garden and patio areas, and the amounts of nonlocal goods recovered from the lots suggested differences in agricultural production, labor organization, and the structure of patron-client relationships among Maya householders living in Mopilá, Cetelac, and Cacalchén. They indicate marked differences in the way people coped with disenfranchisement from land and the uneven extension of credit in the parish. The inhabitants' choices of agrarian-based survival strategies were linked to their community's political situation, control of land ownership, level of integration with the regional economy, and legitimacy in the eyes of the church and state.

Differences in mean house-lot size were statistically significant among the three settlements. The settlement with the lowest rate of population growth, Cetelac, had the largest lots, whereas the settlement with the greatest rate of population growth, Cacalchén, had the smallest house lots.

Differences in the mean number of ancillary features per lot, such as animal pens, gardening features, water storage, or chich piles, were also statistically significant among the three sites. Mopilá had notably fewer animal pens and other features than did Cacalchén and Cetelac. Intensified production and diversification within the settlement zone was most evident in the independent rancho, whose access to and ownership of milpa land was severely restricted by changes in legislation. At Cacalchén, distance from ecclesiastical authority and the inconsistency in collecting tithes probably made animal husbandry an attractive option for augmenting household income. At Cetelac, garden areas within the house lot were also critically important for maintaining household subsistence, because outlying milpa plots were not privately owned and would have been at risk of destruction by cattle. The solution was to expand the size of the garden zone of the house lot, such that the lot itself replaced infield milpa plots. At Cetelac, tithes of hacienda workers were paid by the estate owner, and raising pigs within the house lot was an important supplement to household subsistence. Inhabitants who raised pigs and poultry at Mopilá, however, would have incurred a religious tax. Garden zones within the house lots were large. Mopilá's farmers also maintained sufficient control of privately owned and managed milpa land.

The prevalence of two nonlocal items, glazed ceramics and metal, within the house lots of the three sites was also variable. Householders at Mopilá apparently consumed and discarded many more of these items than did the inhabitants of either Cacalchén or Cetelac. Furthermore, some house lots in Mopilá had notably higher frequencies of these items than did others, suggesting greater economic stratification within the community. Differences in the frequencies of metal and glazed ceramics no doubt are also a function of the length of occupation and stability of household series, which at Mopilá is considerably longer than at the other two sites. It suggests patron-client relationships were structured differently at Mopilá. Greater protections for private ownership of land, opportunities for engaging in wage labor, or acquiring elite patronage may have provided greater access to these goods.

Globalization and the Archaeological Record

The archaeological and historical evidence from Yaxcabá suggests the development of a "resistant adaptation" among Maya agriculturalists in the region. Analysis of settlement patterns reveals a system in which groups of households practiced specific tasks related to agriculture and animal husbandry at distant locales and maintained a degree of long-term residential mobility between these extensive-use locations and permanent settlements.

Yaxcabá and Mopilá (pueblos) were sites used for permanent residence in which a substantial portion of household subsistence production occurs within the settlement itself. Maya householders also used specific places and parcels (many privately owned) away from the settlement for extensive milpa cultivation, apiculture, and stockraising. Such locales were attractive because of the presence of water, good soil (especially on archaeological sites), and other geomorphic features, such as rejolladas, that permitted "locational intensification" (Stone 1996:52–53) of specific production activities. These locations were known as ranchos.

Conditions of population growth, intensification of regional exchange networks, or extraction of household surplus by the state may create conditions that require intensification of household production. Intensification may involve increased supervision of the production process, investment of greater amounts of labor in specific activities, diversifying subsistence resources, or augmenting the production of one commodity over another. These conditions sometimes prompted a group of households to establish residence at rancho locations, and usually the move spanned several generations. If conditions changed, rancho residents might return to the pueblo or cabecera, or the rancho might grow to become a pueblo in its own right. This pattern of land use constitutes a lengthy, mobile subsistence cycle that creates structure in the archaeological record. Some sites demonstrate long household series (spanning several hundred years) that are used for the full range of residential activities associated with tropical agriculture and production for a colonial tributary system. Other sites demonstrate short household series (about one hundred years), often characterized by intensive production in the settlement zone itself, interspersed with periods of abandonment and nonresidential specific-use functions.

During the Colonial period the rancho locations also became ideal places for the practice of avoidance protest. Clandestine religious activities occurred at specific locales "in the monte." Cofradía estates that placed agricultural or other specialized production under the protection of a church-sanctioned sectarian organization, endowed by the Maya elite, often were situated in ranchos. Shifting one's residence to a milperío or ranchería (fleeing to the monte) also distanced the household and its production from civil and ecclesiastical supervision, making the extraction of surplus difficult and inefficient for the governor's agents. Whereas civil and ecclesiastical officials viewed the areas outside of settlements as undifferentiated "monte" or communal village lands, Maya historical and cultural geography was much more precise. Maya-language documents for the Yaxcabá-Sotuta region discuss the former uses, size, characteristics, rulership, ownership, and inheritance of rancho locations back to the conquest (Roys 1939). The mobility inherent in this settlement system presented severe obstacles for the exercise of colonial hegemony.

With the expansion of the Spanish-Creole population to the countryside in the late eighteenth and early nineteenth centuries, rancho locations were purchased or otherwise acquired by the Creole elite. These places were developed and used almost exclusively for the production of a cash crop—cattle. At the same time, Creoles co-opted the political process in Yaxcabá and further limited Maya control of land transfers. A dual economy was established in the parish that progressively removed ranchos from Maya control. Access to such places could be legitimated or restored only by manipulating patron-client relationships.

Establishing share or wage-labor contracts with Creole hacienda owners, manipulating ecclesiastical patronage such that rancho settlements were accorded pueblo status, or swapping patrons were strategies by which Maya farmers maintained ownership of the monte.

The nineteenth-century process of state expansion and Creole appropriation of ranchos is marked archaeologically by the distribution of masonry architecture within Yaxcabá and across the landscape. The proliferation of large-scale, special-function facilities at haciendas (formerly rancho locations) indicates an unprecedented change in settlement pattern and land use. The size and distribution of masonry architecture within haciendas also reflects hierarchical labor organization, suggesting a transition from smallholding to shareholding. These same masonry constructions became prime targets for attack during the war. During this period the population of independent ranchos and pueblos swelled. Restriction of opportunities for dispersal and limitation of agricultural land ownership in the parish induced settlement nucleation. Different communities experienced different pressures and limitations on land use. Consequently, Maya households employed widely divergent tactics to compensate for difficulties of subsistence production.

When the Caste War rebels marched into Yaxcabá in 1848, they likely encountered a divided population with divergent self-interests. The livelihood of some households depended on maintaining relations with Spanish Creoles, the church, or local government, whereas others would be better off if the cattle ranching economy were removed. The struggle of the next twenty years would destroy Yaxcabá's infrastructure and sever the region's ties to the northwest. Yet in the end, the process of state expansion, market integration, and globalization begun in the eighteenth century proved reversible. Access to and ownership of the ranchos and the monte by a vastly reduced Maya population was restored, only to be sanctioned by the government under the agrarian reform law and the distribution of ejidos after the Mexican Revolution.

Epilogue

Today Mérida and the other large cities of the Yucatán peninsula are prospering. International tourism and a healthy national economy have prompted investment in Yucatán's infrastructure and institutions. In Mérida, Valladolid, and Campeche, a new spirit of historical and cultural stewardship has prompted unprecedented historic preservation efforts. Archaeological sites, colonial haciendas, churches, and even Mérida's art deco theaters are being conserved and restored.

In 1999 I returned to Yucatán to attend the wedding of one of my field assistants, who had worked with me in Yaxcabá and Yaxuná and who is now an archaeologist at the Centro INAH Yucatán. The mass and festivities were held in the beautifully restored Hacienda Teya on the outskirts of Mérida. At the reception my friends and I learned of the historic preservation efforts in Yaxcabá. Accordingly, we decided to take a trip back to Yaxcabá to take some photographs and see how things had changed.

In Yaxcabá we encountered the sacristan, who gave us the complete tour of the church. The restoration of the central retablo and the side altars was truly impressive. Repairs had also been made to the structure itself, as well as to the rectory and the hermita of Santa Cruz. We were allowed to see the *camarín* (upstairs room behind the retablo and sanctuary) and the choir-loft, and to climb up in the central tower. The sacristan explained that local benefactors had donated an image of San Pedro to the large church and an image of the Virgin of Guadalupe to the smaller hermita. They would soon rededicate the churches to these new saints. An image of the Virgen del Rosario, a cofradía saint, was kept in the camarín, and people still celebrated her feast day by carrying the saint in procession to Mopilá. From the top of the tower across the jungle canopy, one could see the newly conserved, gleaming white churches in Mopilá and Tabi. The road connecting Yaxcabá to Sotuta had been paved.

We proceeded to Mopilá. The plaza and areas around the church were as overgrown as ever. But inside the church, the retablo had been carefully cleaned and repaired and the floor resurfaced. The baptismal font that we had located at the west edge of the platform had been put back in place, and the elaborately carved basin and pedestal (for holy water) was cleaned and secured.

Back in Yaxcabá, we stopped for a brief visit with one of the farm families who had worked with us on the project and been so helpful during our stay. All the children were grown, and the daughters were married and living in Yaxcabá. The father and his son were still making milpa around Xkekén, and the mother was spending more time on embroidery and marketing her beautiful huipils in Mérida. The father had worked on the restoration in Mopilá. Was there a project? he asked. I explained the purpose of our trip was social. I also asked him why the image of San Mateo, the one with the stone head, and the cross draped with a piece of cloth had been removed from the altar. He seemed surprised—this apparently was a recent development—and he supposed they had been taken for repairs. Why were the reminders of the Caste War, especially those that used to elicit such florid commentary about the past, being removed?

As we continued our journey to Yaxuná, we saw that Cacalchén was still farmed for milpa. Although last year's plots were overgrown, they had exposed one of the adoratorios such that it was visible from the road. Kancabdzonot's church was the most recently restored, and the road between Kancabdzonot and Yaxuná was paved. In Yaxuná we encountered another farmer who had assisted us on our project who accompanied us to the archaeological site. The ball court and related structures in the North Group were completely restored. Our colleague admitted that working with the archaeologists had been difficult for the community. In the end, however, they were able to adjust to the transition from a research project to a restoration effort. He also showed us the new community museum with its exhibit garden of native plants. The town itself was otherwise unchanged. No restoration of the church was planned, and he was rather ambivalent about any such efforts. What the town really needed, he said, was for the government to pave the road between Yaxuná and Piste. Only then would they be able to draw tourists down from Chichén Itzá.

It became clear in the course of the conversation that the most recent episode of economic development was a divisive force within the community. Large archaeological and historical preservation projects raise expectations of new economic development and prosperity. They encourage the intrusion of foreigners in local communities. They also exacerbate factional divisions within and between communities, because there is never enough wage labor to go around. New resources and work opportunities are manipulated by the politically savvy. Some families in

Yaxcabá continue to farm as usual, but do not hesitate to take advantage of opportunities for craft production or wage labor when they are available. They regard recent economic development as beneficial. Some follow wage work to Cancun or Mérida, returning home periodically. Working away from home, however, is stressful and sometimes dangerous, and eventually the household may relocate to the urban center. Others may harbor exalted expectations of the economic prosperity promised by the historic preservation work. They may become dissatisfied and disillusioned when labor contracts end, when local politics preclude their participation in new economic opportunities, or if tourists fail to patronize local attractions.

Consequently, the larger archaeological and historic preservation projects have become classic arenas of struggle in which multilayered resistances are enacted. Footdragging, dissimulation, pilfering, sabotage, and even direct conflict among project personnel are common. Flattery, gift-giving, or other forms of currying favor and patron-swapping are equally frequent. Like the passive forms of protest in the nineteenth century, Maya resistance in Yaxcabá parish today is not strongly polarized among principal actors. Perceptions of self-interest vary radically between communities, between factions, and among households within communities.

On leaving Yaxuná, we went back to Kancabdzonot and from there to Santa María. The road was not paved, and the town appeared just as it had in the mid-1980s—completely tranquil. We located the sacristan who opened the padlock and admitted us to the church. I asked if restoration was planned. He responded that "in fairness" they should renovate Santa María's church next, having just finished Kancabdzonot. Among the engineers who had visited, however, there had been some debate over the feasibility of the project. A couple of the masonry arches that had once supported a cannon-vaulted roof were buckled and ready to collapse. Recent developments, like those in the past, were likely to pass them by. We could not help but notice a magnificent, huipil-draped cross in the center sanctuary, protected behind glass. Another smaller "dressed" cross was placed in a side altar. This church is dedicated not to Santa María but to the Little Holy Cross, or Chan Santa Cruz.

Glossary

Adoratorio—a shrine or small chapel.

Aguada—a shallow depression that provides water; the depressions form permanent ponds in situations where clay has sealed the fissures of the limestone substrate.

Ahcuchcab—a member of a council of officers serving under a batab, head of an extended family group often living in the same neighborhood or barrio.

Ahkin—Maya priest.

Albarrada—dry-laid stone walls, composed of unfaced limestone blocks, used to fence house lots or to construct animal pens.

Alcalde—mayor, justice, or magistrate; top-ranking civil official of the ayuntamiento or the república de indios.

Arbitrios municipales—a schedule of municipal taxes gathered for the support of the town council.

Arriate—a circular surround constructed of rock or masonry that retains soil and aids in the cultivation of herbs, seedlings, and trees by protecting the roots.

Arriero—mule driver.

Asalariado—salaried worker.

Audiencia—an administrative or municipal building that serves the activities of the town council, either the ayuntamiento or the república de indios.

Ayuntamiento—town council.

Batab—headman; a hereditary cacique or chief and governor of a Maya town.

Cabecera—the administrative capital or municipal seat of a civil territorial division, a partido, or a parish.

Cacique—native Maya leader, batab, or halach uinic.

Capitán a guerra—war captain, a Creole government official stationed in each district or partido under the Bourbon intendancy.

Casa de burros—a stable for livestock, especially burros and horses.

Casa de máquinas—a building that houses the machinery of a hacienda or landed estate, especially equipment for crushing sugarcane or extracting fiber from henequen leaves.

Casa principal—principal or main house of a hacienda.

Cenote—collapsed limestone doline that exposes the water table, a natural well.

Chan Santa Cruz—a village (Little Holy Cross) in what is now the state of Quintana Roo, headquarters of the Caste War rebels and the cult of the talking cross, now known as Felipe Carrillo Puerto or Noh Cah Santa Cruz.

Chich—crushed limestone, often used as a building material and floor fill or for roads.

Chilam balam—books based on pre-Columbian Maya codices, reworked by Maya during the colonial period, that describe historical and prophetic events (among other things).

Chiquero—a pig sty.

Cofradía—a religious confraternity that accumulates resources for the annual festival celebrating the patron saint.

Cofradía estate—the property of a religious confraternity, sometimes called "church haciendas," whose produce was used to support the annual celebration of the cofradía's patron saint. They were created through endowments by the Indian elite, who consequently exercised considerable control over the confraternity's activities.

Comisario ejidal—a municipal official charged with overseeing the distribution, use, transfer, and cultivation of a town's communal lands.

Congregación—forced resettlement of dispersed Maya populations into towns.

Creole—a person of European descent born in the New World.

Cruzob—Maya rebels who fought against the Creoles in the Caste War, followers of the talking cross whose center of operations was the village of Chan Santa Cruz.

Cuchcabal—a hierarchically organized political jurisdiction or province, headed by a native Maya leader known as the halach uinic or cacique, that united several Maya towns headed by batabs.

Cuchteel—a group of extended families that lived close to one another, often in the same neighborhood.

Debt peonage—a form of labor organization common on haciendas where Maya laborers became indebted monetarily and socially to the hacienda's owner and thus could not leave the estate. Because debts were inherited and transferable, the patrimonial relationship could extend over several generations, and when the hacienda was sold, laborers' debts (and sometimes the laborers themselves) were passed to the new owner.

Diezmo—a religious tax, a tithe of 10 percent.

Doctrina—catechism.

Encomienda—a grant of the tribute owed by specified Indian towns to an individual Spaniard.

Ejido—village communal lands.

Era—an irrigation berm or channel, usually constructed of masonry.

Estancia—the term for a landed estate used before "hacienda," in Yucatán it usually refers to a small cattle ranch.

Gallinero—a chicken or poultry coop.

Ganado mayor—large or "greater" livestock such as cattle and horses.

Ganado menor—small or "lesser" livestock such as sheep and goats.

Granja—grain storage facility.

Hacienda—a landed estate, usually owned by Creoles, characterized by mixed agricultural and livestock production, permanent infrastructure, and employing large numbers of resident laborers who are often bound to the estate by debt.

Halach uinic—the native Maya leader, cacique, of a cuchcabal or province.

Household—a social group whose members share the activities of production, consumption, resource pooling, reproduction, transmission of knowledge, coresidence, and shared ownership.

Household series—the sequence of households that successively inhabit a given structure or house over a span of more than one generation.

Independent rancho—a settlement of maize farmers situated on open or vacant land apart from other recognized communities. These communities generally were small, ephemeral, and often mobile. Collection of tribute and obventions did not occur with regularity, and independent ranchos were not officially sanctioned by the church or the state.

Jornalero—day laborer, wage worker.

Juez español—judge or justice of the peace, a Creole government official stationed in major towns under the Bourbon intendancy.

Ladino—non-Indian.

League—a linear measurement of 5,000 varas, or about 4 km, the distance one can walk in one hour. A square league measures 43,402 mecates or 1,736 hectares.

Limosnas—alms; obvention; fees paid by Maya for the support of the church.

Lunero—a semipermanent laborer on an hacienda, rancho, or sitio who in return for the use of the land and water of the estate, provided labor rent, one day per week (usually on Monday, lunes, thus the term lunero) to the estate's owner or (more commonly) cultivated a parcel (20 mecates) whose produce was ceded to the estate owner.

Manta—cotton cloth woven by Maya women as tribute.

Mayoral—foreman, usually on a cattle estate.

Mayordomo—steward, custodian.

Mecate—a linear measurement, about 20 m; as a unit of area 1 sq mecate measures 400 sq m.

Milpa—cornfield.

Milpa de caña—a milpa in its second or subsequent year of cultivation, secondary forest land.

Milpa roza—a milpa in its first year of cultivation, primary forest land.

Monte del Rey—"King's forest," public land, all land that was not privately owned, administered by a community or religious confraternity, or designated as village commons.

Noria—a well in which water is pumped to the surface by wind or animal traction. Typically a masonry platform and water tank are constructed adjacent to the well opening to support the pump and store the water.

Obvention—tribute and fees paid by Maya for the support of the church.

Palomar—a dovecote.

Patí—rough or unfinished cotton cloth woven by Maya women as tribute.

Peasant—a rural cultivator whose household surpluses are transferred to a dominant group of rulers who use them to underwrite their own standard of living as well as to feed nonfarmers within a complex, state-level, society.

Peso—a monetary unit; 1 peso = 8 reales.

Pila—a water-storage tank, usually constructed of masonry.

Principal—noble, important Maya leader.

Privately owned rancho—a small, privately owned agricultural estate, usually smaller than an hacienda, used for livestock raising or agricultural pursuits but not characterized by large numbers of resident laborers.

Pueblo—a town, smaller and politically subordinate to the cabecera, also known as a pueblo de visita or an auxiliary. For the most part, inhabitants were maize farmers subject to civil and ecclesiastical supervision and taxation.

Quinta—large residential masonry buildings, usually found in cabeceras and owned and inhabited by Spanish Creoles.

Rajueleado—a decorative treatment used on building exteriors; consists of small stones set into the exterior face of the masonry accompanied by diagonal slashes of the trowel. There is an architectural debate over whether the effect is merely decorative or a surface preparation to make the exterior coat of plaster stick.

Rejollada—sinkhole; a depression formed from the collapse of limestone parent rock that does not reach the water table. Soil accumulates and retains moisture in these depressions, such that they become desirable locales for cultivation.

República de indios—Indian republic, commonwealth; autonomous Indian-controlled municipality.

Real—a monetary unit; 1/8th of a peso.

Regidor—councilman, civil official of the república de indios subordinate to the alcalde.

Repartimiento—a form of labor rationing in which laborers were partitioned among various Spanish enterprises. In Yucatán local products were obtained for market by Spanish entrepreneurs who forced advances of cash and materials on Indians in return for the delivery of cotton cloth and beeswax twice per year.

Revitalization movement—a social movement or revolt, usually organized and directed by a charismatic leader who often justifies advocacy for change or the actions of the movement's members through religious means and/or a return to the "traditional" lifeways of the past. A deliberate, organized, conscious effort by the members of a society to construct a more satisfying culture.

Sascab—calcareous sand that when properly treated with pressure and water forms a hard white marl. Often used to create dwelling floors or for plastering building exteriors.

Servicio personal—personal service labor assessed as part of Maya tribute payments.

Sharecropper—an agriculturalist who cultivates land belonging to another and repays the owner for the use of land and water with a share of the harvest.

Shareholder—agriculturalists who do not own their land and must negotiate share or wage-labor contracts with those who do in order to make a living.

Site structure—the study of spatial patterns among artifacts, ecofacts, features, and structures on archaeological sites.

Sitio—small, often Maya-owned, bee and cattle operation, usually measuring 1 sq league.

Solar—a house lot or yard, usually fenced.

Smallholder—autonomous, subsistence-oriented agriculturalists who practice intensive and sustainable cultivation on land they own or control.

Swidden—a form of extensive shifting cultivation in which land is left fallow for long periods to maintain soil fertility. Cultivation methods often involve slash-and-burn techniques.

Tabardillo—typhus.

Terrenos baldíos—vacant or unworked lands or any land that was not part of village ejidos, community lands, or private property. Previously they were public lands known as crown lands, tierras realengas, or the King's forest, monte del rey, and open to all for use. After 1841, baldíos (including water rights, such as parcels with cenotes) could be sold.

Tierras realengas—"royal lands," public land, all land that was not privately owned, administered by a community or other institution, or designated as village commons.

Tithe farming—method for collecting tithes (diezmos) where entrepreneurs paid a percentage for the right to collect them in specified parishes.

Vara—a linear measurement, 0.838 m.

Zacate—a tall grass, often harvested for animal fodder

Notes

Abbreviations

AGA Archivo General del Arquidiócesis, Mérida
AGEY Archivo General del Estado de Yucatán
AGI Archivo General de Indias
AGN Archivo General de la Nación, México
AME Archivo de la Mitra Emeritense, Mérida
ANEY Archivo Notarial del Estado de Yucatán
BCCA Biblioteca Cresencio Carrillo y Ancona
BM British Museum and British Library, Department of Manuscripts, London
TUL Latin American Library, Tulane University
UNM University of New Mexico, France V. Scholes Collection

Preface

1. See discussion in Andrews and Robles Castellanos 1985:69; and Robles Castellanos and Andrews 1986. Relevant passages in the Chilam Balam of Chumayel indicate that the ruler of Cetelac agreed to pay tribute to the Itzá (Roys 1933:72–75).

2. The original 1549 Map of Mani is located in the Rare Book Collection, Latin American Library, Tulane University, New Orleans. A facsimile was published by Roys (1943:176, 183). The 1600 Map of the Tierras de Sotuta reproduced in Roys's 1939 *The Titles of Ebtun* is part of a bound-manuscript collection known as *Yerbas y hechicerías del Yucatán,* compiled by Juan Pío Pérez, a noted nineteenth-century Yucatecan historian and Mayanist; this work is also part of the Rare Book Collection, Latin American Library, Tulane University. The Map of the Tierras de Sotuta was recopied by Pío Pérez from an earlier source, and the orthography and paleography of the existing map are clearly nineteenth century in date.

3. Maya speakers in this region commonly drop the "l" from most words; thus Cetelac has become Ceteac (see Roys 1939; cf. Roys 1943). The Yaxuná Archaeological Survey was directed by Dr. David Freidel, Southern Methodist University; his account of our first trip to Cetelac appears in Freidel, Schele, and Parker 1993.

4. I use the term "parish," or *parroquia,* of Yaxcabá, because it is the most consistent territorial designation over time. The parish consists of the *cabecera,* Yaxcabá, its

attendant *visitas,* or auxiliary towns of Mopilá, Kancabdzonot, Yaxuná, and Santa María, and the dependent haciendas, ranchos, and *sitios* of these principal settlements. In the nineteenth century, political jurisdictions in Yucatán changed radically. With the implementation of the Bourbon political reforms in 1786, Yaxcabá became part of the Partido de Beneficios Bajos under the intendancy system. After independence, it fell under the jurisdiction of the Partido de Sotuta but was occasionally referred to as the Partido de Yaxcabá. As the new political divisions solidified, Yaxcabá became a *subdelegación* of the Partido de Sotuta within the Departamento de Tekax. In the twentieth century, Yaxcabá was designated a *municipio,* an independent municipality.

5. AME, 1880, Visita a Sotuta. *Visitas Pastorales 1854–1895,* vol. 6. Cathedral Archive, Mérida.

Chapter 1:
Legacies of Resistance

1. Secretaría de Gobernación y Gobierno del Estado de Yucatán, 1988, *Municipios de Yucatán,* Centro Nacional de Estudios Municipales de la Secretaría de Gobernación, Roberto Galván Ramírez, coordinador. Talleres Gráficos de la Nación, México, D.F. Municipio de Yaxcabá, 525–29.

2. *Diario de Yucatán,* June 13, 1999.

3. Most archaeologists would employ a horizontal excavation strategy to acquire data on house-lot site structure. In the Yaxcabá region, however, soils are shallow and exposed bedrock is common. We elected a lower-cost strategy in which we treated surface collection units as single-layer excavations, usually a 5-cm level. This technique allowed greater area coverage without loss of contextual or spatial detail.

Chapter 2:
Agrarian Change and the Caste War

1. Marx quoted in Netting 1993:11; Wells and Joseph 1996:11.

2. For current treatment of historiographic methods, the investigative process of ethnohistorical inquiry, and the ladder of inference for understanding mind-sets, see Barber and Berdan 1998.

3. Dumond's thesis draws from some classic studies in political sociology, notably Skocpol 1979 and Tilly 1978. The idea that peasant rebellions originate with rising expectations that are then cut short has been criticized. Expectations are extremely difficult to measure cross-culturally in the present, and even more so in the past. See also Wolf 1969.

4. The best example is Philip Thompson's (2000:5–7) study of Tekanto. The precondition for employing his methodology, however, is to find "lots of Maya documents." Restall's (1997) work exemplifies how such methodology works at a regional scale. His study encompasses three unrelated communities (Ixil, Tekanto, and Cacalchén) over a long time frame.

5. Some of the most compelling archaeological studies of resistance involve plantation slavery and colonization—situations where the exercise of hegemony is most extreme. See Armstrong 1998; Saunders 1998; and Singleton 1998. Examples of resistant acts in archaeology include caching of presumably stolen items under residences, use of indigenous religious symbols in modified form, use of indigenous technology (especially ceramics) to mark identity, and arrangement of residential space so that some activities are hidden from outsiders.

6. For a classic prehistoric example, see Rene Millon's (1988) discussion of the final days of Teotihuacan.

7. Eunice Uc González, personal communication, 1999. She is an archaeologist at the Centro-INAH, Yucatán, Instituto Nacional de Antropología e Historia, who specializes in archaeological research of caves and cenotes.

Chapter 3:
The Political Economy of Yaxcabá

1. The town of Yaxcabá seems to be a creation of congregación. Although numerous pre-Hispanic settlements are located nearby, especially at Mopilá, Yaxcabá itself lacks evidence of pre-Hispanic occupation. See discussion below in Chapter 4.

2. AGN, 1938, Incorporación a la real corona de las encomiendas de la provincia de Yucatán. Distritos de las reales cajas de Mérida y Campeche. *Boletín del Archivo General de la Nación* (México) 9:456–569. UNM, 1549 Yucatecan encomenderos. Notes on the document from the AGI, Guatemala 128, archive 360, box II-1, Maya, Item 12. Coronado Room, Zimmerman Library, Albuquerque. See also Farriss 1984:158–64.

3. In Yaxcabá, people even went so far as to prove that named sacrificial victims were alive and well (Scholes and Adams 1938:LII–LIII). Although Scholes tends to believe the Sotuta testimony is false, he admits the plausibility of aspects of the testimony. The actual offenses were relatively harmless and consisted of possessing idols, burning copal to idols, asking for a good harvest, asking for success in hunting, and occasionally sacrificing birds and deer. He also suggests that prosecutions are politically motivated to limit local batab power.

4. The disposal of bodies in caves and cenotes is reminiscent of sacrifices to the rain god described in the Book of Chilam Balam of Chumayel (Roys 1933). Archaeological evidence also indicates the prevalence of human remains in cenotes, at Chichén Itzá for example. This form of disposal had the added advantage of hiding the evidence of the sacrifice. Remains of cattle, particularly the skulls, are also commonly found in cenotes, and their presence likely suggests successful cattle theft or rustling.

5. Males between the ages of fourteen and fifty-five paid encomienda tribute, as did women between the ages of twelve and sixty. In 1756, based on a report by Bishop Ignacio de Padilla, the king ordered the governor to stop collecting tribute from women of any age (Garcia Bernal 1972:107). This ruling was not implemented until 1760 (Farriss 1984:41).

6. UNM, 1549 Yucatecan encomenderos. Notes on the document from the AGI, Guatemala 128, archive 360, box II-1, Maya, item 12. Coronado Room, Zimmerman Library, Albuquerque.

7. AME, 1784, Visita a Yaxcabá, Visitas Pastorales 1783–84, vol. 2, exp. 42. Cathedral Archive, Mérida.

8. BM, 1757, Ynforme Anónimo al Governador de Yucatán, Add. 17569.

9. BCCA, 1778, Declaraciones de diezmos en el partido de beneficios altos y bajos, son frutas de setenta y siete colectados en 1778 años. Mérida.

10. AME, 1784, Visita a Yaxcabá, Visitas Pastorales 1783–84, vol. 2, exp. 42. Cathedral Archive, Mérida.

11. BM, Add. 17569. Visita a su obispado por el Yllmo Sor Fr Dn Ygnacio Padilla, 1757. This document states, "Dista de la expresada Villa [Valladolid] 17 leguas, su cura que es el Dm. Don Agustin Cano (electo Racionero de la Catedral de Mérida) ha construido en menos de dos años una primorosa Yglesia de boveda con su crucero y capilla mayor y la concluira perfectamente dentro de dos meses sin haber causado el menor gravamen a los Indios. Esta muy decentamente hornamentada, y proximo a concluir un bello retablo, que estrenara el día de la dedicación de la Yglesia; tiene a distancia de 10 cuadros el Pueblo de Mopilá, una visita de esta administración cuya Yglesia es techada de guano, sus paredes y frontispicio de piedra." The size of the church in Yaxcabá, with its three towers, belies the bishop's comments about the burden of its construction.

12. AME, 1784, Visita a Yaxcabá, Visitas Pastorales 1783–84, vol. 2, exp. 42. Cathedral Archive, Mérida.

13. AME, 1784, Visita a Yaxcabá, Visitas Pastorales 1783–84, vol. 2, exp. 42. Cathedral Archive, Mérida.

14. Robert Patch (1993) discusses the extent to which the term "sharecropper" is applicable to luneros. He is correct that these two labor categories are not quite coterminous in that sharecroppers by definition do not provide labor rent to the landlord. In Yaxcabá, however, it was more common for luneros to pay for land and water rights with a share of the crop. For these reasons, I use the term in this context.

15. UNM, 1809, Relación de los pueblos de Yucatán, con el número de indios tributarios de cada uno, y la cantidad que pagan a la Real Hacienda, según los subdelegados. Notes on the document from the Archivo General de la Nación, México, Tierras 3556. Archive 360, Box II, Yucatán, Item 30, Coronado Room, Zimmerman Library, Albuquerque. In Yaxcabá *indios de pueblo* paid 6.5 reales twice per year, whereas *indios de barrio* paid 3 reales twice per year. Indios de barrio may refer to people from outlying rancho settlements.

16. AGN, 1938, Incorporación a la real corona de las encomiendas de la provincia de Yucatán. Distritos de las reales cajas de Mérida y Campeche. *Boletín del Archivo General de la Nación* (México) 9:456–569.

17. UNM, 1809, Relación de los pueblos de Yucatán, con el número de indios tributarios de cada uno, y la cantidad que pagan a la Real Hacienda, según los subdelegados. Notes on the document from the Archivo General de la Nación, México, Tierras 3556. Archive 360, Box II, Yucatán, Item 30, Coronado Room, Zimmerman Library, Albuquerque.

18. ANEY Notarías, Peniche 1815:347.

19. All population figures presented here are drawn from ecclesiastical sources, specifically the visitas pastorales. AME, 1784, Visita a Yaxcabá, Visitas Pastorales 1783–1784, vol. 2, exp. 42; 1804, Visita a Yaxcabá, Visitas pastorales 1803–1805, vol. 5, exp. 43; 1828, Yaxcabá, Selección Joaquín Arrigunaga Peon, caja 5; 1829 Sotuta, Selección Joaquín Arrigunaga Peon, caja 4. For the period 1784 to 1838, information about population in the parish is remarkably consistent because it was methodically recorded by a single curate, José Bartólome del Granado Baeza. For most years his reports present gross figures for the entire parish distributed among the cabecera and auxiliary towns. Population is broken down among ethnic categories for the years 1798–1815. For 1784, 1804, and 1828, he provides a list of all settlements in the parish, their classifications as pueblo, rancho, or hacienda, their distance from Yaxcabá, and their total population.

20. Although the population of the Yucatán peninsula as a whole begins to recover after 1750, the substantial increase noted in Yaxcabá between 1784 and 1828 is not entirely attributable to internal growth. Migration likely caused some of the increase. Both Hunt (1974) and Dumond (1997) point out that the expansion of commercial agriculture in the northwestern part of the peninsula placed pressure on agriculturalists beginning in the late seventeenth century. Remmers (1981:93) also indicates that for the early nineteenth century the rate of population growth in Yucatán is very low. Nevertheless, between 1794 and 1821 population shifted substantially from the northwestern region to the interior. In 1794 the interior contained 38.7 percent of the peninsula's population, whereas after 1821 this percentage had risen to 51.08.

21. AGEY, 1813, Propios y Arbitrios, Yaxcabá, Proyecto de arbitrios municipales y aprobación del mismo, vol. 2, exp. 18, f. 6.

22. AGEY, 1814, Kancabdzonot, consulta sobre una capitación para los gastos del municipio, Propios y arbitrios, vol. 2, exp. 38, f. 2.

23. BCCA, 1778, Declaraciones de diezmos en el partido de beneficios altos y bajos, son frutas de setenta y siete colectados en 1778 años. Mérida.

24. ANEY Notarías, Peniche 1813:20; Peniche 1815:107; N. del Castillo 1819:291–92; N. del Castillo 1825:154–56; Patron 1829–1830:20–22; Patron 1831:16; Poveda 1831–1833: no foliation.

25. AME, 1797, Pueblo de Yaxcabá. Libro de Cofradías Generales de 1797, no foliation. Cathedral Archive, Mérida.

26. AGEY, 1838, Justicia Civil, Alcaldía Segunda de Peto, Yaxcabá, Demanda promovida por Rodrigo Salazar, albacea del fallecido Francisco del Castillo, por adeudo de una cantidad de dinero, vol. 11, exp. 10; ANEY Notarías, F. del Rio 1838:86–90.

27. AME, 1797, Pueblo de Yaxcabá. Libro de Cofradías Generales de 1797, no foliation. ANEY Notarías, Peniche 1830–1831:232–38; N. del Castillo 1828:223–29. BCCA, 1778, Declaraciones de diezmos en el partido de beneficios altos y bajos, son frutas de setenta y siete colectados en 1778 años.

28. Some details of Granado Baeza's career are presented in Fallon 1979:93–97. This source should be used with caution because the appendix confuses a certain José del Granado Baeza with Bartólome del Granado Baeza. In fact they were the same individual, José Bartólome del Granado Baeza. Fallon indicates that Granado Baeza served

in six separate parishes: Mérida, Tihosuco, Uman, Tixcacaltuyú, Petén Itzá, and finally Yaxcabá. He was born in 1744 to a prominent Valladolid family, one branch of whom settled in Sotuta (Philip Thompson, personal communication, 1999). His *"relación de méritos,"* or list of qualifications, described on application for parish posts are described (in Latin) AME, Concurso a Curatos exp. 29, fs. 32–35. He died at the age of eighty-seven, after serving the parish for forty-one years, and is buried in Yaxcabá's church. "Los Indios de Yucatán," informe dado por el cura de Yaxcabá, was originally written in 1813 and subsequently published in a Mérida literary magazine, the *Registro Yucateco,* in 1845. I thank Terry Rugeley (personal communication, 1999) for historiographic clarifications. See also Rugeley 1997:110–12; Ruz Menéndez 1989.

29. Granado Baeza indicates that these later two practices had ceased, presumably under the Constitution of Cadiz, which banned personal service. Salt extraction would have required sending individuals to the nearest source on the northern coast of Yucatán.

30. The common punishment for sorcery, when discovered, was whipping. See also AGEY, 1845, Fondo Justicia, Ramo Penal, Causa instruida contra Don Pedro Urcelay y Don Gabriel Herrera, Alcaldes de Kancabdzonot, por abusos de autoridad y presunciones de homicidio, vol. 34, exp. 46. This document is mislabeled; the persons named are alcaldes of Chikindzonot. Divination and healing using the saastun continues to the present day.

31. The earliest and largest hacienda, Santa María Nohitzá, dates to 1712 when the license to raise ganado mayor was purchased. ANEY Notarías, N. del Castillo 1819, fs. 76–77.

32. ANEY Notarías, N. del Castillo 1821, fs. 127–29.

33. ANEY Notarías, Patrón 1827–28, fs. 233–43. See also Roys 1939.

34. ANEY Notarías, Peniche 1815:fs. 284–93. See also Rugeley 1997:37.

35. ANEY Notarías, Peniche 1830–1831:fs. 232–38; N. del Castillo 1828:223–29.

36. ANEY Notarías, Peniche 1818:f. 83.

37. ANEY Notarías, N. del Castillo 1818:fs. 251–53.

38. While many scholars would correctly point out that many agricultural strategies are labor intensive, the organization and size of the labor force on Yaxcabá's haciendas is very different from estates that produced sugar or henequen.

39. AME, 1787, Asuntos terminados, vol. 5, exp. 106, 115. BCCA, 1778, Declaraciones de diezmos en el partido de beneficios altos y bajos, son frutas de setenta y siete colectados en 1778 años.

40. The temporary contribución patriótica was 10 reales per year, paid in two installments. AGEY, 1823, Poder ejecutivo, Yaxcabá, Matrícula de la contribución patriótica del pueblo de Yaxcabá, con un plan de egresos de su ayuntamiento, vol. 1, exp. 8, f. 24. See also Dumond 1997:68.

41. AGEY, 1825, Poder ejecutivo, Yaxcabá, Autos de un litigio entre la junta municipal y la república de indios de dicho pueblo, vol. 1, exp. 40, f. 36.

42. I am indebted to Victoria Bricker for her assistance with this document.

43. AGEY, 1835, Poder ejecutivo, Yaxcabá Representación del C. Bartólome Caamal pidiendo se le exceptue del empleo del alcalde del pueblo, vol. 3, exp. 30; 1829, Poder ejecutivo, Kancabdzonot, Renuncia de Juan Pablo Caamal, cacique de Kancabdzonot

y sedignación de Lucíano May, vol. 2, exp. 49, f. 3; 1827, Gobernación, Yaxcabá, sumaria información contra Lázaro Caamal, cacique de Yaxcabá, por ineptitud en el cobro de la contribución personal, vol. 1, exp. 29, f. 4; 1832, Gobernación, Yaxcabá, Designando a Juan Ceh, cacique del pueblo de Yaxcabá por fallecimiento del anterior, vol. 4, exp. 12, f. 2; 1841, Gobernación, Kancabdzonot, Miguel Cámara... presenta la terna para la elección del cacique del pueblo de Kancabdzonot, vol. 4, exp. 95, f. 1; 1841, Gobernación, Yaxcabá, Miguel Cámara... presenta la terna para la elección del cacique del pueblo de Yaxcabá, vol. 4, exp. 96.

44. Güemez Pineda (1991) demonstrates the usefulness of criminal records of the AGEY for identifying resistance. His study of cattle rustling as an everyday form of Maya resistance in northwestern Yucatán during the independence period makes a strong case for patterned, rather than random, clandestine acts against authority. Penal cases for Yaxcabá, however, are relatively scarce. Except for the few incidents cited here in the text, most infractions brought to the attention of authorities related to politically motivated accusations of disturbing the peace (see below) or common crime. Two homicides, one assault, and one case of false imprisonment occurred in the parish during this era (AGEY, 1826, Justicia Penal, vol. 4, exp. 7, Apr. 7–Nov. 9; AGEY, 1832, Justicia, vol. 3, exp. 19, f. 9; AGEY, 1834, Justicia, vol. 11, exp. 22, f. 11; AGEY, 1844, Justicia Penal, caja 26, Kancabdzonot, Feb. 23–Oct. 14). In 1826 Enrique Medina, head of the civic militia, was sentenced to four years of hard labor and road construction for killing Simon Mejicano. In 1844 Francisco May and associates (all Indians) were convicted of killing Dominga Bee in monte surrounding Kancabdzonot. In 1834 a soldier stationed in Yaxcabá, Andres Insuaste, assaulted and badly wounded Santiago Novelo over a debt of 1 real. When the defendant was asked why he attacked Novelo, he claimed he couldn't remember because he was drunk. Finally, in 1832 Juan Nepomuceno Lara was arrested as he was preparing to leave for Bacalar, the officials having "confused him" with a known cattle thief, Felipe Loria. Lara attributed his false arrest to the alcalde's envy of his good fortune. Although these cases suggest that Yaxcabá was not the most tranquil of communities, most accusations and crimes in the documents were perpetrated by Creoles against Creoles, and they do not suggest Maya resistance. In contrast, during this same time period the records of Justicia Penal include several cases for Tiholop and Tihosuco, further south and nearer the geographic origin of the Caste War, for conspiracy, refusing to pay taxes, "revolution," cattle theft, and sorcery (in Chikindzonot, AGEY, 1845, Justicia Penal, vol. 34, exp. 46).

45. AGEY, 1833, Justicia Penal, vol. 3, exp. 46; see also AGEY, 1844, Justicia Penal, caja 26; and AGEY, 1846, vol. 39, exp. 26. While it is possible that public insult to a Creole by an Indian indicates resistance, the documentary evidence indicates that the deputy alcalde was later assaulted by another Creole in 1846. Francisco Mendez punched him in the face while he was drunk, an infraction for which he spent three months in jail.

46. Rugeley (1997:111) indicates that Villamil was also a hypochondriac and preferred Mérida to his parish.

47. AGEY, 1842, Poder Ejecutivo, Ayuntamientos, vol. 2, exp. 41, Expediente sobre una representación del Ayuntamiento de Yaxcabá, sobre irregularidades en el camposanto que atribuye a Don Eusebio Villamil, Cura de dicho población.

48. Today in Yucatán, as well as in previous centuries, most people practice secondary burial. The deceased usually is buried for three years and exhumed after all flesh has decayed. The skeletonized remains are collected and placed in a smaller crypt in the cemetery or church wall.

49. AME, 1845, Asuntos Terminados, vol. 13, exp. 32, Expediente sitando para que el Pro. Dn Juan Pablo Ancona continue de Cura Coadjutor del Pueblo de Yaxcabá. AME, 1845, Asuntos Terminados, vol. 13, exp. 33, Expediente instruidos en que piden varios vecinos de Yaxcabá que su Cura, D. Eusebio Villamil pace a hacerle cargo de su parroquia.

50. AGEY, 1829, Poder Ejecutivo, vol. 2, exp. 31. Copia de las cuentas de fábrica de la Casa Consitorial del pueblo de Yaxcabá, así como tambien de una pieza para el Pócito y el Cuartel de Cívicos, que rindió el ayuntamiento de 1826.

51. Sascab is pulverized limestone that is excavated from subsurface deposits and caves. When treated properly with water and compression, it forms a hard white marl. AGEY, 1840, Poder Ejecutivo, vol. 4, exp. 34. Acta Certificada del Ayuntamiento de Yaxcabá, sobre policia, limpieza de calles y otras obras municipales, Nov. 23, 1840, f. 2. A fine of 1 real was imposed on the owner of any pig found wandering loose.

52. AGEY, 1826, Poder Ejecutivo, vol. 2, exp. 1. Expediente promovido por varios vecinos de Yaxcabá contra el alcalde Claudio Padilla por infracciones a la ley. Oct. 12, 1826, f. 35.

53. AGEY, 1829, Poder Ejecutivo, vol. 2, exp. 32. Diligencias instruidas para la averiguación de unos exesos atribuidos a los oficiales de la milicia cívica de Yaxcabá, por denuncia de unos vecinos interesados. Sept. 13, 1829, f. 16.

54. AGEY, 1842, Poder Ejecutivo, vol. 1, exp. 4. El gobernador declarando nula la elección de J. Tiburcio Días como alcalde primero del ayuntamiento de Yaxcabá. Apr. 29, 1842, f. 8.

55. AGEY, 1842, Poder Ejecutivo, vol. 1, exp. 3. Diligencias practicadas sobre los hechos ocurridos en Yaxcabá, Tabi, Kancabdzonot, y Tixcacaltuyú. Mar. 8, 1842, f. 21. See also Rugeley 1997:143.

56. AGEY, 1846, Fondo Justicia: Penal, vol. 36, exp. 6, Causa instruida contra Tiburcio Días y socios por movimientos tumultuarios y asonada en el pueblo de Yaxcabá. Mar. 5–25, 1846, f. 3.

57. For example, just prior to winning the election for alcalde, José Tiburcio Días sold his hacienda, Nohitzá, to Pascual Espejo, a crony, for 4,000 pesos, of which 1,863 pesos were paid directly to Días and the remaining amount was placed at interest to be awarded to an ecclesiastical benefice. ANEY Notarías, Barbosa, 1845–1846:fs. 82–83.

58. AME, 1828, Visita Pastoral a Yaxcabá, Selección Joaquín Arrigunaga Peon, caja 5; AGEY, 1841, Poder Ejecutivo, Ramo Padrones, vol. 3, exp. 24; vol. 4, exp. 47; vol. 6, exp. 80, Padrón general de los habitantes del pueblo de Kancabdzonot, Santa María, y Yaxcabá. These are three separate censuses that list the names of everyone in each settlement, including affiliated ranchos and haciendas and their occupations. A padrón for Yaxuná that would have included the haciendas Holop, Chacxul, Cetelac, Oxolá, Popolá, and Nohitzá was not located in the AGEY. Thus the 1841

census somewhat underestimates the parish population as a whole, as well as the portion resident on haciendas.

59. Sergio Quezada, personal communication, 1999. He provided the list of places from Juan Pío Pérez's nómina for Yaxcabá; see also Hunt 1974:446 n. 81.

60. Regil and Peon 1853:281–82. The other jurisdictions listed are Tizimin, Tekax, Hecelchakan, Lerma, Seiba, and Carmen, of which Tekax had the next largest number of cattle with 14,542.

61. BCCA, 1845–1847, Registro de las denuncias de terrenos baldíos. I am grateful to Robert Patch for providing the notarial references in the ANEY for several parcels that were subsequently purchased.

62. AGEY, 1841, Poder Ejecutivo, Ramo Padrones, vol. 3, exp. 24; vol. 4, exp. 47; vol. 6, exp. 80, Padrón general de los habitantes del pueblo de Kancabdzonot, Santa María, y Yaxcabá.

63. See Chapter 1 above; also Bricker 1981.

64. When I was doing fieldwork in Yaxcabá in 1988, one elderly man claimed to remember the Caste War and an attack on Yaxcabá. It is most likely that he remembered the liberalist-socialist violence of 1924. Bricker (1981) mentions this individual as well and points out that for the local inhabitants the Caste War was a very protracted conflict.

65. AGEY, 1851, Poder Ejecutivo, Gobernación, Cuartel de Yaxcabá, caja 82, f. 39.

66. AGEY, 1850, Poder Ejecutivo, Gobernación, Manifestación de gravamenes de cumplimiento del decreto del 5 de dic. de 1849, caja 76, f. 2; 1851, Poder Ejecutivo, Gobernación, Secretaría General de Gobierno, Jefatura Política de Sotuta, caja 85, f. 22; 1857, Poder Ejecutivo, Gobernación, Exposición de Propietarios de Sotuta y Yaxcabá, caja 111, f. 2.

67. AGEY, 1851, Poder Ejecutivo, Gobernación, Secretaría General de Gobierno, Jefatura Política de Sotuta, caja 85, f. 22.

68. AGEY, 1852, Poder Ejecutivo, Gobernación, Secretaría General de Gobierno, Jefatura Política de Sotuta, caja 87, f. 5.

69. AGEY, 1857, Poder Ejecutivo, Gobernación, Cacique de Yaxcabá, caja 110, f. 1.

70. AGEY, 1864, Poder Ejecutivo, Hacienda, Plan de Arbitrios de Yaxcabá, caja 141, f. 2.

71. Parish registers of baptisms, marriages, and deaths for Yaxcabá have been lost. Unlike those of Sotuta, they are not extant within the Archivo General del Arzobispado, nor were they recorded on microfilm by the Church of Latter Day Saints, nor are they currently kept in the church in Yaxcabá itself. Granado Baeza undoubtedly kept precise records of these sacraments, but except for the occasional unbound record, information for Yaxcabá begins in the year 1856, mixed with those from Tixcacaltuyú. Later in the 1870s, Yaxcabá parish registers are included with those from Sotuta.

72. AGA, Libro primero de entierros de las parroquias de Tixcacaltuyú y sus anexos que el cura actual y primero despúes de la sublevación del los indios forma a su costa, 1850–1861, José Antonio Monforte.

73. AME, 1880, Visitas Pastorales 1854–95.

74. AGEY, 1886, Poder Ejecutivo, Población, Censos y Padrones, caja 241, 9 folios.

Chapter 4:
Archaeological Settlement Patterns

1. Population figures for Yaxcabá parish as a whole, as well as for individual communities, were presented above in Chapter 3 and will be reprised where necessary. Agricultural production in Yaxcabá has been the subject of several detailed investigations throughout the 1970s and 1980s by the Colegio de Postgraduados en Chapingo, México. See the collection of articles published in Hernández Xolocotzi 1980. Two classic Maya ethnographies of the early twentieth century also describe agricultural practices for villages relatively near Yaxcabá. See Redfield and Villa Rojas 1934; Steggerda 1941.

2. AME, Visitas Pastorales, 1784, 1804, 1828. Another important source for place names is the Registro de las denuncias de terrenos baldíos (BCCA, 1845) and AGEY, 1841, Poder Ejecutivo, Censos y Padrones, Yaxcabá. All of these settlements retain their eighteenth- and nineteenth-century names and are well known to local farmers.

3. See AGEY, 1843, Poder Ejecutivo, Yaxcabá, Secretaría General de Gobierno, Jefatura Política del Partido de Yaxcabá, caja 51, f. 27; AGEY, 1860, Poder Ejecutivo, Gobernación, Petición de los Habitantes de Tabi de pertenecer al partido de Yaxcabá y no al de Sotuta, caja 124, f. 1; AGEY, 1860, Libre Unión, Poder Ejecutivo, Gobernación, Petición de los habitantes de Libre Unión de pertenecer al partido de Yaxcabá y no al de Sotuta, caja 124, f. 1.

4. Specifically we did not survey Santa Rosa, Chich, Chenche, Kancabchen, and Kuxubche. The first three locales are referred to as sitios or haciendas and the last two are described as sitios in the Registro de Terrenos Baldíos and the 1841 census. Santa Rosa is situated west of Yaxcabá and south of Tabi outside of the archaeological region. Kancabchen is north of the hacienda Nohitzá. Hacienda Chich was listed under the jurisdiction of Sotuta in 1845. The hacienda Chenche is located to the east of hacienda Xbac, in Yaxcabá parish proper and is the single site legitimately missing from the archaeological survey. It is a category III site.

5. At the time of the survey (1988–1989), Geographic Positioning System (GPS) technology was relatively new and had not become cost-effective for archaeology. UTMs (Universal Transverse Mercator) were recorded the "old-fashioned" way, using INEGI's 1:50,000 quadrangle maps and by carefully observing distance and direction while traveling to the site. Occasionally it was possible to triangulate among historic and prehistoric communities whose church or temple architecture was visible across the forest canopy.

6. Rajueleado is a decorative treatment used on building exteriors and consists of small stones set into the exterior face of the masonry accompanied by diagonal slashes of the trowel. There is an architectural debate over whether the effect is merely decorative or a surface preparation to make the exterior coat of plaster stick.

7. BM, 1757, Vicita a su obispado por el Yllmo. Sr. Fr. Dn. Ygnacio Padilla, Add. 17569.

8. The hacienda Nohitzá is presently known as the "Rancho El Faisán" and is owned by Juan López, a prosperous cattle rancher. Xuul is the property of Juan Turriza Chan and is also a prosperous cattle-raising establishment. Both of these sites were the property of Pascual Espejo during the Caste War.

9. Some settlements in the parish have the same name. Two communities are called Cacalchén; two are named Santa Cruz; two are called Yaxleulá. In all cases they could be distinguished based on their distance and direction from Yaxcabá recorded in the visitas pastorales. The haciendas Yaxleulá have different patron saints, San José and San Antonio.

10. We initially tried to gather surface collections from each site during the regional survey phase of the project. The results were disappointing; modern and pre-Hispanic material was often mixed with that of the colonial period. Many of the ceramics were not temporally diagnostic. Because ground visibility was poor and the sites were large, it was impossible to acquire a representative sample of surface material without more intensive efforts. Intensive surface collection therefore was reserved for later stages of the project.

11. AGEY, 1841, Poder Ejecutivo, Ramo Padrones, vol. 3, exp. 24; vol. 4, exp. 47; vol. 6, exp. 80, Padrón general de los habitantes del pueblo de Kancabdzonot, Santa María, y Yaxcabá.

12. AME, 1787, Asuntos terminados, vol. 5, exp. 106, 115. BCCA, 1778, Declaraciones de diezmos en el partido de beneficios altos y bajos, son frutas de setenta y siete colectados en 1778 años.

13. Patch (1993:284 n. 23) indicates that in many areas the terms "rancho" and "hacienda" were used interchangeably in the eighteenth century to refer to agricultural estates. By the nineteenth century, the term hacienda had replaced rancho (as well as estancia) in common usage. The term rancho also was used previously and throughout the nineteenth century to mean an unauthorized settlement of Indian agriculturalists.

14. AME, 1797, Pueblo de Yaxcabá, Libro de cofradías generales de 1797, no foliation. ANEY Notarías, Peniche 1830–1831:232–38; N. del Castillo 1828:223–29. BCCA, 1778, Declaraciones de diezmos en el partido de beneficios altos y bajos, son frutas de setenta y siete colectados en 1778 años.

15. See discussion of Kancabdzonot's transformation from a cofradía estate to a pueblo in Chapter 3 above. AME, 1784, 1804, 1828, Visitas Pastorales, Yaxcabá.

16. BCCA, 1845, 1845–1847, Registro de las denuncias de terrenos baldíos. Whether referring to a sitio as a hacienda for the purposes of claiming terreno baldío was a bid for legitimacy is debatable.

17. The third and best documented cofradía estate, Kancabdzonot, is a category II settlement. See Chapter 3, above, for an explanation of changes in its historical classification.

18. Kulimché is located along a road connecting Yaxcabá to the haciendas Kambul and Xbac. Its size may be overestimated because house lots tended to string out along the road, giving the settlement a more elliptical shape.

19. Norias, however, are also present at category II sites (notably Mopilá), and their construction also could be a function of population size.

20. AGEY, 1838, Justicia Civil, Yaxcabá, Demanda promovida por Rodrigo Salazar, albacea del fallecido Francisco del Castillo (vecino de Yaxcabá), por adeudo de una cantidad de dinero, vol. 11, exp. 10; ANEY Notarías, F. del Rio 1836:194–96; F. del Rio 1838:86–90.

21. A notable exception is Philip Thompson's (2000) analysis of landholding and agricultural carrying capacity for Tekanto. Although my analysis parallels many of his assumptions, documentary evidence of Maya landholding in Tekanto is much more detailed than in Yaxcabá.

22. AGEY, 1841, Poder Ejecutivo, Ramo Padrones, vol. 3, exp. 24; vol. 4, exp. 47; vol. 6, exp. 80; Padrón general de los habitantes del pueblo de Kancabdzonot, Santa María, y Yaxcabá.

23. It is not possible to estimate household size from the 1841 census. The census lists names but gives no indication of who resided together.

24. Farmers in the cabecera, pueblos, and independent ranchos list their occupation as "labrador" (farmer); occasionally a person is called a "jornalero" (day laborer). On haciendas, however, individuals not listed as cowboys, foremen, horse-wranglers, or some other specialty usually are described as luneros and only occasionally as labradores. Because people's names also are listed, no individual has been counted twice. For example, a labrador living in rancho Kulimché would not also be listed as a lunero of the hacienda Kambul.

25. The minimum estimate is 2,201 farmers: 1,577 inhabiting the cabecera and the pueblos; 449 living in independent ranchos; and 175 residing on haciendas.

26. ANEY Notarías, F. del Rio 1836:194–96.

27. Patch (1993:144) states that the mean number of cattle on twenty-one estates sampled for the period 1756–1803 was 163 (median 129). I suspect that the mean may be a little too high for Yaxcabá's estates, which tend to be small. In 1778, three haciendas declared tithes on calves: Kambul had 13; Nohitzá 18; and Cetelac had 12. The size of the parent herd, however, remains obscure (BCCA, 1778). I have used Patch's median figure instead, but the estimate may be imprecise.

28. According to Cline (1947:577–79) the smaller municipalities of more than 12 but less than 150 taxpayers originally were permitted 1 sq league. Later that year, these rules were revised again. Settlements of 60 taxpayers were allowed ejidos extending 1,000 varas from the site center. Smaller communities of more than 10 taxpayers were allowed the land on which their houses and buildings stood, plus a zone of 200 varas around the perimeter of the settlement. In 1844 the government also established a tax for making milpa on public lands, village ejidos, or community lands (Cline 1947:576). Every 10 mecates planted on nonprivate land was assessed 1 real, payable to the treasury or municipal fund.

29. BCCA, 1845, 1845–1847, Registro de las denuncias de terrenos baldíos. ANEY Notarías, Barbosa 1845–1846:fs. 26–27, 57–58; Barbosa 1845:f. 119; F. del Rio 1845–1846:fs. 102–4; Barbosa 1847–1849:f. 23. I am grateful to Robert Patch for pointing me to these references. For a regional perspective, see Patch 1985.

30. The modal size of claims in Yaxcabá was 1/4 sq league or 434 ha. Occasional omissions of claim size from the Registro were subsequently specified in the notary records. I have estimated the sizes of only two claims. One was described as an interstice, which I estimated as 1/8 sq league (218 ha), and the other was listed as "un terreno," estimated as 1/4 sq league (434 ha).

31. I am following Thompson's (2000:132–37) methods for estimating land use in Tekanto. Techniques of cultivation in Yucatán vary depending on soil type and

rainfall and also according to population density. Estimates drawn from Yaxcabá itself or nearby communities are most accurate in terms of environmental variability. Estimates drawn from mid-nineteenth-century sources are most accurate in terms of population density, whereas the early-twentieth-century sources pertain to conditions of lower population density. Although Hernández's work in Yaxcabá during the 1970s is further removed in time from the period of study, population density during the 1970s is more similar to mid-nineteenth-century Yaxcabá than the early-twentieth-century ethnographies. Another source of information is Regil and Peon's (1853) indictment of slash-and-burn cultivation methods in mid-nineteenth-century Yucatán, but the data are generalized for Yucatán as a whole.

32. The formula is $a * \frac{(b + c)}{c}$ Where a = plot size; b = number of years fallow; c = number of years cultivation.

33. Unlike many situations today, class did not define race in nineteenth-century Yucatán. One's status as Indian, Spanish, mestizo, or other designation was recognized at baptism and maintained throughout life. This segregation is most apparent in church records, where curates kept separate books of baptisms, marriages, and deaths for Creoles and for Indians. Indians, especially caciques, might become very wealthy, own their own estates, and claim terreno baldío—but they were still "Indians."

Chapter 5:
Archaeological Site Structure
before the Caste War

1. The domesticated American honeybee usually is kept in hollow logs and tree trunks in which the ends are sealed by wooden stoppers held in place with mud mortar. Each log has an opening to permit the bees to enter and leave. The hive logs are stacked on wood racks, protected by a perishable thatched shelter, in the garden zone of the house lot. Honey is harvested four times per year by unplugging the log and extracting a part of the hive from each end, while being careful not to disturb the queen (Redfield and Villa Rojas 1934:48–60). Apiculture using prefabricated wooden boxes also occurs away from the house lot near milpa plots in the Yaxcabá region. These hives require water during the dry season if they are not situated near a natural water source. Such facilities are increasingly colonized by Africanized bees.

2. While we were making surface collections and screening the dirt at Cetelac, we were asked about the disposition of the backdirt under the screens. A number of older children subsequently were sent to collect bags of the finely screened soil for garden use back home. See also Redfield and Villa Rojas 1934:46.

3. We did not find any lost treasure during our survey, but we were asked repeatedly if that was what we were looking for. Any unusual features were interpreted by locals as places where the hacendado hid his valuables. The underground storage rooms built in a sascabera at Cetelac (see below) were one such example of a hiding place.

4. According to Agustino Ku (personal communication, 1989), a Cacalchén native, these two structures do not date to the twentieth century.

5. We did not test the soil in these features for phosphates. Ordinarily, animal-penning features are characterized by very high phosphate levels. Because we were dealing with a surface assemblage (not sealed excavated contexts) in an area characterized by very thin soils that were currently used for slash-and-burn cultivation, phosphate testing was not likely to yield useable results (Barba 1986; Smyth 1990). Several of the pens were built directly on bedrock.

6. Isopleth maps of average sherd weight proved the most useful for locating approximate patio-garden boundaries. Subsequent nonparametric difference of means tests were performed to evaluate whether mean average sherd weight was equal between units in patio versus garden areas for each house lot (Alexander 1993:327–32). For all house lots, the test revealed a significant difference in mean average sherd weight between units collected in patio and garden zones. A principal-components analysis was also employed.

7. The Kruskal Wallis test is a nonparametric alternative to one-way analysis of variance based on the rank transformation of the variable under study. For cases where the assumptions required for one-way analysis of variance are not met, the Kruskal Wallis test evaluates the hypothesis that rank means are equal by calculating the H statistic, which measures the degree to which the various sums of ranks for the variable differ among the groups. The sampling distribution of H approximates the chi square (Blalock 1979; Koopmans 1987:397–404). Tests of patio size and the mean numbers of nonlocal items among the sites should be regarded as preliminary, because small sample size is a concern.

Works Cited

Abrams, Elliot M. 1994. *How the Maya Built Their World: Energetics and Ancient Architecture.* Austin: University of Texas Press.

Abu-Lughod, Lila. 1990. The Romance of Resistance: Tracing Transformations of Power Through Bedoin Women. *American Ethnologist* 17(1): 41–55.

Adas, Michael. 1981. From Avoidance to Confrontation: Peasant Protest in Precolonial and Colonial Southeast Asia. *Comparative Studies in Society and History* 23(2): 217–47.

———. 1986. From Footdragging to Flight: The Evasive History of Peasant Avoidance Protest in South and South-east Asia. *Journal of Peasant Studies* 12(2): 64–86.

Alexander, Rani T. 1993. Colonial Period Archaeology of the Parroquia de Yaxcabá, Yucatán, Mexico: An Ethnohistorical and Site Structural Analysis. Ph.D. dissertation, University of New Mexico.

———. 1997a. Haciendas and Economic Change in Yucatán: Entrepreneurial Strategies in the Parroquia de Yaxcabá, 1775–1850. *Journal of Archaeological Method and Theory* 4(3/4): 331–51.

———. 1997b. Late Colonial Period Settlement Patterns in Yaxcabá Parish, Yucatán, Mexico: Implications for the Distribution of Land and Population Before the Caste War. In *Approaches to the Historical Archaeology of Mexico, Central and South America,* ed. Janine Gasco, Greg Smith, and Patricia Fournier-Garcia, 29–40. Monograph 38. Los Angeles: UCLA Institute of Archaeology.

———. 1998. Community Organization in the Parroquia de Yaxcabá, Yucatán, Mexico, 1750–1847: Implications for Household Adaptation within a Changing Colonial Economy. *Ancient Mesoamerica* 9: 39–54.

———. 1999. Mesoamerican House Lots and Archaeological Site Structure: Problems of Inference in Yaxcabá, Yucatán, Mexico, 1750–1847. In *The Archaeology of Household Activities,* ed. Penelope M. Allison, 78–100. London: Routledge.

———. 2003. Architecture, Haciendas, and Economic Change in Yaxcabá, Yucatán, Mexico. *Ethnohistory* 50(1):191–220.

Allison, Penelope M., ed. 1999. *The Archaeology of Household Activities.* London: Routledge.

Andrews, Anthony. 1991. The Rural Chapels and Churches of Early Colonial Yucatán and Belize: An Archaeological Perspective. In *The Spanish Borderlands in Pan-American Perspective,* ed. David Hurst Thomas, 355–74. Columbian Consequences, vol. 3. Washington, D.C.: Smithsonian Institution Press.

Andrews, Anthony, and Fernando Robles Castellanos. 1985. Chichén Itzá and Coba: An Itza-Maya Standoff in Early Postclassic Yucatán. In *The Lowland Maya Postclassic,* ed. Arlen F. Chase and Prudence M. Rice, 62–72. Austin: University of Texas Press.

Arias Reyes, Luis M. 1980. La Producción Milpera Actual en Yaxcabá, Yucatán. In *Seminario sobre Producción Agrícola en Yucatán,* ed. Efraim Hernández Xolocotzi, 259–304. Mérida: Secretaría de Programación y Presupuesto.

Arias Reyes, Luis M., Ch. Wilver Llanes, Ivan Hernández M., and Geudi Rivas C. 1998. La Horticultura de los Mayas de Yucatán. In *Memorias del Tercer Congreso Internacional de Mayistas,* 580–97. México, D.F.: Universidad Nacional Autónoma de México, Instituto de Investigaciones Filologicas, Centro de Estudios Mayas.

Armstrong, Douglas V. 1998. Cultural Transformation within Enslaved Laborer Communities in the Caribbean. In *Studies in Culture Contact: Interaction, Culture Change, and Archaeology,* ed. James G. Cusick, 378–401. Center for Archaeological Investigations, Occasional Paper No. 25. Carbondale: Southern Illinois University Press.

Arnold, Philip J. III. 1987. The Household Potters of Los Tuxtlas: An Ethnoarchaeological Study of Ceramic Production and Site Structure. Ph.D. dissertation, University of New Mexico.

———. 1990. The Organization of Refuse Disposal and Ceramic Production Within Contemporary Mexican Houselots. *American Anthropologist* 92: 915–32.

———. 1991. *Domestic Ceramic Production and Spatial Organization: A Mexican Case Study in Ethnoarchaeology.* Cambridge: Cambridge University Press.

Ashmore, Wendy. 1981. Some Issues of Method and Theory in Lowland Maya Settlement Archaeology. In *Lowland Maya Settlement Patterns,* ed. Wendy Ashmore, 37–69. Albuquerque: University of New Mexico Press.

Ashmore, Wendy, and Richard R. Wilk. 1988. Household and Community in the Mesoamerican Past. In *Household and Community in the Mesoamerican Past,* ed. Richard R. Wilk and Wendy Ashmore, 1–27. Albuquerque: University of New Mexico Press.

Barba, Luis. 1986. La Química en el Estudio de Areas de Actividad. In *Unidades Habitacionales Mesoamericanas y sus Areas de Actividad,* ed. Linda Manzanilla, 21–39. México, D.F.: Instituto de Investigaciones Antropológicas, Universidad Nacional Autónoma de México

Barber, Russell J., and Frances F. Berdan. 1998. *The Emperor's Mirror: Understanding Cultures through Primary Sources.* Tucson: University of Arizona Press.

Barth, Fredrik. 1966. *Models of Social Organization.* Royal Anthropological Institute, Occasional Papers No. 23, London.

———. 1967. Economic Spheres in Darfur. In *Themes in Economic Anthropology,* ed. Raymond Firth. London: Tavistock.

Binford, Lewis R. 1968. Archaeological Perspectives. In *New Perspectives in Archeology,* ed. Sally R. Binford and Lewis R. Binford, 5–32. Chicago: Aldine.

———. 1987. Researching Ambiguity: Frames of Reference and Site Structure. In *Method and Theory for Activity Area Research: An Ethnoarchaeological Approach,* ed. Susan Kent, 449–512. New York: Columbia University Press.

———. 2001. *Constructing Frames of Reference: An Analytical Method for Archaeological Theory Building Using Hunter-Gatherer and Environmental Data Sets.* Berkeley: University of California Press.

Blalock, Hubert M. 1979. *Social Statistics.* 2d ed. New York: McGraw-Hill.

Blanton, Richard E. 1994. *Houses and Households: A Comparative Study.* New York: Plenum Press.

Borah, Woodrow. 1951. *New Spain's Century of Depression.* Iberoamericana No. 35. Berkeley: University of California Press.

Boserup, Ester. 1965. *The Conditions of Agricultural Growth; The Economics of Agrarian Change under Population Pressure.* New York: Aldine.

Bracamonte y Sosa, Pedro. 1984. Haciendas, ranchos y pueblos en Yucatán (1821–1847). *Boletín de la Escuela de Ciencias Antropológicas de la Universidad de Yucatán* 11: 3–21.

———. 1988. Haciendas y Ganados en el Noroeste de Yucatán, 1800–1850. *Historia Mexicana* 37(4): 613–39.

———. 1990. Sociedades de Sirvientes y Uso del Espacio en las Haciendas de Yucatán 1800–1860. *Historia Mexicana* 40(1): 53–77.

———. 1993. *Amos y Sirvientes, Las Haciendas de Yucatán 1789–1860.* Mérida: Universidad Autónoma de Yucatán.

Brading, David A. 1977. The Hacienda as an Investment. In *Haciendas and Plantations in Latin American History,* ed. Robert G. Keith, 135–40. New York: Homes and Meier Publishers, Inc.

Brannon, Jeffery T., and Gilbert M. Joseph, eds. 1991. *Land, Labor, and Capital in Modern Yucatán: Essays in Regional History and Political Economy.* Tuscaloosa: University of Alabama Press.

Braudel, Fernand. 1984. *Civilization and Capitalism 15th–18th Century: Vol. III, The Perspective of the World.* London: Collins.

Bretos, Miguel. 1992. *Iglesias de Yucatán.* Mérida: Producción Editorial Dante.

Bricker, Victoria R. 1977. The Caste War of Yucatán: The History of a Myth and the Myth of History. In *Anthropology and History in Yucatán,* ed. Grant D. Jones, 251–58. Austin: University of Texas Press.

———. 1981. *The Indian Christ, the Indian King.* Austin: University of Texas Press.

Brumfiel, Elizabeth M. 1993. The Economic Anthropology of the State: An Introduction. In *The Economic Anthropology of the State,* ed. Elizabeth M. Brumfiel, 1–16. Monographs in Economic Anthropology, vol. 11. Lanham, Md.: University Press of America.

Brumfiel, Elizabeth M., and Timothy K. Earle. 1987. Specialization, Exchange, and Complex Societies. In *Specialization, Exchange, and Complex Societies,* ed. Elizabeth M. Brumfiel and Timothy K. Earle, 1–9. Cambridge: Cambridge University Press.

Castañeda, Quetzil. 1996. *In the Museum of Maya Culture: Touring Chichén Itzá.* Minneapolis: University of Minnesota Press.

Chamberlain, Robert S. 1948. *The Conquest and Colonization of Yucatán, 1517–1550.* Washington, D.C.: Carnegie Institution of Washington Publication No. 582.

Charlton, Thomas H. 1972. *Post-Conquest Developments in the Teotihuacan Valley, Mexico.* Report No. 5. Office of the State Archaeologist, Iowa City.

———. 1986. Socioeconomic Dimension of Urban-Rural Relations in the Colonial Period Basin of Mexico. In *Ethnohistory,* ed. Ronald Spores, 122–33. Supplement to the *Handbook of Middle American Indians,* vol. 4, general editor, Victoria R. Bricker. Austin: University of Texas Press.

———. 2003. On Agrarian Landholdings in Post-Conquest Rural Mesoamerica. *Ethnohistory* 50(1): 221–30.

Chayanov, A. V. 1986. Peasant Farm Organization. In *A. V. Chayanov on the Theory of Peasant Economy,* ed. Basile Kerblay, Daniel Thorner, and R. E. F. Smith, 29–269. Madison: University of Wisconsin Press.

Chuchiak, John F. 1994. In the Path of the Raingod Chac: The Persistence of Paganism and Mayan Resistance to the Franciscans' Missionary Efforts in Yucatán, 1546–1786. MA thesis, Tulane University.

Claessen, Henri J. M., and Pieter van de Velde. 1991. Introduction. In *Early State Economics,* ed. Henri J. M. Claessen and Pieter van de Velde, 1–29. Political and Legal Anthropology, vol. 8. New Brunswick, N.J.: Transaction Publishers.

Clarke, David L. 1972. A Provisional Model of an Iron Age Society and its Settlement System. In *Models in Archaeology,* ed. David L. Clarke, 801–69. London: Methuen and Co. Ltd.

———. 1977. Spatial Information in Archaeology. In *Spatial Archaeology,* ed. David L. Clarke, 1–32. London: Academic Press.

Cline, Howard F. 1947. Related Studies in Early Nineteenth Century Yucatecan Social History. In *Microfilm Collection of Manuscripts on Middle American Cultural Anthropology.* University of Chicago Library, Chicago.

———. 1972. Introduction: Reflections on Ethnohistory. In *Guide to Ethnohistorical Sources, Part 1,* ed. Robert Wauchope, 3–16. *Handbook of Middle American Indians,* vol. 12. Austin: University of Texas Press.

Coale, Ansley J., and Paul Demeny. 1966. *Regional Model Life Tables and Stable Populations.* Princeton, N.J.: Princeton University Press.

Cook, Sherburne F., and Woodrow Borah. 1979. *Essays in Population History: Mexico and the Caribbean.* 3 vols. Berkeley: University of California Press.

Cowgill, George L. 1988. Onward and Upward with Collapse. In *The Collapse of Ancient States and Civilizations,* ed. Norman Yoffee and George L. Cowgill, 244–76. Tucson: University of Arizona Press.

Deal, Michael. 1985. Household Pottery Disposal in the Maya Highlands: An Ethnoarchaeological Interpretation. *Journal of Anthropological Archaeology* 4: 243–91.

———. 1998. *Pottery Ethnoarchaeology in the Central Maya Highlands.* Salt Lake City: University of Utah Press.

Dewar, Robert E. 1984. Environmental Productivity, Population Regulation, and Carrying Capacity. *American Anthropologist* 86: 601–14.

Drennan, Robert D. 1988. Household Location and Compact versus Dispersed Settlement in Prehispanic Mesoamerica. In *Household and Community in the Mesoamerican Past,* ed. Richard R. Wilk and Wendy Ashmore, 273–93. Albuquerque: University of New Mexico Press.

Dumond, Carol S., and Don E. Dumond. 1982. *Demography and Parish Affairs in Yucatán, 1797–1897.* University of Oregon Anthropological Papers No. 27. Portland: University of Oregon Press.

Dumond, Don E. 1985. The Talking Crosses of Yucatán: A New Look at Their History. *Ethnohistory* 32(4): 291–308.

———. 1997. *The Machete and the Cross: Campesino Rebellion in Yucatán.* Lincoln: University of Nebraska Press.

Dunning, Nicholas P. 1996. A Reexamination of Regional Variability in the Prehistoric Agricultural Landscape. In *The Managed Mosaic: Ancient Maya Agriculture and Resource Use,* ed. Scott L. Fedick, 53–68. Salt Lake City: University of Utah Press.

Fallon, Michael J. 1979. The Secular Clergy in the Diocese of Yucatán: 1750–1800. Ph.D. dissertation, Catholic University of America.

Farriss, Nancy M. 1978. Nucleation versus Dispersal: The Dynamics of Population Movement in Colonial Yucatán. *Hispanic American Historical Review* 58: 187–216.

———. 1984. *Maya Society Under Colonial Rule: The Collective Enterprise of Survival.* Princeton, N.J.: Princeton University Press.

Faust, Betty Bernice. 1998. *Mexican Rural Development and the Plumed Serpent: Technology and Maya Cosmology in the Tropical Forest of Campeche, Mexico.* Westport, Conn.: Bergin & Garvey.

Fedick, Scott L. 1996. Introduction: New Perspectives on Ancient Maya Agriculture and Resource Use. In *The Managed Mosaic: Ancient Maya Agriculture and Resource Use,* ed. Scott L. Fedick, 1–14. Salt Lake City: University of Utah Press.

Flannery, Kent V., ed. 1982. *Maya Subsistence: Studies in Memory of Dennis E. Puleston.* New York: Academic Press.

Florescano, Enrique. 1977. The Problem of Hacienda Markets. In *Haciendas and Plantations in Latin American History,* ed. Robert G. Keith, 128–34. New York: Homes and Meier Publishers, Inc.

———. 1987. The Hacienda in New Spain. In *Colonial Spanish America,* ed. Leslie Bethell, 250–85. Cambridge: Cambridge University Press.

Fortes, Meyer. 1958. Introduction. In *The Developmental Cycle in Domestic Groups,* ed. Jack Goody, 1–14. Cambridge: Cambridge University Press.

Freidel, David A. 1983. Political Systems in the Lowland Yucatán: Dynamics and Structure in Maya Settlement. In *Prehistoric Settlement Patterns: Essays in Honor of Gordon R. Willey,* ed. Evon Z. Vogt and Richard M. Leventhal, 375–86. Albuquerque: University of New Mexico Press.

Freidel, David A., and Jeremy A. Sabloff. 1984. *Cozumel: Late Maya Settlement Patterns.* New York: Academic Press.

Freidel, David A., Linda Schele, and Joy Parker. 1993. *Maya Cosmos: Three Thousand Years on the Shaman's Path.* New York: W. W. Morrow.

Fry, Robert E. 1985. Revitalization Movements Among the Postclassic Lowland Maya. In *The Lowland Maya Postclassic,* ed. Arlen F. Chase and Prudence M. Rice, 126–41. Austin: University of Texas Press.

Garcia Bernal, Manuela Cristina. 1972. *La Sociedad de Yucatán, 1700–1750.* Sevilla: Escuela de Estudios Hispano-Americanos.

———. 1978. *Población y Encomienda en Yucatán bajo los Austrias.* Sevilla: Escuela de Estudios Hispano-Americanos.

Garza Tarzona de González, Silvia, and Edward B. Kurjack. 1980. *Atlas Arqueológico del Estado de Yucatán.* 2 vols. México: Centro Regional del Sureste, SEP-INAH.

Gasco, Janine. 1987. Economic Organization in Colonial Soconusco, New Spain: Local and External Influences. In *Research in Economic Anthropology,* vol. 8, ed. Barry Isaac, 105–37. Greenwich, Conn.: JAI Press.

———. 1992. Material Culture and Colonial Indian Society in Southern Mesoamerica: The View from Coastal Chiapas, Mexico. *Historical Archaeology* 26: 67–74.

Geertz, Clifford. 1963. *Agricultural Involution: The Process of Ecological Change in Indonesia.* Berkeley: University of California Press.

Gerhard, Peter. 1979. *The Southeast Frontier of New Spain.* Princeton, N.J.: Princeton University Press.

Gibson, Charles. 1964. *The Aztecs Under Spanish Rule: A History of the Indians of the Valley of Mexico, 1519–1810*. Stanford, Calif.: Stanford University Press.

Gómez-Pompa, Arturo, Jose Salvador Flores, and Mario Aliphat Fernández. 1990. The Sacred Cacao Groves of the Maya. *Latin American Antiquity* 1:247–257.

González y González, Luis. 1973. *Invitación a Microhistoria*. México, D. F.

Goody, Jack, ed. 1958. *The Developmental Cycle in Domestic Groups*. Cambridge: Cambridge University Press.

Granado Baeza, Bartólome Jose. 1845. Los Indios de Yucatán. *Registro Yucateco* 1: 165–78.

Gross, Daniel, George Eiten, Nancy M. Flowers, Francisca M. Levi, Madeline Lattman Ritter, and Dennis W. Werner. 1979. Ecology and Acculturation Among Native Peoples of Central Brazil. *Science* 206: 1043–50.

Güemez Pineda, Arturo. 1991. Everyday Forms of Mayan Resistance: Cattle Rustling in Northwestern Yucatán, 1821–1847. In *Land, Labor and Capital in Modern Yucatán: Essays in Regional History and Political Economy,* ed. Jeffery T. Brannon and Gilbert M. Joseph, 18–50. Tuscaloosa: University of Alabama.

———. 1994. *Liberalismo en Tierras del Caminante, Yucatán, 1812–1840*. Zamora: El Colegio de Michoacán.

Guha, Ranajit. 1983. *Elementary Aspects of Peasant Insurgency in Colonial India*. Delhi: Oxford University Press.

———, ed. 1997. *Dominance Without Hegemony: History and Power in Colonial India*. Cambridge, Mass.: Harvard University Press.

Halstead, Paul, and John O'Shea. 1989. Introduction: Cultural Responses to Risk and Uncertainty. In *Bad Year Economics: Cultural Responses to Risk and Uncertainty,* ed. Paul Halstead and John O'Shea, 1–7. Cambridge: Cambridge University Press.

Hammel, E. A. 1984. On the *** of Studying Household Form and Function. In *Households: Comparative and Historical Studies of the Domestic Group,* ed. Robert McC. Netting, Richard R. Wilk, and Eric J. Arnould, 29–43. Berkeley: University of California Press.

Hanks, William. 1990. *Referential Practice: Language and Lived Space Among the Maya*. Chicago: University of Chicago Press.

Hanson, Craig A. 1996. The Hispanic Horizon in Yucatán: A Model of Franciscan Missionization. *Ancient Mesoamerica* 6: 15–28.

Hanson, Craig A., William M. Ringle, and Sharon Bennett. 1994. The Colonial Community of Ek Balam, Yucatán, Mexico. Paper presented at the 59th Annual Meeting of the Society for American Archaeology, Anaheim, Calif.

Harrington, Raymond P. 1982. The Secular Clergy in the Diocese of Merida de Yucatán: 1780–1850: Their Origins, Careers, Wealth, and Activities. Ph.D. dissertation, The Catholic University of America.

Hassig, Ross. 1985. *Trade, Tribute, and Transportation: The Sixteenth-Century Political Economy of the Valley of Mexico.* Norman: University of Oklahoma Press.

Hayami, Yurjiro, and Masao Kikuchi. 1982. *Asian Village Economy at the Crossroads: An Economic Approach to Institutional Change.* Tokyo: University of Tokyo Press.

Hayden, Brian, and Aubrey Cannon. 1983. Where the Garbage Goes: Refuse Disposal in the Maya Highlands. *Journal of Anthropological Archaeology* 2: 117–63.

———. 1984. *The Structure of Material Systems: Ethnoarchaeology in the Maya Highlands.* Society for American Archaeology Paper No. 3. Society for American Archaeology, Washington, D.C.

Hayden, Brian, and Rob Gargett. 1990. Big Man, Big Heart? *Ancient Mesoamerica* 1: 3–20.

Hellmuth, Nicholas. 1977. Cholti-Lacandon (Chiapas) and Petén Itzá Agriculture, Settlement Pattern and Population. In *Social Process in Maya Prehistory: Studies in Honour of Sir Eric Thompson,* ed. Norman Hammond, 421–48. New York: Academic Press.

Hernández Xolocotzi, Efraim, ed. 1980. *Seminario sobre Producción Agrícola en Yucatán.* Mérida: Secretaría de Programación y Presupuesto (SPP).

Hill, J. N., and R. K. Evans. 1972. A Model for Classification and Typology. In *Models in Archaeology,* ed. David L. Clarke, 231–73. London: Methuen & Co. Ltd.

Hirth, Kenneth G. 1993. The Household as an Analytical Unit: Problems in Method and Theory. In *Prehispanic Domestic Units in Western Mesoamerica: Studies of the Household, Compound, and Residence,* ed. Robert S. Santley and Kenneth G. Hirth, 21–36. Boca Raton, La.: CRC Press.

Hunt, Marta Espejo-Ponce. 1974. Colonial Yucatán: Town and Region in the Seventeenth Century. Ph.D. dissertation, Department of History, University of California, Los Angeles.

Isphording, W. C., and E. M. Wilson. 1973. Weathering Process and Physical Subdivisions of Northern Yucatán. *Proceedings of the Association of American Geographers* 5: 117–20.

Izquierdo, Ana Luisa. 1988. Documentos de la Division del Beneficio de Yaxcabá: El Castigo a una Idolatria. *Estudios de Cultura Maya* 17: 161–95.

Johnson, Allen W. 1971. *Sharecroppers of the Sertão: Economics and Dependence on a Brazilian Plantation.* Stanford, Calif.: Stanford University Press.

Jones, David M. 1980. *The Archaeology of Nineteenth Century Haciendas and Ranchos of Otumba and Apan, Basin of Mexico.* Post-Conquest Developments in the Teotihuacan Valley, Mexico, Part 5, Research Report No. 2. Mesoamerican Research Colloquium, Department of Anthropology, University of Iowa, Iowa City.

Jones, Grant D. 1989. *Maya Resistance to Spanish Rule: Time and History on a Colonial Frontier.* Albuquerque: University of New Mexico Press.

―――. 1998. *The Conquest of the Last Maya Kingdom.* Stanford, Calif.: Stanford University Press.

Joseph, Gilbert M. 1985. From Caste War to Class War: The Historiography of Modern Yucatán (c. 1750–1940). *Hispanic American Historical Review* 65(1): 111–34.

―――. 1988. *Revolution from Without: Yucatán, México, and the United States 1880–1924.* Durham, N.C.: Duke University Press.

―――. 1991. On the Trail of Latin American Bandits: A Reexamination of Peasant Resistance. *Latin American Research Review* 25(3): 7–53.

―――. 1998. The United States, Feuding Elites, and Rural Revolt in Yucatán, 1836–1915. In *Rural Revolt in Mexico: U.S. Intervention and the Domain of Subaltern Politics,* ed. Daniel Nugent, 173–206. Durham, N.C.: Duke University Press.

Joseph, Gilbert M., and Daniel Nugent, eds. 1994. *Everyday Forms of State Formation: Revolution and Negotiation of Rule in Modern Mexico.* Durham, N.C.: Duke University Press.

Kepecs, Susan, and Sylvianne Boucher. 1996. The Cultivation of Rejolladas and Stonelands: New Evidence from Northeast Yucatán. In *The Managed Mosaic: Ancient Maya Agriculture and Resource Use,* ed. Scott L. Fedick, 69–91. Salt Lake City: University of Utah Press.

Killion, Thomas W. 1987. Agriculture and Residential Site Structure Among Campesinos in Southern Veracruz Mexico: Building a Foundation for Archaeological Inference. Ph.D. dissertation, Department of Anthropology, University of New Mexico.

―――. 1990. Cultivation Intensity and Residential Site Structure: An Ethnoarchaeological Examination of Peasant Agriculture in the Sierra de los Tuxtlas, Veracruz, Mexico. *Latin American Antiquity* 1: 191–215.

―――. 1992. The Archaeology of Settlement Agriculture. In *Gardens of Prehistory: The Archaeology of Settlement Agriculture in Greater Mesoamerica,* ed. Thomas W. Killion, 1–13. Tuscaloosa: University of Alabama Press.

Killion, Thomas W., Jeremy A. Sabloff, Gair Tourtellot, and Nicholas P. Dunning. 1989. Intensive Surface Collection of Residential Clusters at Terminal Classic, Sayil, Yucatán, Mexico. *Journal of Field Archaeology* 16: 273–94.

Kirch, Patrick V. 1994. *The Wet and the Dry: Irrigation and Agricultural Intensification in Polynesia.* Chicago: University of Chicago Press.

Koopmans, Lambert H. 1987. *Introduction to Contemporary Statistical Methods.* 2d ed. Boston: PWS-Kent.

Kyle, Chris. 2003. Land, Labor, and the Chilapa Market: A New Look at the 1840s Peasant Wars in Central Guerrero. *Ethnohistory* 50(1):89-130.

La Motta, Vincent M., and Michael B. Schiffer. 1999. Formation Processes of House Floor Assemblages. In *The Archaeology of Household Activities,* ed. Penelope M. Allison, 19–29. London: Routledge.

Little, Peter D. 1987. Domestic Production and Regional Markets in Northern Kenya. *American Ethnologist* 14: 295–308.

López de Cogolludo, Diego. 1954. *Historia de Yucatán.* 4th ed. 3 vols. Comisión de Historia, Campeche.

MacLeod, Murdo J. 1973. *Spanish Central America: A Socio-Economic History.* Berkeley: University of California Press.

Manzanilla, Linda, and Luis Barba. 1990. The Study of Activities in Classic Households: Two Case Studies from Cobá and Teotihuacan. *Ancient Mesoamerica* 1: 41–49.

Marcus, Joyce. 1982. The Plant World of the Sixteenth- and Seventeenth-Century Lowland Maya. In *Maya Subsistence: Studies in Memory of Dennis E. Puleston,* ed. Kent V. Flannery, 239–73. New York: Academic Press.

————. 1993. Ancient Maya Political Organization. In *Lowland Maya Civilization in the Eighth Century A.D.: A Symposium at Dumbarton Oaks, 7th and 8th October 1989,* ed. Jeremy A. Sabloff and John S. Henderson, 111–83. Washington, D.C.: Dumbarton Oaks.

McAnany, Patricia A. 1995. *Living with the Ancestors: Kinship and Kingship in Ancient Maya Society.* Austin: University of Texas Press.

McCay, Bonnie J., and James M. Acheson, eds. 1987. *The Question of the Commons: The Culture and Ecology of Communal Resources.* Tucson: University of Arizona Press.

Millet Cámara, Luis. 1984. De las Estancias y Haciendas en el Yucatán Colonial. In *Hacienda y Cambio Social en Yucatán.* Colección Raices. Mérida: Instituto Nacional de Antropología e História.

————. 1985. Las Haciendas de Yucatán. *Cuadernos de Arquitectura Virreinal* 2: 34–41.

Millon, René. 1988. The Last Years of Teotihuacan Dominance. In *The Collapse of Ancient States and Civilizations,* ed. Norman Yoffee and George L. Cowgill, 102–64. Tucson: University of Arizona Press.

Moore, Jerry D., and Janine L. Gasco. 1990. Perishable Structures and Serial Dwellings from Coastal Chiapas: Implications for the Archaeology of Households. *Ancient Mesoamerica* 1: 205–12.

Morley, Sylvanus G., and George W. Brainerd. 1956. *The Ancient Maya.* Stanford, Calif.: Stanford University Press.

Morrison, Kathleen D. 1994. The Intensification of Production: Archaeological Approaches. *Journal of Archaeological Method and Theory* 1: 111–59.

————. 1996. Typological Schemes and Agricultural Change: Beyond Boserup in Precolonial South India. *Current Anthropology* 37: 583–608.

———. 2001. Coercion, Resistance, and Hierarchy: Local Processes and Imperial Strategies in the Vijayanagara Empire. In *Empires: Perspectives from Archaeology and History,* ed. Susan E. Alcock, Terrence N. D'Altroy, Kathleen D. Morrison, and Carla M. Sinopoli, 252–278. Cambridge: Cambridge University Press.

Murdock, George P. 1949. *Social Structure.* New York: MacMillan.

Nations, James D., and Ronald B. Nigh. 1980. The Evolutionary Potential of Lacandon Maya Sustained-Yield Tropical Forest Agriculture. *Journal of Anthropological Research* 36: 1–30.

Netting, Robert McC. 1993. *Smallholders, Householders: Farm Families and the Ecology of Intensive Sustainable Agriculture.* Stanford, Calif.: Stanford University Press.

Netting, Robert McC., Richard R. Wilk, and Eric J. Arnould. 1984. Introduction. In *Households: Comparative and Historical Studies of the Domestic Group,* ed. Robert McC. Netting, Richard R. Wilk, and Eric J. Arnould, xiii–xxxviii. Berkeley: University of California Press.

Nichols, Christopher. 2003. Solares in Tekax: The Impact of the Sugar Industry on a Nineteenth Century Yucatecan Town. *Ethnohistory* 50(1):161–189.

Nugent, Daniel, ed. 1998. *Rural Revolt in Mexico: U.S. Intervention and the Domain of Subaltern Politics.* Durham, N.C.: Duke University Press.

Ortner, Sherry B. 1995. Resistance and the Problem of Ethnographic Refusal. *Comparative Studies in Society and History* 37(1): 173–93.

Paso y Troncoso, Francisco del. 1939. *Epistolaria de Nueva España 1505–1818, Tomo V, 1547–1549.* México: Antigua Libreria Robredo de Jose Porrua e Hijos.

Patch, Robert W. 1979. *A Colonial Regime: Maya and Spaniard in Yucatán.* Ph.D. dissertation published by University Microfilms International.

———. 1985. Agrarian Change in Eighteenth-Century Yucatán. *Hispanic American Historical Review* 65(1): 21–49.

———. 1991. Decolonization, the Agrarian Problem, and the Origins of the Caste War, 1812–1847. In *Land, Labor and Capital in Modern Yucatán: Essays in Regional History and Political Economy,* ed. Jeffery T. Brannon and Gilbert M. Joseph. Tuscaloosa: University of Alabama Press.

———. 1993. *Maya and Spaniard in Yucatán.* Stanford, Calif.: Stanford University Press.

———. 1998. Culture, Community, and "Rebellion" in the Yucatec Maya Uprising of 1761. In *Native Resistance and the Pax Colonial in New Spain,* ed. Susan Schroeder, 67–83. Lincoln: University of Nebraska Press.

Pool Novelo, Luciano. 1980. El Estudio de los Suelos Calcimórficos con Relación a la Producción Maicera. In *Seminario Sobre Producción Agrícola en Yucatán,* ed. Efraim Hernández Xolocotzi, 393–424. Mérida: Secretaria de Programación y Presupuesto (SPP).

Pyburn, K. Anne. 1998. Smallholders in the Maya Lowlands: Homage to a Garden Variety Ethnographer. *Human Ecology* 26(2): 267–86.

Quezada, Sergio. 1985. Encomienda, Cabildo y Gubernatura Indigena en Yucatán, 1541–1583. *Historia Mexicana* 34(4): 662–84.

———. 1993. *Pueblos y Caciques Yucatecos, 1550–1580.* México, D.F.: El Colegio de México.

Re-Cruz, Alicia. 1996. *The Two Milpas of Chan Kom: Scenarios of a Maya Village Life.* Albany: State University of New York Press.

Redfield, Robert, and Alfonso Villa Rojas. 1934. *Chan Kom: A Maya Village.* Washington, D.C.: Carnegie Institution of Washington Publication No. 448.

Reed, Nelson. 1964. *The Caste War of Yucatán.* Stanford, Calif.: Stanford University Press.

———. 2001. *The Caste War of Yucatán.* Rev. ed. Stanford, Calif.: Stanford University Press.

Regil, Jose M., and Alonso Manuel Peon. 1853. Estadistica de Yucatán. R. Sociedad de Geografía y Estadistica pamphlet located in the Rare Book Collection of Tulane University Latin American Library, New Orleans, La.

Relaciones Histórico-Geográficos. 1983. *Relaciones Histórico-Geográficas de la Governación de Yucatán (Mérida, Valladolid, y Tabasco).* 2 vols. México, D.F.: Universidad Nacional Autónoma de México.

Remmers, Lawrence J. 1981. Henequen, the Caste War and Economy of Yucatán, 1846–1883: The Roots of Dependence in a Mexican Region. Ph. D. dissertation, University of California, Los Angeles.

Restall, Matthew. 1997. *The Maya World: Yucatec Culture and Society 1550–1850.* Stanford, Calif.: Stanford University Press.

———. 1998. *Maya Conquistador.* Boston: Beacon.

Restauración de los Retablos Coloniales. *Diario de Yucatán,* June 13, 1999.

Rico-Gray, Victor, Jose G. Garcia-Franco, Alexandra Chemas, Armando Puch, and Paulino Sima. 1990. Species Composition, Similarity and Structure of Mayan Homegardens in Texpeual and Tixcacaltuyúb, Yucatán, Mexico. *Economic Botany* 44(4): 470–87.

Ringle, William M., and E. Wyllys Andrews V. 1988. Formative Residences at Komchen, Yucatán, Mexico. In *Household and Community in the Mesoamerican Past,* ed. Richard R. Wilk and Wendy Ashmore, 171–97. Albuquerque: University of New Mexico Press.

Robinson, David J., ed. 1990. *Migration in Colonial Spanish America.* Cambridge: Cambridge University Press.

Robles Castellanos, Fernando, and Anthony P. Andrews. 1986. A Review and Synthesis of Recent Postclassic Archaeology in Northern Yucatan. In *Late Lowland Maya Civilization: Classic to Postclassic,* ed. Jeremy A. Sabloff and E. Wyllys Andrews V, 53–98. Albuquerque: University of New Mexico Press.

Roys, Ralph L. 1933. *The Book of Chilam Balam of Chumayel.* Washington, D.C.: Carnegie Institution of Washington Publication No. 438.

———. 1939. *The Titles of Ebtun.* Washington, D.C.: Carnegie Institution of Washington Publication No. 505.

———. 1943. *The Indian Background of Colonial Yucatan.* Washington, D.C.: Carnegie Institution of Washington Publication No. 548.

———. 1952. *Conquest Sites and the Subsequent Destruction of Maya Architecture in the Interior of Northern Yucatan.* Washington, D.C.: Carnegie Institution of Washington Contributions to American Anthropology and History No. 54.

———. 1957. *The Political Geography of the Yucatan Maya.* Washington, D.C.: Carnegie Institution of Washington Publication No. 613.

Rugeley, Terry. 1997. *Yucatán's Maya Peasantry and the Origins of the Caste War.* Austin: University of Texas Press.

Ruz, Mario Humberto. 1979. El Añil en el Yucatán del Siglo XVI. *Estudios de Cultura Maya* 12: 111–56.

Ruz Menéndez, Rodolfo. 1989. Los Indios de Yucatán de Bartólome del Granado Baeza. *Revista de la Universidad de Yucatán* 4(168): 52–63.

Sahlins, Marshall. 1972. *Stone Age Economics.* New York: Aldine de Gruyter.

Sanders, William T., and Thomas W. Killion. 1992. Factors Affecting Settlement Agriculture in the Ethnographic and Historic Record of Mesoamerica. In *Gardens in Prehistory: The Archaeology of Settlement Agriculture in Greater Mesoamerica,* ed. Thomas W. Killion, 14–31. Tuscaloosa: University of Alabama Press.

Sanders, William T., Jeffrey Parsons, and Robert S. Santley. 1979. *The Basin of Mexico: Ecological Processes in the Evolution of a Civilization.* New York: Academic Press.

Sanders, William T., and David Webster. 1978. Unilinealism, Multilinealism, and the Evolution of Complex Societies. In *Social Archaeology, Beyond Subsistence and Dating,* ed. Charles L. Redman, M. J. Berman, E. V. Curtin, W. T. Langhorne Jr., N. M. Versaggi, and J. C. Wanser, 249–302. New York: Academic Press.

Santley, Robert S. 1993. Late Formative Period Society at Loma Torremote: A Consideration of the Redistribution versus the Great Provider Models as a Basis for the Emergence of Complexity in the Basin of Mexico. In *Prehispanic Domestic Units in Western Mesoamerica: Studies of the Household, Compound, and Residence,* ed. Robert S. Santley and Kenneth G. Hirth, 67–86. Boca Raton, La.: CRC Press.

Santley, Robert S., and Kenneth G. Hirth. 1993. Household Studies in Western Mesoamerica. In *Prehispanic Domestic Units in Western Mesoamerica: Studies of the Household Compound and Residence,* ed. Robert Santley and Kenneth G. Hirth, 3–17. Boca Raton, La.: CRC Press.

Saunders, Rebecca. 1998. Forced Relocation, Power Relations, and Culture Contact in the Missions of La Florida. In *Studies in Culture Contact: Interaction, Culture Change, and Archaeology,* ed. James G. Cusick, 402–29. Center for Archaeological Investigations, Occasional Paper No. 25. Carbondale: Southern Illinois University Press.

Schiffer, Michael B. 1976. *Behavioral Archaeology.* New York: Academic Press.

———. 1987. *Formation Processes of the Archaeological Record.* Albuquerque: University of New Mexico Press.

Schmidt, Peter. 1980. La Producción Agrícola Prehistórica de los Mayas. In *Seminario Sobre Producción Agrícola en Yucatán,* ed. Efraim Hernández Xolocotzi, 39–82. Mérida: Secretaria de Programación y Presupuesto (SPP).

Scholes, France V., and Eleanor B. Adams. 1938. *Don Diego Quijada Alcalde Mayor de Yucatan, 1561–1565.* 2 vols. México, D.F.: Antigua Libreria Robredo de Jose Porrua e Hijos.

Scholes, France V., Carlos R. Menendez, J. Ignacio Rubio Mañe, and Eleanor B. Adams. 1938. *Documentos para la História de Yucatán.* 3 vols. Mérida: Companía Tipográfica Yucateca.

Scholes, France V., and Ralph L. Roys. 1938. Fray Diego de Landa and the Problem of Idolatry in Yucatán. Washington, D.C.: Cooperation in Research, Carnegie Institution of Washington Publication, No. 501, pp. 585–620.

Schwartz, Glenn M., and Steven E. Falconer, eds. 1994. *Archaeological Views from the Countryside: Village Communities in Early Complex Societies.* Washington, D.C.: Smithsonian Institution Press.

Scott, James C. 1976. *The Moral Economy of the Peasant: Subsistence and Revolution in Southeast Asia.* New Haven, Conn.: Yale University Press.

———. 1985. *Weapons of the Weak: Everyday Forms of Peasant Resistance.* New Haven, Conn.: Yale University Press.

———. 1990. *Domination and the Arts of Resistance: Hidden Transcripts.* New Haven, Conn.: Yale University Press.

Scott, James C., and Benedict J. Kerkvliet. 1977. How Traditional Rural Patrons Lose Legitimacy: A Theory with Special Reference to Southeast Asia. In *Friends, Followers, and Factions: A Reader in Political Clientelism,* ed. Steffen W. Schmidt, Laura Guasti, Carl H. Landé, and James C. Scott. Berkeley: University of California Press.

Secretaría de Gobernación y Gobierno, Estado de Yucatán. 1988. *Municipios de Yucatán.* Centro Nacional de Estudios Municipales de la Secretaría de Gobernación, Roberto Galván Ramírez, coordinador. México, D.F.: Talleres Gráficos de la Nación.

Sharer, Robert J. 1994. *The Ancient Maya.* 5th ed. Stanford, Calif.: Stanford University Press.

Singleton, Theresa A. 1998. Cultural Interaction and African American Identity in Plantation Archaeology. In *Studies in Culture Contact: Interaction, Culture Change, and Archaeology,* ed. James G. Cusick, 172–88. Center for Archaeological Investigations, Occasional Paper No. 25. Carbondale: Southern Illinois University Press.

Skocpol, Theda. 1979. *States and Social Revolutions: A Comparative Analysis of France, Russia, and China.* Cambridge: Cambridge University Press.

Small, David, and Nicola Tannenbaum, eds. 1999. *At the Interface: Households and Beyond.* Lanham, Md.: University Press of America.

Smith, Jane, Immanuel Wallerstein, and H. D. Evers, eds. 1984. *Households and the World Economy.* London: Sage Publications.

Smith, Michael E. 1992. Braudel's Temporal Rhythms and Chronology Theory in Archaeology. In *Archaeology, Annales, and Ethnohistory,* ed. A. Bernard Knapp, 23–34. Cambridge: Cambridge University Press.

Smyth, Michael. 1988. Domestic Storage Behavior in the Puuc Region of Yucatan, Mexico: An Ethnoarchaeological Investigation. Ph.D. dissertation, University of New Mexico.

———. 1990. Maize Storage Among the Puuc Maya: The Development of an Archaeological Method. *Ancient Mesoamerica* 1: 51–69.

Stanford, Lois. 1991. Peasant Resistance in the International Market: Theory and Practice in Michoacán, Mexico. *Research in Economic Anthropology* 13: 67–91.

Steggerda, Morris. 1941. *Maya Indians of Yucatán.* Washington, D.C.: Carnegie Institution of Washington Publication No. 531.

Stein, Gil J. 1998. World System Theory and Alternative Modes of Interaction in the Archaeology of Culture Contact. In *Studies in Culture Contact: Interaction, Culture Change, and Archaeology,* ed. James G. Cusick, 220–55. Center for Archaeological Investigations, Occasional Paper No. 25. Carbondale: Southern Illinois University Press.

———. 1999. *Rethinking World-Systems: Diasporas, Colonies, and Interaction in Uruk Mesopotamia.* Tucson: University of Arizona Press.

Stern, Steve J. 1987. New Approaches to the Study of Peasant Rebellion and Consciousness: Implication of the Andean Experience. In *Resistance, Rebellion, and Consciousness in the Andean Peasant World, 18th to 20th Centuries,* ed. Steve J. Stern, 3–25. Madison: University of Wisconsin Press.

Stevens, Rayfred L. 1964. The Soils of Middle America and Their Relation to Indian Peoples and Cultures. In *Natural Environment and Early Cultures,* ed. Robert C. West, 265–315. *Handbook of Middle American Indians,* vol. 1, general editor, Robert Wauchope. Austin: University of Texas Press.

Stier, Frances. 1982. Domestic Economy: Land Labor, and Wealth in a San Blas Community. *American Ethnologist* 9: 519–37.

Stone, Glenn D. 1996. *Settlement Ecology: The Social and Spatial Organization of Kofyar Agriculture.* Tucson: University of Arizona Press.

Strickon, Arnold. 1965. Hacienda and Plantation in Yucatán: An Historical-Ecological Consideration of the Folk-Urban Continuum in Yucatán. *América Indígena* 25: 35–65.

Sullivan, Paul. 1989. *Unfinished Conversations: Mayas and Foreigners Between Two Wars.* Berkeley: University of California Press.

Tedlock, Dennis. 1993. Torture in the Archives: Mayans Meet Europeans. *American Anthropologist* 95(1): 139–52.

Thompson, J. Eric S. 1970. *Maya History and Religion.* Norman: University of Oklahoma Press.

Thompson, Philip C. 1978. Tekanto in the Eighteenth Century. Ph.D. dissertation, Tulane University.

————. 2000. *Tekanto, a Maya town in Colonial Yucatán.* Middle America Research Institute Publication No. 67. Tulane University, New Orleans, La.

Tilly, Charles. 1978. *From Mobilization to Revolution.* Reading, Mass.: Addison-Wesley Publishing Co.

Tourtellot, Gair, Jeremy A. Sabloff, Patricia A. McAnany, Thomas W. Killion, Nicholas P. Dunning, Kelli Carmean, Rafael Cobos Palma, Christopher D. Dore, Fahmel Beyer, Sandra L. López Varela, Carlos Perez Alvarez, Susan J. Wurtzburg, and Michael P. Smyth. 1989. *Archaeological Investigations at Sayil, Yucatán, Mexico, Phase II: The 1987 Field Season.* Anthropological Papers. University of Pittsburgh, Pittsburgh, Pa.

Tozzer, Alfred M. 1941. *Landa's Relación de las Cosas de Yucatán.* Papers of the Peabody Museum of Archaeology and Ethnology, vol. 18. Trustees of Harvard University, Cambridge, Mass.

Turner, B. L. II, and Charles H. Miksicek. 1984. Economic Plant Species Associated with Prehistoric Agriculture in the Maya Lowlands. *Economic Botany* 38(2): 179–93.

Turner, B. L. II, and Peter D. Harrison. 1978. Implications from Agriculture for Maya Prehistory. In *Pre-Hispanic Maya Agriculture,* ed. Peter D. Harrison and B. L. Turner II, 246–69. Albuquerque: University of New Mexico Press.

Turner, Ellen S., Norman I. Turner, and Richard E. W. Adams. 1981. Volumetric Assessment, Rank Ordering, and Maya Civic Centers. In *Lowland Maya Settlement Patterns,* ed. Wendy Ashmore, 71–88. Albuquerque: University of New Mexico Press.

Vara Morán, Adelaido. 1980. La Dinámica de la Milpa en Yucatán: El Solar. In *Seminario Sobre Producción Agrícola en Yucatán,* ed. Efraim Hernández Xolocotzi, 305–42. Mérida: Secretaria de Programación y Presupuesto (SPP).

Vivó Escoto, Jorge A. 1964. Weather and Climate of Mexico and Central America. In *Natural Environment and Early Cultures,* ed. Robert C. West, 187–215. *Handbook of Middle American Indians,* vol. 1, general editor, Robert Wauchope. Austin: University of Texas Press.

Wagner, Philip L. 1964. Natural Vegetation of Middle America. In *Natural Environment and Early Cultures,* ed. Robert C. West, 216–64. *Handbook of Middle American Indians,* vol. 1, general editor, Robert Wauchope. Austin: University of Texas Press.

Wallace, Anthony F. C. 1956. Revitalization Movements. *American Anthropologist* 58: 264–81.

Wallerstein, Immanuel. 1974. *The Modern World-System.* New York: Academic Press.

Wallerstein, Immanuel, and Jane Smith. 1992. Households as an Institution of the World Economy. In *Creating and Transforming Households: The Constraints of the World Economy,* ed. Jane Smith and Immanuel Wallerstein, 3–23. Cambridge: Cambridge University Press.

Wells, Alan, and Gilbert M. Joseph. 1996. *Summer of Discontent, Seasons of Upheaval: Elite Politics and Rural Insurgency in Yucatán, 1876–1915.* Stanford, Calif.: Stanford University Press.

West, Robert C. 1964. Surface Configuration and Associated Geology of Middle America. In *Natural Environment and Early Cultures,* ed. Robert C. West, 33–83. *Handbook of Middle American Indians,* vol. 1, general editor, Robert Wauchope. Austin: University of Texas Press.

Wilk, Richard R. 1983. Little House in the Jungle: The Causes of Variation in House Size Among Modern Kekchi Maya. *Journal of Anthropological Archaeology* 2: 99–116.

———. 1984. Households in Process: Agricultural Change and Domestic Transformation Among the Kekchi Maya of Belize. In *Households: Comparative and Historical Studies of the Domestic Group,* ed. Richard R. Wilk, Robert McC. Netting, and Eric J. Arnould, 217–44. Berkeley: University of California Press.

———. 1991. *Household Ecology: Economic Change and Domestic Life Among the Kekchi Maya in Belize.* Tucson: University of Arizona Press.

Wilk, Richard R., and Robert McC. Netting. 1984. Households: Changing Forms and Functions. In *Households: Comparative and Historical Studies of the Domestic Group,* ed. Richard R. Wilk, Robert McC. Netting, and Eric J. Arnould, 1–28. Berkeley: University of California Press.

Wilk, Richard R., and William L. Rathje. 1982. Household Archaeology. *American Behavioral Scientist* 25(6): 617–39.

Wilk, Richard R., and Michael B. Schiffer. 1979. The Archaeology of Vacant Lots in Tucson, Arizona. *American Antiquity* 44(3): 530–36.

Wilken, Gene C. 1971. Food-Producing Systems Available to the Ancient Maya. *American Antiquity* 36: 432–38.

Willey, Gordon R. 1953. *Prehistoric Settlement Patterns in the Viru Valley, Peru.* Bureau of American Ethnology Bulletin No. 155. Washington, D.C.: Smithsonian Institution Press.

Wolf, Eric R. 1956. Aspects of Group Relations in a Complex Society: Mexico. *American Anthropologist* 58: 1065–78.

———. 1969. *Peasant Wars of the Twentieth Century.* New York: Harper & Row.

———. 1982. *Europe and the People Without History.* Berkeley: University of California Press.

———. 1990. Distinguished Lecture: Facing Power—Old Insights, New Questions. *American Anthropologist* 92: 586–96.

Wolf, Eric R., and Sidney W. Mintz. 1957. Haciendas and Plantations in Middle America and the Antilles. *Social and Economic Studies* 6: 380–411.

Wood, W. R., and D. L. Johnson. 1978. A Survey of Disturbance Processes in Archaeological Site Formation. In *Advances in Archaeological Method and Theory,* vol. 1, ed. Michael B. Schiffer, 315–81. New York: Academic Press.

Index